PORTRAIT OF AN AGE

George Malcolm Young was born in 1882. He was a Fellow of All Souls College, Oxford, and served for many years as a trustee of the National Portrait Gallery and the British Museum. 'I was born', he wrote, 'when the Queen had still nearly nineteen years to reign; I saw her twice, Gladstone once; I well remember the death of Newman and Tennyson, and my earliest recollection of the Abbey brings back the flowers fresh on Browning's grave. But if I place myself in 1900, and then look forward thirty-six years, and backward for as many, I feel doubtful whether the changes made in the earlier time were not greater than anything I have seen since. I am speaking of changes in men's minds, and I cannot in my own time observe anything of greater consequence than the dethronement of ancient faith by natural science and historical criticism, and the transition from oligarchic to democratic representation.' G. M. Young died in 1959.

Also by G. M. Young

Early Victorian England (ed.)
The Good Society
Burke
Charles I and Cromwell: An Essay
Daylight and Champaign
Government of Britain
Mr Gladstone
Rights and Duties in the Modern State
Scott and History
Stanley Baldwin
Today and Yesterday: Collected Essays and Addresses
Last Essays

PORTRAIT OF AN AGE

G. M. Young

Servants talk about People: Gentlefolk discuss Things
Victorian Precept

Second Edition

PHOENIX
PRESS

5 UPPER SAINT MARTIN'S LANE
LONDON
WC2H 9EA

A PHOENIX PRESS PAPERBACK

First published in Great Britain
by Oxford University Press in 1936
This paperback edition published in 2002
by Phoenix Press,
a division of The Orion Publishing Group Ltd,
Orion House, 5 Upper St Martin's Lane,
London WC2H 9EA

Phoenix Press
Sterling Publishing Co Inc
387 Park Avenue South
New York
NY 10016–8810
USA

A CIP catalogue record for this book
is available from the British Library.

Set by Deltatype Ltd, Birkenhead, Merseyside
Printed and bound in Great Britain by
Clays Ltd, St Ives plc

ISBN 1 84212 598 2

INTRODUCTION

In the First War, partly from curiosity and partly from comfort, I set myself to study the course and outcome of the great Napoleonic struggle. When Waterloo had been fought and won, I went on to the years of peace and distress which followed, and so to the collapse of Tory domination in 1830, to the Reform Bill and the New Poor Law, to the England of young Gladstone, young Tennyson, young Darwin: of the Oxford Movement: of the Benthamites: of Factory Inspectors and School Inspectors: of Chadwick and Horner: of *Sybil* and the People's Charter. As I read, my picture of Victorian England grew clearer, and it was a very different picture from the one at that time commonly accepted by popular opinion and set out by popular writers. So, in a fit of wrath over what seemed to me a preposterous misreading of the age, I wrote an Essay[1] which was intended as a manifesto, or perhaps an outline for others to fill in. I had had little or no experience of writing, and the Essay was in places sadly crude, and in places badly rhetorical. But it did, I found, induce some readers to reconsider their ideas, and re-orientate their attitudes: ideas and attitudes generated rather by an emotional antipathy to the Victorian Age than by any insight into its historic significance. So when Oxford asked me to plan a book on *Early Victorian England*, to match those on *Shakespeare's England* and *Johnson's England*, I felt I was committed to do my best, and I think I can justify my rashness by saying that I persuaded Sir John Clapham to write the chapter on 'Work and Wages'.

For myself I reserved the final, summary chapter, to be called

[1] Published as '*Victorian History*', in *Selected Modern Essays*: Second Series (The World's Classics, No. 406. Oxford University Press, 1932).

v

'Portrait of an Age 1831 to 1865', the Reform Bill and the death of Palmerston being, as it were, the natural limits of the period. In the Essay of which I have spoken, I had, somewhat paternally, exhorted young historians to study the methods of the great masters. I followed my own advice with the result that my first draft rapidly degenerated into a flat imitation of Macaulay's Third Chapter. It went into the fire. The second was more promising, but, as I was thinking it into shape, I found myself asking, what is this chapter really about? For that matter, what is History about? And the conclusion I reached was that the real, central theme of History is not what happened, but what people felt about it when it was happening: in Philip Sidney's phrase, 'the affects, the whispering, the motions of the people'; in Maitland's, 'men's common thought of common things'; in mine, 'the conversation of the people who counted.' Who were they? What were the assumptions behind their talk? And what came of it all? Then 'the boy born in 1810' offered himself as the interpreter of that talk, and my first paragraph wrote itself.

I had always been convinced that Victorianism was a myth, engendered by the long life of the sovereign and of her most illustrious subjects. I was constantly being told that the Victorians did this, or the Victorians thought that, while my own difficulty was to find anything on which they agreed: any assumption which was not at some time or other fiercely challenged. 'Victorian History', I had said, 'is before all things a history of opinion. To see ideas embodying themselves in parties and institutions: institutions and parties closing in upon ideas: to show old barriers sometimes sapped, and sometimes stormed, by new opinions: positions once thought impregnable abandoned overnight, and forces once thought negligible advancing to unforeseen victories, that is to understand Victorian history.' And the historian must be in sympathy with them all.

So conceived, my final draft did not dissatisfy me. I thought the outlines were true, the incidents fairly selected, the omissions justified, though I might with advantage have found space for the Mutiny and the transfer of India to the Crown. But, when I was asked to expand my chapter into a survey of the whole reign, I found myself involved in difficulties which I could not always master. I see now that I should have carried my book to 1914 and treated Late Victorian and Edwardian England as the *ancien régime* of the England in which I was writing. I could then have shown, more clearly than I have, the ecumenical significance of the age, revealed not only in the foundation of the great Dominions but in that marvellous network of commerce and finance which may truly be called a World Economy, and which was created by the genius, and sustained by the strength of Victorian England. That is what I should try to set out if I were beginning afresh. But as the greatest of our masters has said, 'where error is irreparable, repentance is useless'.

G. M. Y.

1952

ἀρεταὶ δ' αἰεὶ μεγάλαι πολύμυθοι·
βαιὰ δ' ἐν μακροῖσι ποικίλλειν
ἀκοὰ σοφοῖς.

Portrait of an Age

I

A boy born in 1810, in time to have seen the rejoicings after
Waterloo and the canal boats carrying the wounded to hospital,
to remember the crowds cheering for Queen Caroline, and to
have felt that the light had gone out of the world when Byron
died, entered manhood with the ground rocking under his feet
as it had rocked in 1789. Paris had risen against the Bourbons;
Bologna against the Pope; Poland against Russia; the Belgians
against the Dutch. Even in well-drilled Germany little dynasts
were shaking on their thrones, and Niebuhr, who had seen one
world revolution, sickened and died from fear of another. At
home, forty years of Tory domination were ending in panic and
dismay; Ireland, unappeased by Catholic Emancipation, was
smouldering with rebellion; from Kent to Dorset the skies were
alight with burning ricks. A young man looking for some creed
by which to steer at such a time might, with the Utilitarians,
hold by the laws of political economy and the greatest happiness
of the greatest number; he might simply believe in the Whigs,
the Middle Classes, and the Reform Bill; or he might, with
difficulty, still be a Tory. But atmosphere is more than creed,
and, whichever way his temperament led him, he found himself
at every turn controlled, and animated, by the imponderable
pressure of the Evangelical discipline and the almost universal
faith in progress.

Evangelical theology rests on a profound apprehension of the
contrary states: of Nature and of Grace; one meriting eternal
wrath, the other intended for eternal happiness. Naked and
helpless, the soul acknowledges its worthlessness before God and
the justice of God's infinite displeasure, and then, taking hold of
salvation in Christ, passes from darkness into a light which

makes more fearful the destiny of those unhappy beings who remain without. This is Vital Religion. But the power of Evangelicalism as a directing force lay less in the hopes and terrors it inspired, then in its rigorous logic, 'the eternal microscope' with which it pursued its argument into the recesses of the heart, and the details of daily life, giving to every action its individual value in this life, and its infinite consequence in the next. Nor could it escape the notice of a converted man, whose calling brought him into frequent contact with the world, that the virtues of a Christian after the Evangelical model were easily exchangeable with the virtues of a successful merchant or a rising manufacturer, and that a more than casual analogy could be established between Grace and Corruption and the Respectable and the Low. To be serious, to redeem the time, to abstain from gambling, to remember the Sabbath day to keep it holy, to limit the gratification of the senses to the pleasures of a table lawfully earned and the embraces of a wife lawfully wedded, are virtues for which the reward is not laid up in heaven only. The world is very evil. An unguarded look, a word, a gesture, a picture, or a novel, might plant a seed of corruption in the most innocent heart, and the same word or gesture might betray a lingering affinity with the class below.

The discipline of children was becoming milder, because it was touched with that tenderness for all helpless things which we see increasing throughout the eighteenth century, and with that novel interest in the spectacle of the opening mind which was a characteristic product of the Revolutionary years. But it was, perhaps for the same reason, more vigilant; and moral, or social, anxiety made it for girls at least more oppressive.[1] Yet if, with Rosalind and Beatrice in our eye, we recall Dryden's saying about 'the old Elizabeth way for maids to be seen and not heard', we shall realize how easy it is to misunderstand our grandmothers. The notable Victorian woman is a blend of the great lady and the intellectual woman, not yet professional, and

[1] But any one who supposes that there was such a thing as a 'Victorian' family or 'Victorian' father should meditate Norris of Bemerton's *Spiritual Counsel*, 1694, or *The Ladies' Calling* (Oxford University Press, 1673).

we can graduate the proportions until, at the opposite ends of the scale, we encounter the limiting instances of the Queen herself and Harriet Martineau. In Mrs Grote, who would have been a far more effective Member of Parliament than her husband, who sat with her red stockings higher than her head, discomfited a dinner-party by saying 'disembowelled' quite bold and plain, and knew when a hoop was off a pail in the back kitchen, the great lady is formidably ascendant; in Mrs Austin the intellectual woman. In Mrs Austin's daughter, Lady Duff Gordon, in Lady Eastlake – another product of the high secluded culture of the provinces – and, with the emphasis of genius, in Miss Nightingale, the kind achieves its balance.

But for working use the eighteenth century had conceived a standard type of womanhood, sensitive and enduring, at once frailer and finer than the man[1] – in a word, Amelia – and this type, repeated and articulated in a thousand novels, had blended insensibly with the more positive type evolved, in a humanitarian age, by the persuasive working of a religion of duty. Helen Pendennis in fiction, Mrs Tennyson in life, might serve as examples; Miss Nightingale's caustic allusion to 'woman's particular worth and general missionariness' as a corrective. In making up the account of English morals in the nineteenth century it is necessary to bear in mind that the most influential women were reared in an atmosphere which made them instinctively Custodians of the Standard. The two who had most aptitude and most capacity for rebellion were fanatics, Charlotte Brontë for the moral, Harriet Martineau for the economic law. Mary Wollstonecraft left, unhappily, no equal successor, and George Sand could never have grown in English soil. Thus it came about that the pagan ethic which, when faith in God and Immortality had gone, carried into the next, the agnostic, age and evangelical faith in duty and renunciation,

[1] God! she is like a milk-white lamb that bleats
For man's protection.

God! indeed. But this is Keats (1817), and is Rousseau's Sophie rather than Fielding's Sophia. One does not easily picture Emma Woodhouse (1816) bleating for Keats.

3

was a woman's ethic. George Eliot's rank in literature has, perhaps, not yet been determined: in the history of ideas her place is fixed. She is the moralist of the Victorian revolution.

That the ethic could be so transposed from a Christian to a Stoic key shows how native the discipline was. It had its roots deep down in the habits of a northern race,[1] vigorous and self-controlled, not sensitive but not unkindly, in country rectories and manor houses, in the congregations of City churches, in the meeting houses of Yorkshire clothing towns. It rose and spread with the advance of the class which principally sustained it: Wesley and his followers carried it into regions which the old churches had hardly touched; Wilberforce and Hannah More brought wit and fashion to its support; Cowper brought poetry. By the beginning of the nineteenth century virtue was advancing on a broad invincible front. The French wars made England insular, and conscious of its insularity, as it had not been since the Conquest. The Evangelicals gave to the island a creed which was at once the basis of its morality and the justification of its wealth and power, and, with the creed, that sense of being an Elect People which, set to a more blatant tune, became a principal element in Late Victorian Imperialism. By about 1830 their work was done. They had driven the grosser kinds of cruelty, extravagance, and profligacy underground. They had established a certain level of behaviour for all who wished to stand well with their fellows. In moralizing society they had made social disapproval a force which the boldest sinner might fear.

By the beginning of the Victorian age the faith was already hardening into a code. Evangelicalism at war with habit and indifference, with vice and brutality, with slavery, duelling, and bull-baiting, was a very different thing from Evangelicalism grown complacent, fashionable, superior. Even its charity had acquired what a Yorkshire manufacturer once grimly styled a 'diffusive, itinerant quality'. The impulses it had quickened showed at their best in the upper ranks of society, where they

[1] I may refer to Hazlitt's contrast of Northern and Southern manners in *Hot and Cold* (Plain Speaker).

had been absorbed into an older tradition of humour, culture, and public duty; or at the Universities, where they blended with new currents of intellectual eagerness and delight. The piety of a fine scholar like Peel or a haughty Border lord like Graham, of Gladstone or Sidney Herbert, had not much in common with the soul-saving theology of the money-making witness-bearers, those serious people whose indifference to national affairs Bright was one day to deplore. But, morally, their way of life was the same. Evangelicalism had imposed on society, even on classes which were indifferent to its religious basis and unaffected by its economic appeal, its code of Sabbath observance, responsibility, and philanthropy; of discipline in the home, regularity in affairs; it had created a most effective technique of agitation, of private persuasion and social persecution. On one of its sides, Victorian history is the story of the English mind employing the energy imparted by Evangelical conviction to rid itself of the restraints which Evangelicalism had laid on the senses[1] and the intellect; on amusement, enjoyment, art; on curiosity, on criticism, on science.

2

The Evangelical discipline, secularized as respectability, was the strongest binding force in a nation which without it might have broken up, as it had already broken loose. For a generation and more the static conception of society[2] had been dissolving

---

[1] Kingsley (who described Shelley as a lewd vegetarian) correctly diagnosed Byron as an Evangelical gone wrong. Byron's objection to mixed bathing, even when the parties are married, as 'very indelicate', comes from his Venetian period.

[2] As explained, for example, by an Irish judge in 1798. 'Society consists of noblemen, baronets, knights, esquires, gentlemen, yeomen, tradesmen and artificers.' The jury found that, as the subject had ceased to be a breeches maker without

because society itself was dissolving. 'A nobleman, a gentleman, a yeoman,' Cromwell told one of his Parliaments, 'that is a good interest.' But the good interest was splitting into a hundred aristocracies and a hundred democracies, button-makers and gentlemen button-makers,[1] all heels and elbows, jostling, pushing, snubbing, presuming. On the whole, the articulate classes, whose writings and conversation make opinion, were gainers by the change – it has been estimated, for example, that between 1815 and 1830 the purchasing capacity of the classes above the wage-earning level was all but doubled – and the Victorian belief in progress was buttoned on the complacency which comes of steadily rising incomes and steadily improving security. Mixed with this, no doubt, was the vulgar pride in mere quantity, the thoughtless exultation of a crowd in motion. But no one can read for long in the literature of the thirties and forties without touching a finer and deeper pride, portentously draped in tables of trade and revenue and the publications of the Useful Knowledge Society, but glowing with the authentic sense of war and victory, man against nature, and reason against the traditions of the elders.

Great things are done when men and mountains meet.

To travellers descending from the moorlands, the smoke and roar of Lancashire seemed like the smoke and roar of a battle-field, and the discipline of the factories like the discipline of a great army. It is hardly an accident that the first history of the Renaissance came from Liverpool[2] and that the most conspic-uous memorial of the Utilitarians is a History of Greece. Across the ages, the modern Englishman recognized his peers.

But we must be careful if we are to keep the picture true, not to view the early Victorian age of production through that distorting medium, the late Victorian age of finance. Science touched the imagination by its tangible results. It was immersed

becoming a gentleman, he must be a yeoman.
[1] For whom there were separate doors in the Birmingham taverns.
[2] 'The historian of the Age of Leo (Roscoe) has brought into cultivation the extensive tract of Chatmoss.' (Mrs Barbauld, 1811.)

in matter, and it conformed directly to the Augustan canon of historic progress by its immediate contribution to the 'order, regularity, and refinement of life'. Romance and the Revolution bred ideas of human purpose which only slowly permeated the English mind. Even in 1830 – far more powerfully in 1840 – they were beginning to work. But the common intelligence was still dominated by the solid humanism of the Augustans, to which the Eighteenth Proposition of Oxford Liberalism would have seemed a self-evident truth:

> Virtue is the child of Knowledge: Vice of Ignorance: therefore education, periodical literature, railroad travelling, ventilation, and the arts of life, when fully carried out, serve to make a population moral and happy.[1]

'The objects of this Society', so ran the prospectus of the Rochdale Pioneers, 'are the moral and intellectual advancement of its members. It provides them with groceries, butcher's meat, drapery goods, clothes and clogs.' Gas-lighting of the streets was hardly an improvement so much as a revolution in public security;[2] cheap cotton goods in personal cleanliness, colza lamps in domestic comfort. Finance, the manipulation of wealth and credit as things by themselves, three or four degrees removed from the visible crop or ore, was an adjunct. Production was the thing itself.

A generation which has come to take invention for granted and is, perhaps, more sensitive to its mischief than its benefits, cannot easily recover the glory of an age when knowledge, and with it power, seemed to have been released for an illimitable destiny.[3] The Englishman might reluctantly allow that in social

---

[1] Newman, *Apologia*, Note A. But what does *serve* mean? The almost magical effect of ventilation on the moral habits (temper and sobriety) of a poor quarter was demonstrated again and again.

[2] 'Without presuming to play on words,' said the Lambeth magistrate 'I regard gas as essential to an enlightened police.' It was once proposed to illuminate thieves' quarters with lamps of a special construction so that law-abiding pedestrians should pass by on the other side.

[3] The admiration of Bacon, almost amounting to a rediscovery, is very characteristic of the period. So is the Utilitarian preference for the more scholastic, less imaginative Hobbes. When his editor, Molesworth, stood for Southwark the

amenity the French, in care for the well-being of the people the Prussians, went beyond him. He might at moments be chilled by the aesthetic failure of his time, so profuse and yet so mean: alienated by its ethical assurance, at once so pretentious and so narrow. In a petulant mood, he would talk, with Grote, of the Age of Steam and Cant, but all the while he knew that in the essential business of humanity, the mastery of brute nature by intelligence, he had outstripped the world, and the Machine was the emblem and the instrument of his triumph. The patriotism of early Victorian England, not yet blooded by the Crimean War and the Indian Mutiny, irritated by Napoleon III, or exalted by the vision of empire, was at heart a pride in human capacity, which time had led to fruition in England; and in the great humanist, who brought all history to glorify the age of which he was the most honoured child, it heard its own voice speaking.[1]

To articulate the creed of progress, to state its evidences and draw out its implications, was the mission of that remarkable group of men variously known as the Utilitarians, or the Philosophic Radicals. In discipleship or reaction no young mind of the thirties could escape their influence. Bentham's alliance with James Mill, Mill's friendship with Malthus and Ricardo, had created a party, almost a sect, with formularies as compact as the Evangelical theology, and conclusions not less inexorable. However far the Benthamite discipline went, he would find the old sage had been there before him; every trail was blazed, every pitfall marked, and in every path stood a lion, the Sinister Interest of Privilege. Between rulers and ruled there exists an inherent antagonism[2] which can only be resolved if rulers and

populace paraded the streets shouting NO OBBS.

[1] *Il a son orgueil d'homme.* Taine's fine saying of Macaulay is true of his whole age. 'That wicked XVIII century' died hard: under his Romantic ornament Macaulay is through and through Augustan; and contemporary critics (Brougham and Harriet Martineau are examples) reproduce against him the charges which the early Romantics had laid against Gibbon – materialism and want of philosophy.

[2] Translate this into economic terms, substitute for the antagonism of rulers and ruled the antagonism of employers and employed, and some curious conclusions will follow which the Socialists of the next age were ready to draw.

ruled are identified by means of universal suffrage and the ballot-box, and the identity is preserved by publicity and a cheap press.[1] The sovereignty thus created is to be exercised through a carefully balanced system: of Parliament to legislate, central organs to direct, local organs to execute. On the question of Women's Suffrage, the Utilitarians were somewhat inconsistently divided; Bentham, a flirtatious old bachelor, being more logical than James Mill, who, in spite of Malthus, had begotten more children than he could afford on a female whom he despised. On all other matters, above all on the sovereign authority of Economic Law, they spoke with one voice.

Reduced from an aspiration to a schedule, progress might seem a gloomy business for the mass of mankind. It rests on competition, and always and everywhere competition is reducing the profits of the employer, and the wages of the workman, to the level of bare subsistence. Only the landowner, the common enemy of all, continually profits by the growing demand for sites, and for food, because, always and everywhere, population is pressing on the means to live. Such is the law. But Nature has not left her children without all hope of escaping the fate to which her mathematics seem to have consigned them. By industry, and abstinence, the employer may enlarge the market for his goods; by industry, and continence, the workman may increase the purchasing power, and limit the numbers, of his class: progress, like salvation, is the reward of virtue; of diligence and self-education; of providence and self-control; and all the evolutionary speculation of the next age, has for background Malthus's Stoic vision of that remote, austere, divinity 'whose purpose is ever to bring a mind out of the clod'.

In the early thirties the Philosophic Radicals were a portent, men whose meetings were watched, the spearhead of a

---

[1] 'The principle of human nature, upon which the necessity of government is founded, the propensity of one man to possess himself of the objects of desire at the cost of another, leads on, by infallible sequence, not only to that degree of plunder which leaves the members (except the instruments and recipients) the bare means of subsistence, but to that degree of cruelty which is necessary to keep in existence the most intense terrors.' – James Mill on Government.

revolution beginning with the ballot and going on, Heaven knew how far, to compulsory education and a federated Empire. Then, frigid and scholastic, as a party they fade from the view. The popular Radicals, hotter against Church and Lords, and readier champions of the unprivileged and the opposed, made more noise; and people preferred the Tories. Grote lived to decline a peerage; when the ballot was at last conceded in 1872 John Mill had decided that he did not want it and had moved on to proportional representation instead; Leader vanished into an aesthetic Italian exile; Molesworth's features are more familiar at Ottawa than his name at Westminster. The case for Free Trade was taken out of their hands by men who had learnt their economics in the counting-house, their logic on the platform, and their rhetoric in the pulpit.[1] But they had done inestimable service. They came down into a world where medieval prejudice, Tudor Law, Stuart economics, and Hanoverian patronage still luxuriated in wild confusion, and by the straight and narrow paths they cut we are walking still. The Gladstonian Liberals have gone where the Peelites followed the Canningites; the Evangelical creed long ago foundering on the Impregnable Rock of Holy Scripture, and the great Whig name has not been heard for fifty years. But it would be hard to find any corner of our public life where the spirit of Bentham is not working to-day.

It is dangerous to force historic movements into exaggerated symmetry. But the parallel operation of Evangelicalism and Utilitarianism cannot be ignored. Their classics, Malthus on *Population* and Wilberforce's *Practical View*, appeared almost simultaneously, one in 1797, the other in 1798. Their greatest victories in public affairs, the Abolition of Slavery and the Reform of the Poor Law, were won in 1833 and 1834. When a distracted Government threw the Old Poor Law at a Royal Commission, the Benthamites rose to the height of their opportunity. The Secretary of the Commission was Edwin

---

[1] The supersession of Charles Villiers by Cobden, Bright, and W. J. Fox is typical.

Chadwick, whom the Patriarch had selected to be his apostle to the new age, and in his hands there was no fear lest the faith should grow cold. Born in 1800, in a Lancashire farmhouse where the children were washed all over, every day, the mainspring of Chadwick's career seems to have been a desire to wash the people of England all over, every day, by administrative order. In practical capacity Chadwick was the greatest, in the character of his mind, in the machine-like simplicity of his ideas and the inexhaustible fertility of his applications, the most typical of the Benthamites. Napoleon III once asked him what he thought of his improvements in Paris. 'Sir,' he answered, 'it was said of Augustus that he found Rome brick and left it marble. May it be said of you that you found Paris stinking and left it sweet.' It might stand for Chadwick's epitaph. He found England stinking. If he did not leave it sweet, the fault was certainly not his. Through the Poor Law Commission, the Benthamite formula inquiry, legislation, execution, inspection, and report – was incorporated in our working constitution. It was rounded off by the invention of the Public Audit and the Grant-in-aid to tighten central control and stimulate local activity. But the corresponding formula for unofficial effort – information, agitation, the parent society, the local branch, the picture,[1] and the handbill – had been discovered by the Evangelicals and humanitarians in their warfare against slavery, and by them it was imparted to the Chartists and the Free Trade League.

The Evangelical and Utilitarian movements both rested on a body of doctrine which to question was impious or irrational; in both cases the doctrine was the reflection of an exceptional experience, the religious experience of a nation undergoing a moral revival, its social experience during a revolution in the methods of production; and in both cases a larger view was certain to show that neither was a more than provisional

---

[1] For example, the fine colour prints by Smith after Morland, of the shipwrecked crew entertained by natives, whom they return to carry into slavery.

synthesis. In the meantime they furnished England with a code and a great company of interpreters: with their almost Genevan rigour, and almost Latin clarity, they imposed themselves like foreign task-masters on the large, ironic English mind, and their great doctrines were all too readily snipped into texts for the guidance of those who did not wish to think at all, and the repression of those who wished to think for themselves, into Cant for Practical Men and Cant for Serious Men. Finally, they were alike in this, that each imparted its peculiar virtue: the Evangelicals their zeal for holiness, the Utilitarians their faith in reason, to the movements, even to the reactions which sprang out of them, to Tractarians and Agnostics who denied their introspective ethic, to Tories and Socialists who challenged their conception of the competitive State.

3

Much of accident goes to the making of history, even the history of thought, which might seem to be most exempt from contingencies. The Victorian record would have been very different if Canning had lived to the years of Palmerston, if the new writers had grown up under the shadow of Byron, Keats, and Shelley. But the old men lived and the young men died. A strange pause followed their departure, and the great Victorian lights rose into a sky which, but for the rapid blaze of Bulwer Lytton, was vacant. Tennyson and Macaulay, Carlyle and Newman, Gladstone and Disraeli, Arnold and Dickens appear above the horizon together. In Sydney Smith's stately compliments to the Graduate of Oxford,[1] the eighteenth century

[1] 'He said [*Modern Painters*, I] was a work of transcendent talent, presented the most original views in the most elegant language, and would work a complete

bows itself off the stage and introduces its successor. With the appearance of *Vanity Fair* in 1847, the constellation is complete and the stars are named. It was part of the felicity of the fifties to possess a literature which was at once topical, contemporary, and classic; to meet the Immortals in the streets, and to read them with added zest for the encounter.

Anchored to its twofold faith in goodness and progress, the early Victorian mind swung wide to the alternating currents of sentiment and party spite, but the virulence of the Press,[1] and the gush of the popular novel were play on the surface of a deep assurance. There are whimperings, sometimes bellowings, of self-pity, but defiance was no longer the mode. The greater and better part of English society accepted the social structure and moral objectives of the nation, as a community of families, all rising, or to be raised, to a higher respectability. To those postulates their criticism of life was not directed: they were satisfied, not indeed with the world as it was, for they were all, in their way, reformers, but as it would become by the application of those reasoned and tested principles which made up the scheme of progress and salvation.

Poised and convinced, they could indulge, too, in a licence of feeling impossible to a generation bred in doubt, and they could take their ease in an innocent vulgarity which to a later age would have been a hard-worked and calculated Bohemianism. They could swagger and they could be maudlin. In public they could be reserved, for they were a slow and wary race, and reserve is at once the defence of the wise and the refuge of the stupid. But cynicism and superciliousness, the stigmata of a beaten age and a waning class, were alien to the hopeful, if anxious, generation which had taken the future into its hands. In their exuberance and facility, the earlier Victorians, with

revolution in the world of taste.' (*Praeterita*: Chapter ix.)
[1] It was a Cambridge joke that

> The abysmal deeps of personality

meant *The Times*.

their flowing and scented hair, gleaming jewellery and resplend-
ent waistcoats, were nearer to the later Elizabethans; they were
not ashamed; and, like the Elizabethans, their sense of the
worthwhileness of everything – themselves, their age, and their
country: what the Evangelicals called seriousness; the Arnoldians, earnestness; Bagehot, most happily, eagerness – over-
flowed in sentiment and invective, loud laughter, and sudden
reproof. Once at Bowood, when Tom Moore was singing, one
by one the audience slipped away in sobs; finally, the poet
himself broke down and bolted, and the old Marquis was left
alone. We are in an age when, if brides sometimes swooned at
the altar, Ministers sometimes wept at the Table; when the sight
of an infant school could reduce a civil servant to a passion of
tears; and one undergraduate has to prepare another undergraduate for the news that a third undergraduate has doubts
about the Blessed Trinity – an age of flashing eyes and curling
lips, more easily touched, more easily shocked, more ready to
spurn, to flaunt, to admire, and, above all, to preach.

A young man brought up in a careful home might have
heard, whether delivered or read aloud, a thousand sermons; an
active clergyman was a social asset to a rising neighbourhood,
his popularity a source of spiritual danger to himself. The form
of preachers was canvassed like the form of public entertainers,
and the circulation of some Victorian sermons is a thing to fill a
moderate writer with despair. If we consider the effect,
beginning in childhood, of all the preachers on all the
congregations, of men loud or unctuous, authoritative or
persuasive, speaking out of a body of acknowledged truth to the
respectful audience below them, we shall see why the homiletic
cadence, more briefly Cant, is so persistent in Victorian oratory
and literature. It sufficed to persuade the lower middle classes
that Tupper was a poet and the upper middle classes that
Emerson was a philosopher. Mr Gladstone formed his style by
reading sermons aloud, and his diaries are full of self-delivered
homilies.[1] Old Sir Robert Peel trained his son to repeat every

[1] He once delivered an address on Preaching (City Temple, March 22, 1877).

Sunday the discourse he had just heard, a practice to which he owed his astonishing recollection of his opponents' arguments and something, perhaps, of the unction of his own replies. The sermon was the standard vehicle of serious truth, and to the expositions and injunctions of their writers and statesmen the Victorian public brought the same hopeful determination to be instructed, and to be elevated, which held them attentive to the pleadings, denunciations, and commonplaces of their preachers.

The body of acknowledged truth, out of which this early Victorian literature speaks, appears, at first sight, to consist of little more than all those dogmas which a victorious middle class had imposed on the nation. There is not much in it which the Compleat English Tradesman could not understand, and still less that he would not approve; as he could not understand Browning, Browning had to wait outside. But to take the height of the Victorian classics we must view them from the waste land of dreary goodness, useful information, and tired humour, stretching all about them, and no one who has surveyed the exploration will underrate the genius which could raise such a fabric on such foundations. The world desired to be instructed: it was given Grote and Thirlwall, Milman and Macaulay, Lyell's *Principles of Geology*, Mill's *Logic*, Mill's *Political Economy*; to be elevated: it had *Past and Present*, *Modern Painters*, and *In Memoriam*; it asked for theology and got Newman, for education and got Arnold. Out of the Minerva Press came Disraeli, out of the horseplay of sentimental Cockneys, Dickens.

It is only necessary to set these names down in order to realize what potent agencies of dissolution were working in the early Victorian years. English society was poised on a double paradox which its critics, within and without, called hypocrisy. Its practical ideals were at odds with its religious professions, and its religious belief was at issue with its intelligence. We, for example, should probably count an employer who kept children of nine working nine hours a day in a temperature of 98 degrees as, at least, a very stupid man. If he went farther and insisted that, when they wished to lift up their hearts in song, it must not be in carnal ditties like 'A Frog He Would A' Wooing Go', but in hymns –

> By cool Siloam's glassy rill
> How sweet the lily grows,
> How sweet the scent upon the hill
> Of Sharon's dewy rose –

we might credit him with a touch of diabolical humour. We should be wrong in a matter where it is both important and difficult to go right. He may have been a low hypocrite who slept with pretty mill girls on the sly. He may have been a kindly and intelligent man who had convinced himself that only by production, kept down to the lowest cost, could the country be fed, and that the sufferings of the poor in this present time were not worthy to be compared with the glory which should be revealed in them hereafter. Or, like most of us, he may have been something in between: borne along partly by conviction, partly by example, and neither disposed nor able to analyse ideas which proved themselves by their material results. Cheap labour meant high profits; respectable workpeople meant good work.[1]

It could not last. It was impossible to maintain for ever the position that Christian responsibility was a duty everywhere except in economic life, and that strength and vigour, the control of nature by science, of events by prudence, are good things everywhere except in the hands of the State: not less impossible to suppose that the criticism which was unravelling the constitution of the rocks and the legends of antiquity, would always consent to stand in respectful submission before the conventions, or the documents, of contemporary Protestantism. So long as the fear of subversion persisted, criticism could not

---

[1] In the eighteenth century the mill often furnished the millowner's harem: in our period rarely. I cannot resist the conclusion that the current religion did sometimes act as a provocative to sadism. A ghastly story came out in the Courts of a private tutor who prayed with a backward pupil, beat him to a jelly, kissed him, and left him to die. The connexion between religious professions and fraudulent dealing started many criminals on the downward path – or so they assured the prison chaplains. But, again, this is an old story. In *Areopagitica* the City Man and his Religion almost twists a smile from Milton.

act with freedom: clerisy[1] and *bourgeoisie* stood together, and, where they differed, the clerisy, on the whole, preserved a loyal silence. Indeed, in State affairs they did not differ greatly. When, in his tract on Chartism, Carlyle essayed to translate the verities into practice, he had nothing to suggest that half the parsons in the land did not know already: that everybody should be sent to school and the odd man to the colonies. In religion they were coming to differ deeply, as the strong surviving vein of Augustan rationalism was reinforced by the conclusions of Victorian science. But the sanctions of orthodoxy were still formidable, and in a world where *Prometheus Unbound* might be judicially held to be a blasphemous libel,[2] a certain economy in the communication of unbelief was evidently advisable.

The sense of being under a Code accompanies us through the early Victorian decades. To the age of revolt, which runs from Rousseau to Shelley, succeeds the age of acquiescence; the Titans are dead, or they have been tamed. It seems as if speculation had ceased; there is an answer to every question and usually the answer is no, Milman is ostracized for calling Abraham a sheik; Miss Mitford is publicly reproved for calling a pudding a roly-poly; old lords have to guard their words for fear of shocking young lords, and a Member of Parliament wishing to say contracted pelvis must put it in the decent obscurity of a learned language. A Parliamentary Committee, who asked a factory woman if she had ever miscarried, brought on themselves the anger of *The Times* for violating the principles which should preside over such inquiries, 'a dread of ridicule and an anxious avoidance of indecency', and *The Economist*, a paper of exceptional intelligence, declined to go into the details of the Public Health Bill of 1847 and fill its columns with a number of unpleasant words. A guilty conscience has never betrayed itself by a more superior sniff. Absurdity and impropriety, like domesticated dragons, guard the stability of society and the

---

[1] Coleridge's useful word for the educated classes acting as a body.
[2] As *Queen Mab* actually was found to be in 1841.

peace of the home, and absurdity seems to mean any way of
thinking, impropriety any way of behaving, which may impair
the comfort, impeach the dignity, and weaken the defence of the
middle class. We remember with surprise that we are dealing
with a race which had once, and not so long ago, been famous
in its island for an independence and even eccentricity which it
now only displayed abroad, and we ask what has happened to
make it submit its behaviour, its language, and its ideas to this
drastic and vigilant censorship.

4

Every period of history may be interpreted in various ways, and
the richer it is in event or thought the more numerous will be
the interpretations. Early Victorian history might be read as the
formation in the thirties of a Marxian *bourgeoisie* which never
came into existence, the re-emergence in the forties of a more
ancient tradition, a sense of the past and a sense of social
coherence, which never fulfilled its promise, and a compromise
between the two which possessed no ultimate principle of
stability.[1] But we must all the time remember that the
Victorian age is only the island counterpart of a secular
movement, as significant as the turn from the Greek middle
ages in the time of Socrates or the Latin middle ages at the
Renaissance. Twice the European mind had been carried to the
verge, and twice it had been baffled. In the nineteenth century it
won the top and saw stretching before it that endless new world
which Bacon had sighted, or imagined, where nothing need
remain unknown, and for everything that is known there is
something that can be done; the world of organized thought
where even modern scientific man was only the rudiments of

[1] The three phases are conveniently marked by Miss Martineau's *Illustrations of
Political Economy*, *Coningsby*, and Bagehot's *English Constitution*.

what man might be. But European currents have a way of changing their direction when they touch our shores: it was so with the Renaissance, it was so with the Reformation. We borrowed our Party names from France and Spain; only Radical is all our own.[1] But the Conservative Party is a far more vital element in the State than a Parti Conservateur, and Continental Liberalism had little to teach a people who counted their freedom not by revolutions but by dynasties. 'You see,' said Mackintosh, when the latest French pamphlet on Liberty was exhibited for his admiration, 'in England we take all that for granted.' Of Continental Socialism we may say we gave as good as we took, and the Nationalism, which was to glorify the heroisms and to poison the conflicts of a century, made little appeal to a race which had no memories of foreign oppression to brood over, and is always more disposed to grudge the cost of its victories than to spend fresh money in avenging its defeats. On the other hand, the special and domestic preoccupations which give the European movement its English colour, being of a kind which our peculiar and isolated history had engendered, the call of the sea, the constant embarrassment of English policy by Irish agitation, the persistence of the religious interest into a secularist age, aristocracy into a commercial age, and monarchy into a radical age, cannot be expounded in European terms.

To all these themes, the ground-tone was given by the growth of population, the result of many combining tendencies, humanitarian and scientific, which since the middle of the eighteenth century had operated with ever-increasing force.[2] In 1730 it seems that of every four children born in London three failed to reach their fifth birthday. A hundred years of improvement had almost reversed the proportion.[3] Life was

---

[1] Possibly Communism, which is claimed, as a colloquial inspiration, for Mr Barmby of Hanwell. He must be distinguished from Mr Baume, who planned a Communist University at Colney Hatch.

[2] It was a European phenomenon. The French death-rate seems to have fallen from 39 to 29 between 1780 and 1820.

[3] This is London over all. The infantile mortality about 1840 was – upper classes 1/10; middle classes 1/6; lower classes 1/4. In Manchester and Leeds the mortality under 5 was about 57/100.

safer and longer, and every census was swelled by the numbers of babies who now grew up, young people who now lived into manhood, old people who lingered on the earth which a hundred years before they would have quitted in middle life. But if the process was a just ground for pride, the results could not be contemplated without deep apprehension, and the gravity of the problem was at once demonstrated and accentuated by the state of Ireland, from which, crossing St George's Channel at deck cargo rates, the starving Papists swarmed by thousands to gather the harvest in English fields or fill the slums of English towns. Those who traced them home, in books, or by the new tourist route to Killarney, and heard or saw for themselves the worse-than-animal wretchedness of a people withal so intelligent and so chaste, might well ask themselves what relief was in prospect unless Nature intervened and ordained depopulation on a scale from which Cromwell might have shrunk, and whether the misery of Ireland was not a foreshadowing of the doom of England herself.[1]

The only visible relief was by way of emigration, and already some minds had been fired by the thoughts of the great spaces waiting to be peopled or, with an even larger sweep of the imagination, by the picture of a vast Eastern Empire ruled from Australia. But the English of 1830, with six generations of the Law of Settlement behind them, were not easily up-rooted, and, publicly, the only restraint that could be recommended was late marriage and the abolition of those provisions of the Poor Law which set a premium on reckless unions. There was much active, if furtive, discussion of birth-control in Radical circles: John Mill was once in trouble for poking pamphlets down area

---

[1] Down to the French wars England had been on balance a wheat-exporting country. After Waterloo it was plain that the balance had been reversed and that foreign wheat, though there were still years when the import only amounted to a few days' consumption, was normally required to make good the English harvest. The sliding scale of 1828 was contrived to steady home prices, and therefore rents, while admitting foreign supplies as they were needed: in theory the Radicals preferred Free Trade, in theory the Whigs were for a fixed duty; but in the early thirties the issue was not raised, the schism between the commercial and landed interests was latent and speculative.

railings; and one writer proposed that instruction in the subject should be included in the rules of all Trade Unions.[1] But contraception did not seriously affect the birth-rate until, in the seventies, it returned from America, to which it had been carried by the younger Owen. Malthus had raised a spectre which could be neither ignored nor laid.

More immediately significant than the growth of population waits aggregation in great towns. Down to the French wars the moral habit of society was definitely patrician and rural, and had still much of the ease, the tolerance, and the humour which belongs to a life lived in security and not divorced from nature. What differences existed in the lives and outlook of a gentleman, a yeoman, and a cottager were mitigated by their common subjection to the ebb and flow of the world, the seasons, and the hours. In correspondence with its traditional structure, the traditional culture and morality of England were based on the patriarchal village family of all degrees: the father worked, the mother saw to the house, the food, and the clothes; from the parents the children learnt the crafts and industries necessary for their livelihood, and on Sundays they went together, great and small, to worship in the village church. To this picture English sentiment clung, as Roman sentiment saw in the Sabine farm the home of virtue and national greatness. It inspired our poetry; it controlled our art; for long it obstructed, perhaps it still obstructs, the formation of a true philosophy of urban life.

But all the while Industrialism had been coming over England like a climatic change; the French wars masked the consequences till they became almost unmanageable. It is possible to imagine, with Robert Owen, an orderly evolution of the rural village into the industrial township, given the conditions which he enjoyed at New Lanark, a limited size and a resident, paternal employer. Belper under the Strutts, Bolton under the Ashworths, the cosy houses and flourishing gardens of

[1] Wade in his *History of the Middle Classes* (if indeed I have correctly interpreted his mysterious hintings). Place gave instruction at Charing Cross; Mrs Grote, I suspect, more than instruction to her village neighbours. Croker's attack on Miss Martineau was quite unpardonable, but it is fairly clear that Miss Martineau did not know what she was talking about.

South Hetton, to which foreign visitors were carried with special pride, the playing fields of Price's Candle Works, the Lancashire village where Coningsby met Edith, all have some affinity with the Owenite Utopia, bold peasants, rosy children, smoking joints, games on the green; Merrie England, in a word, engaged in a flourishing export trade in coal and cotton.[1] But any possibility of a general development along these lines had already been lost in the change-over from water to steam power, in the consequent growth of the great urban aggregates, and the visible splitting of society, for which the Enclosures had created a rural precedent, into possessors and proletariat. The employers were moving into the country; their officials following them into the suburbs; the better workmen lived in the better streets; the mixed multitude of labour, native or Irish, was huddled in slums and cellars, sometimes newly run up by speculative builders, sometimes, like the labyrinth round Soho and Seven Dials, deserted tenements of the upper classes. In a well-managed village with a responsible landlord and an active parson, with allotments for the men and a school for the children, the old institutions and restraints might still hold good; in a neglected village, and in that increasing part of the population which now lived in great towns, they were perishing. Off work, the men could only lounge and drink; the girls learnt neither to cook nor to sew. Lying outside the orbit of the old ruling class, neglected by their natural leaders, the industrial territories were growing up as best they might, undrained, unpoliced, ungoverned, and unschooled.

Yet the physical separation was not so complete that the world beyond the pale could be ignored, and the Evangelical ascesis was imposed on a generation to which the spectacle of bodily existence was at once obstrusive and abhorrent. Physically, the national type was changing; the ruddy, careless Englishman of the eighteenth century, turbulent but placable, as

---

[1] I have read an Owenite fancy of the thirties in which the world is organized as a federation of Garden Cities. One episode is the return of a delegation, clad in chitons, from Bavaria, where, if I remember right, they have been showing their German brethren how to lay a drain.

ready with his friendship as his fists, seemed to be making way for a pallid, sullen stock, twisted in mind and body. And if the eye which ranged with such complacency over the palaces of Regent's Park, the thronging masts of wide-wayed Liverpool, the roaring looms of hundred-grated Leeds, descended to a closer view, of Finsbury, say, or Ancoats, it would have observed that the breeding ground of the new race was such that in truth it could breed nothing else. The life within the factory or the mine was doubtless rigorous, and to children often cruel, but the human frame is immensely resilient, and with such care as many good employers took, the working hours of a labourer's life were probably his happiest. But the imagination can hardly apprehend the horror in which thousands of families a hundred years ago were born, dragged out their ghastly lives, and died: the drinking water brown with faecal particles, the corpses kept unburied for a fortnight in a festering London August; mortified limbs quivering with maggots; courts where not a weed would grow, and sleeping-dens afloat with sewage.[1]

And while the new proletariat was falling below the median line of improving decency on one side, the middle classes were rising above it on the other, becoming progressively more regular, more sober, more clean in body, more delicate in speech. But not only were the middle classes drawing apart from the poor, each stratum, in a steady competition, was drawing away from the stratum next below, accentuating its newly acquired refinements, and enforcing them with censorious vigilance. The capriciousness, the over-emphasis, of Victorian propriety betrays its source. When we have set aside all that

---

[1] The following figures tell their own tale:

Expectation of Life at Birth

	Bath	Rutland	Wilts.	Derby	Truro	Leeds	Manchester	Liverpool
Gentlefolk	55	52	50	49	40	45	38	35
Traders & farmers	37	41	48	38	33	27	20	22
Labourers	25	38	33	21	28	19	17	15

In London the mortality was twice as great in the East End as in the West. In adjacent streets it varied from 38 to 12.

England shared with New England, all that nineteenth-century England had in common with nineteenth-century France[1] and Germany, and all that the England of Victoria had in common with the England of George III[2] and Edward VIII, there remains this peculiar element, what Clough called 'an almost animal sensibility of conscience', this super-morality of the nerves and the senses, of bodily repulsion and social alarm.

Cleanliness is next to godliness. The Victorian insistence, whenever the poor are the topic, on neatness, tidiness, the well-brushed frock and the well-swept room, is significant. 'The English', Treitschke once told a class at Berlin, 'think Soap is Civilization.' Neatness is the outward sign of a conscious Respectability, and Respectability is the name of that common level of behaviour which all families ought to reach and on which they can meet without disgust. The Respectable man in every class is one whose ways bear looking into, who need not slink or hide or keep his door barred against visitors, the parson, or the dun, who lives in the eye of his neighbours and can count on the approval of the great and the obedience of the humble. 'The middle classes know', Lord Shaftesbury once said, 'that the safety of their lives and property depends upon their having round them a peaceful, happy, and moral population.' To induce, therefore, some modicum of cleanliness and foresight, to find some substitute for savage sport and savage drinking, to attract the children to school and the parents to church, to awaken some slight interest in books and the world beyond the end of the streets, on such limited, necessary ends as these was bent that enormous apparatus of early Victorian philanthropy: of individual effort by squires and parsons and their wives and daughters,[3] of organized effort by Hospital Committees, City

---

[1] Much nonsense about 'the Victorians' is dissipated by the reflection that it was the French Government that prosecuted *Madame Bovary*.

[2] In 1804 Crabb Robinson wrote from Germany: 'To express what we should call Puritanism in language, and excess of delicacy in matters of physical love, the word Engländerei has been coined.'

[3] As early as the twenties, the young lady in the country was expected to do her district-visiting seriously, with a register and account book. It is, I think, true to say that the pruriency which we find so offensive in Victorian morals (the Blush-to-the-

Missions, Savings Banks, Mechanics' Institutes, and Dispensaries, by institutions of every creed and size and object, from the Coal Club, the Blanket Club, and the Ladies' Child Bed Linen Club up to the great societies for the diffusion of useful knowledge, religious knowledge, education, and temperance, and the provision of additional Curates. Respectability was at once a select status and a universal motive. Like Roman citizenship, it could be indefinitely extended, and every extension fortified the State.

5

In 1830 one aspect, and not the least formidable, of the new civilization, was suddenly forced on every mind. For half a generation, the cholera had been wandering at large across Asia and eastern Europe. It spread, in spite of the most active precautions, into Germany; from Hamburg it crossed to Sunderland; in a few weeks it was in London. Measures were hastily improvised to meet a visitation which might, for all that science could tell, be as destructive as the Great Plague. A Central Board of Health was established in London; local boards in the provinces; a day of fasting and humiliation was proclaimed. Of the local boards the most active was in Manchester, and the report of their secretary – it is only thirty pages long – is one of the cardinal documents of Victorian history. For the first time the actual condition of a great urban population was exposed to view. There was no reason to suppose that Manchester was any worse than other towns, and the inevitable conclusion was that an increasing portion of the population of England was living under conditions which were

Cheek-of-the-Young-Person business) is mainly an urban, and therefore middle-class, characteristic. There could not have been much about the 'facts of life' that a country girl who taught in school and visited in cottages did not know.

not only a negation of civilized existence, but a menace to civilized society.

Nor, it seemed, was the country-side in better condition. The Labourers' Rising of 1830 served, like the cholera, to call attention to a problem which without it might have been neglected till it was too late. The land was breaking under the burden of the poor rate, and the administration of the Poor Law was degrading the labourer whom it was designed to support. But the rural problem was simplicity itself compared with the problem of the towns. Let the able-bodied man be given the choice of earning his own living or going into the workhouse, and then, if he still cannot find work on the land, send him to the factory or the colonies. So long as the Poor Law Commissioners were at work in the south, pauperism, disappeared as by magic. But, as they moved northwards, unexpected difficulties appeared. 'We grasped the nettle all right,' one of them, ruefully acknowledged, 'but it was the wrong nettle.' Machinery had so reduced the value of labour that at any moment the workman might find himself starving in the midst of a plenty which his own hands had helped to create. But the urban problem could not be solved by marching the unemployed in and out of the workhouse as times were bad or good. That rural England was over-populated, the slow increase, in some counties a decline, through the years of prosperity proved. Industrial England was neither over-populated nor under-populated, but periodically over- and under-employed.

Unemployment was beyond the scope of any ideas which Early Victorian reformers had at their command, largely because they had no word for it.[1] Their language and their minds were dominated by the Malthusian conception of over-population. Sanitation and education were within their reach. But these are remedies which need time to do their work, and in the interim the catastrophe might have happened. A fermentation unknown to an earlier England was stirring in the

---

[1] It only becomes common in the eighties. Thornton's (very able) *Treatise on Overpopulation* (1845) is really an analysis of unemployment.

commons. Eighteenth-century society was stable, and felt itself to be stable. From the Revolution to the fall of the Bastille, the thought of subversion, of any social crisis more serious than an election riot or a no-popery riot, never entered the mind of Governments. From Waterloo to 1848 it was hardly ever absent. Looking back from the serene and splendid noon of mid-Victorian propriety, Kingsley wrote of the years when 'young lads believed (and not so wrongly) that the masses were their natural enemies and that they might have to fight, any year or any day, for the safety of their property and the honour of their sisters'. Young lads will believe anything. But men old enough to remember the French Revolution, or the Committees of Secrecy and the Six Acts of 1819, had their fears, too, when they reflected that as the country became more and more dependent on machines, its stability turned more and more on the subordination and goodwill of the savage masses which tended them.

To fortify the State against these and all other perils by admitting the respectable class as a body to the franchise was the purpose of the Reform Bill. For two years, beginning with the Paris Revolution of July 1830, England lived in a sustained intensity of excitement unknown since 1641. But when the dust had settled down Tories might have asked themselves what they had been afraid of, Radicals what they had been fighting for. Never was a revolution effected with more economy in change. The right of the magnate to appoint the representatives of the lesser boroughs had gone: his influence, if he chose to exercise it with discretion and decorum, was hardly impaired, and it soon appeared that if there was less rioting and less bribery at an election, there was still much bribery, and more intimidation, and election day was still a carnival which usually ended in a fight. Open voting kept the tenant under his landlord's eye; the tradesman under his customer's; and in every county the fifty-pound tenants at will, prudently enfranchised by a Tory amendment, made a solid block of dependable voters. The country was satisfied: even the Radicals accepted the Reform Bill as a fair instalment of their demands without pressing to know when the other instalments – the ballot, one man one vote, one vote one value – would be paid.[1]

The reforming impulse of the Whigs was exhausted with the passing of the Municipal Reform Act of 1835. The reorganization of the Judicature which Brougham ought to have effected in 1833 was left for Selborne in 1873. Graham, their best administrator, Stanley their best debater, left them. Lord Grey gave up; Lord Melbourne lounged along. The genial Althorp, who kept the Commons in good temper, was taken from them to the Lords. Harried by the Irish, baited by the Radicals, blocked by the Peers, divided among themselves, equally unable to pass their Bills or balance their budgets, the Whigs sank in public esteem and dragged Parliament with them. Their one admitted success did them as much harm as their numerous failures. They kept Ireland quiet, but their pacts with O'Connell seemed to English opinion a disgraceful subservience to a rebel. They accepted Penny Postage, but on a falling revenue it sent their finance to pieces. Palmerston, marching steadily and buoyantly on a line of his own, brightened their last days with a diplomatic triumph over France and a naval victory over Mehemet Ali, of which, perhaps, in the long run, the most that can be said is that it gave England something to think of beside the misery of 1840. All through the thirties we are aware of a growing disaffection, of which Carlyle and Dickens are mouthpieces, with the delays and irrelevancies[2] of parliamentary

---

[1] The figures of the first registration show how oligarchical the new Constitution was:

| Counties, England | 345,000 | Scotland 33,000. |
| Boroughs, England | 275,000 | Scotland 31,000. |

The £10 householder in town was in effect a man with £150 a year and upward: without exaggerating it, as the Tories were inclined to do, one must still remember that Reform did disenfranchise a large number of working men. Boroughs of 200 and 300 voters were still common: Thetford had 146. In very general terms one might say that from 1832 to 1867 one man in six had a vote, after 1867 one in three. In the same period over fifty returns were set aside for malpractices. *Electorate* is a L.V. word: *constituency* which appeared (colloquially) for the first time in 1830/1 originally meant *the whole body of electors*: then, *a particular body*.

[2] And mysteries. The procedural history of Parliament is a struggle between an old principle (freedom of debate) and a new one (to make a programme and get

We declare, then, that nothing has yet happened to mitigate those apprehensions which within the last fortnight we have from day to day expressed, of evil likely to befal the new reign, if the probable causes of it should not be well examined and prepared against. The very depth and fulness of his loyal attachment to his QUEEN ought to make a virtuous Englishman so much the more solicitous to protect her from perils of which it is scarcely in the nature of things that she should of herself be conscious.

The proceedings of yesterday have not dispelled our fears; but, on the contrary, much tended to enhance them. Subscribing to all that has been announced as to the correct and becoming manner in which HER MAJESTY, on this first performance of a public duty, read the declaration composed for her, and demeaned herself before the members of her Council, we are still bound to regard that declaration on the same constitutional ground which governs the construction of KINGS' speeches to Parliament—as merely the declaration of the Minister by whom it was framed. And who is that Minister? No other than Lord MELBOURNE, the Whig slave of the Radical JOSEPH HUME, and of the anti-Saxon Papist, O'CONNELL—the same Lord MELBOURNE, who has for these two last years and more been levying open war against, or trickily undermining, the ancient laws, the fundamental institutions, and the Protestant monarchy of Great Britain. Has he (under the tuition of Middlesex JOSEPH) turned black into white? Has this Whig-Radical " Ethiopian changed his skin? "—" this " leper" of Popery " his spots ?"

The Times *celebrates the Queen's Ascension*, 21 *June* 1837

The decision of the Cabinet is no longer a secret. Parliament, it is confidently reported, is to be summoned for the first week in January; and the Royal Speech will, it is added, recommend an immediate consideration of the Corn Laws, preparatory to their total repeal. Sir ROBERT PEEL in one house, and the Duke of WELLINGTON in the other, will, we are told, be prepared to give immediate effect to the recommendation thus conveyed.

An announcement of such immeasurable importance, and to the larger portion of the community so unspeakably gratifying, almost precludes the possibility of comment. No pen can keep pace with the reflections which must spontaneously crowd upon every thoughtful and sensitive mind. They who have long desired this change, and have long traced its manifold bearings on the welfare and happiness of the world, will in one moment see the realization of that fair prospect, and will hardly endure to be informed of what they already behold. The approaching event, therefore, which we this day communicate to our readers, must be left to speak for itself.

From The Times, 4 *December* 1845

30

government, which, as the years went on, seemed to be degenerating more and more into an unseemly scuffle between Ins and Outs. The political satire of Dickens is tedious and ignorant. But it registers, what *Past and Present* conveys more passionately, the disillusionment which followed on the hopes of 1830.

Socially, the first reformed Parliaments were hardly distinguishable from their predecessors. The days of extravagant expenditure, when the poll was open for three weeks and a candidate might spend, as the virtuous and religious Acland did in Devon, £80,000 on four contests, were over and done with. But an election might easily cost a candidate £5,000.[1] The just influence of landed property was preserved, and the old humanity of the South was still politically ascendant over the new industry of the North. The Whigs had introduced a self-adjusting device into the constitution, but it worked slowly. So late as 1845 three notes of exclamation were required to convey Prince Albert's amazement at the thought of Cobden in the Cabinet. The Tories had learnt by experience to adopt capacity from whatever quarter it appeared: they admitted Peel, the son of a cotton-spinner; Canning, whose mother was an actress; and Huskisson, whose origin, if possibly more respectable, was even more obscure. The Whigs in exile had drawn closer together and farther from the main stream of English life; they came from the eighteenth century, where privilege was taken for granted, and they brought the eighteenth century with them; and one result of the Reform was to give England, growing more and more resentful of privilege, the most aristocratic Government that any one could remember, and to set the Lords almost in equipoise with the Commons. And all the while, with a suspicious, but obedient, party behind him – 150 in '32, 250 in

through it). In the thirties, freedom exercised through (*a*) a multitude of formal stages, (*b*) irrelevant amendments on going into Committee or adjourning, was in the ascendant. The public, intensely interested in Parliament, was in consequence often baffled to know what Parliament was doing or why.

[1] Bringing voters to the poll (abolished in 1885) was the main item. The commonest malpractice was impersonation. In one borough election in 1838, out of 310 votes given, 109 were challenged on that ground.

'34, 300 in '37 – Peel was biding his time. With the return of the Conservatives in 1841 and the impending grapple of Land and Industry, Parliament recovered its standing as the debating-place of public issues, and, what to the new electorate was even more important, as the guardian of the public purse. The country preferred an Income tax from Peel to one deficit more from Baring.

Until 1834 the traveller approaching London over Westminster Bridge saw on his left a foreshore where watermen lounged among their boats: behind it a walled garden fronting a low range of red-brick Tudor houses. At the far left the chapel of St Stephen projected almost to the water's edge, and high above all stretched the grey roof of the Hall. The towers of the Abbey were just visible behind. After the fire of 1834 the Commons found room in the old House of Lords, the Peers sat in the Painted Chamber, while the palace of Barry and Pugin was rising to overshadow both Abbey and Hall: the Lords entered their new house in 1847: the Commons in 1852. Business commonly began at four, mornings being kept for Committees, with questions, few, but often involving voluminous reply, and followed by some desultory conversation, and the presentation of petitions. These opportunities for demagogic eloquence, which at one time threatened to overwhelm the House, were cautiously restricted, and finally abolished in 1843. Two nights were reserved for Government business. Lord John Russell tried to get a third and was refused. Party allegiance was loose, party management dexterous and sharp. Private members had more freedom and opportunity than in a modern Parliament, and much legislation was drafted, introduced, and carried from the back benches.[1] After the first few speeches the audience scattered to dinner and left the bores in possession. From nine the attendance and the excitement increased. There was no eleven o'clock rule, and often the sun was up before the

---

[1] The career of Ewart (son of Mr Gladstone's godfather) is typical. He was in Parliament thirty-four years. He carried three important bills (capital punishment, defence of felons, public libraries) besides being very active on free trade, schools of design, and competitive examination. But he was never in office.

G.M. Young

Commons, with parched throats and throbbing heads, escaped
to enjoy, if they could, the majestic spectacle of London from
the bridges, before the smoke had risen to make every street
dark and every face dirty.

The manners of Parliament in the thirties seem to have been
the worst on record, and they were not improved when, in 1835,
the Whigs, in their brief interval of Opposition, chose to put out
a strong Speaker, Manners Sutton, and put in a weak one,
Abercromby.[1] Under his amiable governance, with the windows shut – and the stench of the Thames made it impossible to
keep them open – the mooings, cat-calls, and cock-crows, what
O'Connell once called the 'beastly bellowings', of the faithful
Commons, could be heard fifty yards away. The eloquence
which could master such an audience was of a new kind. The
great rhetorical tradition which begins with Halifax and runs
through Pitt and Canning, sent up an expiring flash in
Macaulay. The modern manner was less declamatory and more
closely reasoned: we might call it more conventional if we
remember that conversation still kept some of the amplitude of
an earlier day.[2] Speeches were very long, but the contentions
over the currency and the fiscal system had created a new style,
of which Huskisson was the first exponent, Peel the most
specious master, and which Mr Gladstone wielded like a Tenth
Muse: knowledge of the facts and an apt handling of figures was
now the surest proof of capacity, and among the most
memorable feats of Victorian oratory are speeches on finance.

In this development Parliament reflected a movement in the
national mind. It was the business of the thirties to transfer the
treatment of affairs from a polemical to a statistical basis, from
Humbug to Humdrum.[3] In 1830 there were hardly any figures

[1] Lord John Russell urged the view, which fortunately did not become canonical,
that the Speaker should always be in sympathy with the majority.
[2] The Brookfields in the fifties claimed to have introduced the new style of
conversation, brisk and allusive. Mrs Carlyle used to torture London parties with the
elaboration of her anecdotes.
[3] As a symbol of the age, one might cite the Lords' Report on 'the expediency of

to work on. Even the Census was still far from perfect: in that of 1831 the acreage of England is given twice over, with a discrepancy as large as Berkshire. Imports were still reckoned by Official Values based on the prices of 1690. But statistical inquiry, fostered very largely by the development of the Insurance business, was a passion of the times. The Statistical department of the Board of Trade was founded in 1832; the department of the Registrar-General in 1838; the Royal Statistical Society sprang out of the Cambridge meeting of the British Association of 1833. Two private compilations of the thirties, McCulloch's *Statistical Account of the British Empire*[1] and Porter's *Progress of the Nation*, are still the best approach to Victorian history. Then come the great inquiries, by Parliamentary Committees or Royal Commissions, following the Poor Law Commission of 1832. To Sydney Smith it seemed that the world had been saved from the flood to be handed over to barristers of six years' standing, and a Prussian visitor apprehended that the object of the Whigs was to Germanize England by means of Royal Commissions. In a few years the public mind had been flooded with facts and figures bearing on every branch of the national life, except agriculture: the collection of agricultural statistics was resisted till the sixties. No community in history had ever been submitted to so searching an examination.[2] Copied or summarized in the Press, the Blue Books created a new attitude to affairs; they provided fresh topics for novelists and fresh themes for poets. *Sybil* is a Blue Book in fiction; *The Cry of the Children* a Blue Book in verse. With

Discontinuing the present Mode of Engrossing Acts of Parliament in Black Letter and substituting a Plain Round Hand'. But until Lord Thring took it in hand, the actual drafting of statues came far short of these good intentions.

[1] Which gives more space to Oxford than to Canada. *Empire* in E. V. English is stylistic for *realm, kingdom,* and imports no overseas reference. 'Dog's Hole Lane has been widened! Main drainage has been installed! Soon X will take her rightful place among the Cities of the Empire!' I quote from memory from the history of some 'glad aspiring little burg'.

[2] The Parliamentary papers were first put on sale in 1835; division lists first published in 1836.

the parliamentary inquiries must be ranged the local investigations made by individuals, societies, and municipalities. I have
spoken of Kay-Shuttleworth's Report on Manchester. In a few
years a score of great towns, Bristol, Westminster, Southwark,
Hull, Liverpool, Leeds, had all been put through the same mill
and with much the same results.[1] Douglas Jerrold, who had
once produced an unsuccessful play called *The Factory Girl*,
complained that in 1833 no one was thinking about the poor
and in 1839 on one was thinking about anything else. But in
1839 the depths had not been sounded.

6

The years following the Reform Act were for the towns a time
of quiet prosperity, which culminated in the golden harvest of
1835. Towards the end of 1836 a warning shiver ran through the
commercial world: over-production and speculation were producing their natural consequences. There was a parallel
depression in America, and the European States were raising
their tariffs. Lancashire went on half-time; the harvest of 1838
failed; gold was exported to buy food, and the Bank of England
was barely saved from default by credits in Paris and Hamburg.
That a bad period was approaching was evident. But few could
have guessed through what misery the country would have to
pass before the clouds lifted again. In Stockport nearly a fourth
of the houses were empty. Thousands of families were living on
relief administered at the rate of a shilling a head. Out of 15,000
persons visited, not one in ten was fully employed. Wages had
fallen from a pound and more to 7s.6d.; the average weekly
income was less than 1s.6d. Manchester and Bolton were in like

[1] The impulse came from the Statistical Society of Manchester, which, as a
control experiment, also investigated Rutland. Leeds was, I believe, the first
municipality to investigate itself.

case: the Potteries, the Black Country, the cloth towns of the west, all told the same tale. It was the background of Chartism and the Free Trade League.

The Chartists wished to make a revolution: the Leaguers asserted that the revolution had happened, and drew out the consequences. Lancashire, the home of the movement, was the most typical product of the new civilization, and it needed little argument to prove that Lancashire could not live without imported cotton, could not maintain her increasing population without expanding markets, could not expand her markets unless the foreigner was kept in funds by the sale of food to England. Did the workshop of the world need a hobby farm, with a subsidized gentry to manage it, especially a gentry which was beginning to show an inconvenient interest in factory children, and the tendency of the fourteen hour day *minuere et contrahere pelvem*?[1] The League was founded in January 1839. For the first years of its existence it was fighting on two fronts, against the Protectionists and against the Chartists. Free Trade lecturers ran the double risk whenever they stood up in a market-place of being fined by the magistrate and ducked by the mob. To hungry men the prospect of relief by Free Trade was more remote than the prospect of relief by direct action, and it was as easy to represent the League as a coalition of mill-owners bent on reducing their wages bill, as a coalition of democrats bent on destroying the landed interest. 'You are a Chartist, Sir; you are a leveller,' the Home Secretary shouted at the respectable Mr Ashworth, manufacturer, when he came on a Free Trade deputation. The self-protective instinct of the aristocracy felt in the League its most dangerous enemy. But the instinct of society as a whole was more sensitive to the growing menace of Chartism.

The political creed of the Chartists was an amplification of the Radical formula, one man one vote, one vote one value. How they were going to get the vote was not so clear, and what

[1] Lord John Manners let the cat out of the bag when he talked, apropos of a Factory Bill, of 'putting a curb on the manufacturing interest and making it know its rider'.

they were going to do with it remained, even to themselves, unknown. Judged by what they did, they might be considered a body of decent, hardly used, and not particularly intelligent men, whose allegiance, given with equal readiness to high-minded leaders like Lovett and Hetherington and to pitiful demagogues like Feargus O'Connor, would probably be at the service of the first Conservative or Liberal who showed that he deserved it. Judged by what they said, or by what O'Connor, 'false, malignant, and cowardly', said for them, both their objects and their methods seemed to involve a bloody progress from confiscation, through anarchy, to famine and a dictatorship. The Socialism of Robert Owen, the doctrine that industrialism was not an impersonal force to be adored or bewailed, but a way of life to be controlled by co-operation, had gone underground. The young Queen was gracious to him for her father's sake, who had been his friend in the days when Napoleon had studied his projects in Elba, and Castlereagh had laid them before Congresses. But his mind was failing, and to most people Owenism meant a crazy multiplication of Trade Unions with long names, and the combination of economic heresy with irreligion and sexual depravity. 'You tell us', a Parliamentary Committee once said to a clergyman, 'that the railway navvies are mostly infidels. Would you say that they are also socialists?' 'In practice, yes; because though most of them appear to have wives, few of them are really married.' The more intelligent workmen professed a belated rationalism,[1] nourished on the writings of Tom Paine, with which often went, for philosophy, and wondrous addiction to the phrenology of George Combe.[2] The older sects meant little to the working

[1] The term Secularism was invented by Holyoake and first appears in his paper, *The Reasoner*, 1846. The badge of the Secularist was the defiance of Sabbatarian restrictions.

[2] Which was shared by Cobden. Phrenology was regularly taught in Mechanics' Institutes, and did, I think, help to keep the idea of personality alive under the steam-roller of respectablity. Otherwise, science (for want of apparatus) did not much affect the workman. The culture of the self-educated man was still literary. He began with the Bible and its commentators and worked up through Milton to the economists, philosophers, and historians. This was of some importance politically. If the speeches of Bright, Gladstone, or Disraeli *ad Quirites* are examined, they will be found to imply

classes. The Wesleyans, whose service in humanizing the masses were handsomely recognized by authority, on principle held aloof from political contests; and Chartism, which disgusted fair-minded men by the violence of its invective, terrified a still larger class by its supposed designs, not only on movable property, but on religion and the family. Yet there was much silent sympathy with the Chartists as men; if the new rich had been their only enemies, many young gentlemen would have been glad to strike a blow for the old poor. Young England was a sincere if boyish gesture of goodwill, and to play King Richard to somebody else's Wat Tyler has always been a Tory fancy.

How far the mass of the workpeople were at any time seriously engaged is a question not easy to answer. The Londoners, who were most closely allied with the Parliamentary Radicals, stood for caution and constitutional methods. The admixture of cheap Irish labour and cheap Irish rhetoric alienated the Englishman, and the party of physical force were unlucky in their choice of military advisers. In no age are Count Chopski and Colonel Macerone names to conjure with in English working circles. The Convention summoned to London withdrew to the less frigid air of Birmingham: it was known that Lancashire was arming; regiments were recalled from Ireland, the army was increased by 7,000 men, a White Guard instituted, and Sir Charles Napier, a wise and sympathetic choice, was sent to take command of the Northern Division. In 1839 the Charter was presented and rejected: the Convention considered a general strike and a march on London. There was no strike; no one marched, and the insurgents had to be content with a wild riot in Birmingham. In a few weeks 400 Chartists were in prison, and the revolution ended in a splutter of musketry and a dozen men killed outside the Queen's Hotel, Newport. Chartism, though there was some brief, fierce rioting in 1842, when the Charter was again presented and rejected, was effectively dead.

It is impossible to gauge the danger of a revolution which

a considerable body of literary culture common to the speaker and at least a great part of his audience.

refused to happen. But in estimating the alarm we must allow
for the melodramatic streak in the early Victorian temperament. When Wellington said on the morrow of the riots that no
town sacked in war presented such a spectacle as Birmingham,
he did not mean that he had gone to see it for himself, any more
than when Lord Shaftesbury said that *Ecce Homo* was the foulest
book ever vomited from the jaws of hell, he meant that he had
read all the others. Events, like books, still came widely spaced,
with time between to set the imagination working; and that
generation was still overshadowed by the revolutionary years
and read itself in their volcanic light. In 1840 there were many
men living who could recall the flight of the French nobility.
The sacking of Bristol was still fresh in all memories, and
England had hardly the elements of a civil force capable of
stopping disorder before it reaches the point where factories are
burnt and the troops must shoot.

London was provided for by the Peelers and the mounted
patrol who kept order within five miles of Charing Cross. The
parish had its constable, and the police of the boroughs were
reinforced in emergencies by specials: on election days and
other occasions of riot the specials might be numbered by
hundreds. There were five hundred private associations for the
prosecution of felons; but there was no county police;[1] and
the mainstay of the public peace was not the constable but the
yeoman, and behind the yeoman, though cautiously and
reluctantly employed, the soldier. Lord John Russell, accounting
to the Queen for the progress of the Tories at the elections of
1838, added that the Military had in all cases conducted
themselves with great temper and judgement. They were
employed on even humbler duties: once, at least, troops were
called out to enforce the Act of 1823 and save a poor ox from
being baited on his way to market. England as a whole, and the

---

[1] This is not without its bearing on Victorian psychology. With 25,000 vagrants
on the pad, and all the village idiots at large, the unprotected female really had
something to be afraid of.

country gentlemen in particular, were highly suspicious of anything in the nature of a national police, and the Act of 1839 went no further than to permit the Justices of a County to appoint a Chief Constable and form a police force if they so desired. The boroughs already had the power. But in that alarming year it was discovered that neither Birmingham nor Manchester could maintain a paid force, and an emergency detachment had to be sent from London. So sensitive was the feeling of sound constitutionalists in the matter of police, that Lord John, having sent London constables to Bradford to help with a Poor Law riot, decided on reflection to withdraw them and enjoined the magistrates to use dragoons instead. The Permissive Act of 1839 was generalized by the Compulsory Act of 1856. The interval had been well employed. Essex selected as Chief Constable a retired Naval Officer. He very soon made it appear that a paid constabulary was not only more efficient but actually cheaper than the gratuitous service of Dogberry and Verges. One by one the counties adopted the model he had devised, and all that was necessary in '56 was to bring the laggards into line. There are many famous men to whom England owes less than she owes to Captain M'Hardy, Chief Constable of Essex.

But his career, and his achievement, are typical of a general rule. The English administration was made by administrators throwing out their lines until they met and formed a system. In the fustian phrase which exasperated clear-headed Radicals, it was not made, it grew. In 1830, except for the collection and management of the revenue, for defence, and the transmission of letters, there was hardly anything which a Frenchman or a Prussian would have recognized as an administration. The national expenditure was £50,000,000, of which the debt absorbed £29,000,000, defence £15,000,000, leaving £16,000,000 only for collection, for the Crown, and the whole civil service. The total and the proportions did not vary greatly till the Crimean War. But by 1860 the cost of defence was £26,000,000, the balance for civil purposes £15,000,000. These figures, which point to the emergence of the armed administrative State, show also with what a slight equipment early Victorian government operated. Local revenue was about a quarter of Imperial, and on an average one-half went in the relief of the poor. The rest was spent on Police, Bridges, and Highways; on Lunatics; on the upkeep of Parish Churches. The Church rate, an inconsiderable sum, but the occasion of much agitation and some painless martyrdom, was persistently evaded, made voluntary in 1853, and abolished in 1868.

The Civil Servants who ran this light machinery were of two sorts: clerks, infallible in accounts, writing a fair hand, the repository of precedent; gentlemen, or the protégés of gentlemen, of the political class, whose position when young might be anything from a copying clerk to a private secretary, and who when old were rather assistants and advisers to an executive chief than executants themselves. There was much routine, so much that by the time the juniors were seniors they were usually unfit for anything else, and the higher posts had to be filled from outside. But almost everything that rose above routine was, except at the Treasury, policy, requiring the personal attention of the Minister: the intermediate sphere of administration did not exist, because there were hardly any laws to administer. Readers of Disraeli's novels must sometimes have been puzzled by the importance of the Under-Secretaries as a class. When the Cabinet was open only to birth, to exceptional genius or exceptional influence, men of excellent gifts had to be content, and were content, with Under-Secretaryships, and the unbroken Tory régime had given some of them a very long innings. Croker was of this class, so was 'gray-headed, financial' Herries; and the Whigs of 1827 could not master their wrath when they were asked to accept as a Cabinet colleague a fellow whom they had always looked upon as a Tory clerk. A Treasury official in Early Victorian English means a Junior Lord.

Well on into the reign the line between politics and administration could be crossed and recrossed as it was by Endymion. Cornewall Lewis was a Civil Servant for fourteen years before he entered Parliament, where he reached Cabinet rank in eight. Benjamin Hawes from Parliamentary Secretary became Permanent Secretary to the War Office. William Blamire made his mark in Parliament with a speech on tithes, and was given a post which made him, in effect, for twenty years a non-parliamentary Minister of Agriculture. But the dismissal of the Under-Secretaries with their chiefs in 1830, and inexperiences of the new Whig Ministers, and the reform of the Poor Law, made a fresh departure. The Benthamite conception of a trained staff dealing with specific problems entered the Civil Service at the very point where the Civil Service impinged most forcibly on the public. The Poor Law filled the whole horizon in 1834. And here, there, and everywhere were Chadwick's young crusaders, the Assistant Commissioners, scouring the country in stage-coaches or post-chaises, or beating up against the storm on ponies in the Weald, returning to London, their wallets stuffed with the Tabular Data so dear to philosophic Radicals, to draft their sovereign's decrees declaring the Union and stating his austere principles of administration, and then back to see that they were carried out. It was an exciting life. Once they had to be protected with cavalry. When they appeared at Todmorden, Fielden rang his factory bells and beat them out of town. In so splendid and imperial a manner did the English Civil Servant first take his place in the national life.[1]

The Radicals had conceived the possibility of applying disinterested intelligence to social problems. Chadwick realized the idea and created the organ of application. The administrative temper was in being before there was an administration to give it effect. The Poor Law schools at Norwood were taken as a model by the new Education Department. The Poor Law

---

[1] The distinction between administrative and clerical duties which lies at the root of the Northcote-Trevelyan reforms in '53 was carried out at the Poor Law Commission from the first. James Mill had already introduced it at the India House. The confusion of functions reached its height at Dublin Castle, where the duties of the Under-Secretary were, *inter alia*, to deputize for the Lord-Lieutenant, to docket incoming letters in red ink, to advise on all criminal business, and to see that the stationery was not wasted.

framework was adopted in 1838 for the registration of births, marriages, deaths, and the causes of death. In the same year a London vestry, baffled by an outbreak of fever, turned to the Poor Law Board for help, a step from which descends by regular stages the Health Board of 1848, the Local Government Board of 1870, the existing Ministry of Health. What was growing up, in fact, in the thirties, under the vigorous impulsion of Chadwick and Kay and the bewildered gaze of Ministers, was a Public Welfare Service, which was bound sooner or later to demand compulsory powers, and to receive them as soon as the public mind was sufficiently moved, enlightened, or alarmed.

But the rapid growth of our administrative services is on the whole due less to head-quarters than to the Inspectorate. Inspection was in the air: the Factory Inspectors of 1834 were followed by the Prison Inspectors, and these by the School Inspectors, the Railway Inspectors, and the Mines Inspectors. The Inspectors, like the higher officials, were often men of mature experience who came to their duties with ideas already formed. Leonard Horner, whose reports underlie so much of our industrial legislation, was nearing fifty when he entered the Factory department, and was already a man of note in education and science. Hugh Tremenheere, joining the Education department at thirty-five, had fourteen Acts of Parliament to his credit when he retired. With them must be ranked the specialists in public health; above all, Southwood Smith and John Simon. Smith, a Unitarian minister, whose devotional writings must have had some singular quality to be admired both by Wordsworth and Byron, came late to the profession of medicine, but he found his place at once with an Essay on Fever. Cholera was a visitor: typhus a resident who Southwood Smith believed could be expelled. Joining forces with Chadwick he became, in effect, Medical Adviser to the Poor Law Commission. His junior, Simon, a cultivated surgeon of French descent, a connoisseur and the friend of Ruskin, covered in his official life the development of the Board of Health into the

Local Government Board, of which he was the first medical officer. In the careers of men like these, or of Arthur Hassell, who took the adulteration of food for his province, we see the impact of the educated intelligence on the amorphous, greedy fabric of the new civilization, and I know nothing which brings the epic quality of the early Victorian warfare against barbarism into such vivid relief as the reports, eloquent, impassioned, and precise, which from 1848 onwards Simon addressed to the Corporation of the City of London.

7

The thirty years from Waterloo have the unity and, at times, the intensity of a great drama. Castlereagh and Canning adjusted our insular relations to the Old World and the New. The Reform Act and the Municipal Reform Act gave the islands a rational political framework; steam unified their economic structure. Of all these processes, the Repeal of the Corn Laws in 1846 was the logical and historical culmination. The operations of the League, which had gone with a swing all through the bad years, flagged with the return of prosperity in 1843 and the absorption of the unemployed by the railway boom; by 1845 manufacturers did not know where to turn for hands. Peel himself was slowly moving towards Free Trade in corn, but he was restrained, not by a political, but by an economic scruple: the belief that cheap food meant low wages and that the loss of rents to the land-owner would be followed with no compensating advantage to the working classes. When this doubt was resolved his way grew clear. The great Budget of 1842, in which he had swept away the accumulated muddles of the Whigs and raised an income tax to lower the customs, marks the opening stage of classical Victorian finance. Incidentally, the sliding scale of 1828, which had refused to slide, was readjusted. In 1845 he repeated his stroke, and circumstances were gradually imposing a larger policy on his mind. Of his young men, Gladstone, Lincoln, Canning, Ramsay were Free Traders already, and Peel, behind the repellent front which he turned to the world, and which, indeed, cost him his life, was exceptionally sensitive to the ideas, and the sufferings, of others. The prosperity of the mid-forties had not spread to the villages; whatever the cause, the consequences were plain enough: 'I be protected and I be starving.' One good harvest more, to keep the League quiet, and he would go to the country as a Free Trader, with the compensating offer of a credit for the re-conditioning of the land and the absorption of the next wave of unemployment, and return with the middle-class Conservatism he had created, solidly based on the gratitude of the towns and the regeneration of the farming interest. The disaster which depopulated Ireland shattered the Conservative party on the threshold of a generation of power.[1]

The Irish difficulty went deeper than the philosophy of the age could reach. The twin cell of English life, the squire administering what everybody recognizes as law and the parson preaching what everybody acknowledges to be religion, had no meaning in a country where the squire was usually an invader and the parson always a heretic. England had staked the good government of Ireland on a double speculation, that the Irish would conform to the Protestant establishment and that they would accept the English use of landlord, farmer, and labourer. The Irishry preferred to misgovern themselves as Catholics and small-holders, and the Englishry, after a few generations, were all too ready to take up the part of tribal chiefs. To analyse the Irish trouble into racial, religious, and agrarian is impossible because in Irish history these three are one, and when England

---

[1] Peel's long-distance programme will be found in a memorandum by Prince Albert, Christmas 1845. His character is not easy to read, because his mastery of Parliamentary methods masked an intense dislike of the party system, while his frigid efficiency covered an almost passionate concern for the welfare of the people. On his last ride an acquaintance, who recognized his horse as a bolter, was afraid to warn him, but in a begging letter-writer's list of people most likely to be touched for a fiver, Peel's name was found with good Queen Adelaide and Dickens.

had conceded Catholic emancipation against her own Protestants, and insisted on agrarian reform against the Irish landlords, and both in vain, the logic of history left her no alternative but to concede all the rest, never quite understanding what it was the Irish wanted or why they wanted it.

Thus throughout the nineteenth century Ireland was an uneasy place in the body politic which could be neither forgotten nor assuaged. In the thirties it is tithes and crime. The establishment was a grievance which an English government might alleviate if it could not remove. Disorder was a pestilence which it was bound to stamp out. Hence the history of Lord Grey's Government is taken up very largely with Irish Church bills and Irish coercion bills. On the whole the Whigs were successful, mainly because they sent two honest gentlemen, Drummond and Ebrington, to the Castle and left them alone, and in '41 they handed over to their successors an Ireland neither prosperous nor contented, but at least reasonably quiet. The nationalist agitation which sprang up suddenly in the following years, round Gavan Duffy and his friends, was unexpected. Had it fallen a little earlier so as to coincide with the Chartist movement in England, and if O'Connell could have overcome his aversion to physical force, the results might have been memorable. But in 1839 Ireland was so peaceful that soldiers could be spared for England, and in 1843 England was in such good humour that they could be safely sent to Ireland. On October 5 a great demonstration was to assemble at Clontarf; it was proclaimed and O'Connell arrested. Convicted, almost of course, by a Protestant Dublin jury, he was set at liberty by the House of Lords. The incident added a phrase to the language – Lord Denman saying that trial by jury as practised in this case was 'a delusion, a mockery, and a snare', and the Nationalist movement died down.[1] Peel's Government used their victory not unwisely. They issued a Royal Commission of Enquiry into Irish land tenure and, in the teeth of a frantic Protestant opposition, they carried their proposal to

[1] And split up, the split being signalized by the foundation of the *United Irishman* in opposition to *The Nation*.

LONDON, WEDNESDAY, JULY 3, 1850.

Sir ROBERT PEEL is no more. After three days of excessive suffering, at a few minutes past eleven last night, the greatest statesman of his time quitted the scene in which he had performed so conspicuous a part. Even the anxiety and the rumours which have penetrated every household since the first alarming intelligence will have failed to prepare the country for the deplorable result. Except, indeed, in the field of battle, never was the transition from life to death so marked and so touching. On Friday the House of Commons, which for more than forty years has witnessed the triumphs and reverses of the great Conservative chief, was filled with an extraordinary assemblage anxious for the result of a great political crisis. Sir ROBERT addressed them with an ability and a spirit which recalled his more youthful efforts, and more powerful days. It was the first occasion for four years that elicited any serious or direct opposition to the policy of HER MAJESTY's present advisers, and, not to reopen a debate full of mistakes and crosspurposes, it must be allowed that the speech was at least an admirable defence of the principles on which Sir ROBERT and his colleagues had ever proceeded. He sat down, as our report says, amid " loud and long-" continued cheering." Within a few hours the statesman who had commanded the applause of that listening senate was a wreck of life and strength, shattered, feeble, restless, and agonized. The feverish interval is past. That heart has ceased to beat ; that tongue is ever still. That ardent spirit and capacious intellect are now in another and an unknown world.

From The Times, 3 *July* 1850

LATEST INTELLIGENCE.

THE FALL
OF
SEBASTOPOL.

WAR DEPARTMENT, SEPT. 10.

Lord Panmure has received the following telegraphic despatch from General Simpson, dated

"CRIMEA, SEPT. 9.

" Sebastopol is in the possession of the allies.

" The enemy, during the night and this morning, have evacuated the south side, after exploding their magazines and setting fire to the whole of the town.

" All the men-of-war were burnt during the night, with the exception of three steamers, which are plying about the harbour.

" The bridge communicating with the north side is broken."

Sir Charles Wood has received the following despatch from Sir E. Lyons :—

" During the night the Russians have sunk all the remainder of the line-of-battle ships in Sebastopol harbour."

WAR DEPARTMENT, SEPT. 10.

Lord Panmure has received the following telegraphic despatch from General Simpson, dated

" CRIMEA, SEPT. 10.

" The casualties, I regret to say, are somewhat heavy.

" No General officer killed.

" Names shall be sent as soon as possible."

From The Times, 11 *September* 1855

48

increase the grant for training Irish priests at Maynooth. On the report of the Commission, a classic document for the history of the Irish question, they introduced a Bill to secure compensation for improving tenants. The Lords objected and the Bill was withdrawn for further consideration. The occasion had passed and it did not return.

Early in August 1845, at the end of a successful session, with a thriving country and a full exchequer, Peel received a letter from a potato-dealer, warning him that the crop was diseased and the disease spreading. Half the population of Ireland lived on potatoes, and by the beginning of October it was doubtful whether half the crop would be saved. England had been accustomed to take on an average of 2,000,000 quarters of wheat from Ireland. It looked as if she would have to send 2,000,000 quarters to keep the Irish alive, and the English harvest was short. It was out of the question to ask the English to pay duty both on the corn they ate themselves, and on the corn they bought for the Irish: equally impossible to suppose that the Corn Laws, once suspended, could ever be reimposed, or that the Conservative party, as it stood, would ever consent to repeal them. Peel, with the support of the Whigs and with a fragment of his own party, undertook to admit foreign corn at a nominal fixed duty.[1] Supported by imminent famine, the arguments of the League could not be answered: they could only be opposed. It seemed as if nature, which was solving the Irish problem in the sense of the economists by killing off the surplus population, would solve an English problem in the sense of the Radicals by killing off the superfluous landlords. In fact, it did no harm to the English gentry, and it made the Irish problem insoluble. The Encumbered Estates thrown on the market were bought up by investors who proceeded to reorganize them economically by wholesale evictions, and for years hardly a ship sailed to the west without its freight of exiles

---

[1] It is characteristic of Early Victorian manners that in the Cabinet paper announcing his conversion, Peel can hardly bring himself to call That Root by its proper name. It was observed that in all prayers offered up for our Irish brethren, potatoes were never mentioned.

carrying to America an unappeasable passion for vengeance on the dispossessor.

Yet there was never an Irish tragedy without its satyric afterpiece. In 1848, Smith O'Brien, a respectable and humourless Member of Parliament who seems to have been drawn to Repeal by simple despair of the Union, was caught levying war on the Queen's Majesty in the widow McCormack's cabbage garden. The campaign was brief, as O'Brien had forgotten to provide his army with anything to eat. He was sentenced to the usual penalty, which was at once commuted to transportation. With the maddening logic which Irishmen have at command he argued that as he had not been convicted of anything deserving transportation, he must be pardoned or he must be hanged. The Law Officers admitted his contention, and a short Act had to be passed providing that, in spite of the earnest expectation of the creatures, O'Brien and others in like case might lawfully be required to remain alive.

8

Later Victorians, to whom Free Trade had become a habit of mind, tended almost instinctively to divide the century into the years before and after 1846. But in the sixties one social observer laid his finger not on the Repeal of the Corn Laws in '46, but on the Factory Act of '47, as the turning-point of the age and, with our longer perspective, we can hardly doubt that he was right. Of facts which, in Gibbon's phrase, are dominant in the general system, by far the most significant in this period is the emergence of a new State philosophy, of which the overt tokens are the Factory Act, the Public Health Acts,[1] and the Education Minute of 1846. The great inquiries of the thirties

[1] The principal are: Baths and Washhouses Act '46 and '47; Town Improvements Clauses '47; Public Health '48; Lodging Houses '51; Burials '52.

and forties were the Nemesis of the middle-class victory of 1830; an unreformed Parliament would never have persisted in them, and they led, silently and inevitably, to a conception of the State and its relations to its subjects which the electors of the first Reformed Parliaments would almost unanimously have repudiated. The cataclysm of 1830 proved to have been the beginning of a slow evolution, by which, while an aristocratic fabric was quietly permeated with Radical ideas, an individualistic society was unobtrusively-schooled in the ways of State control. Engels's *Condition of the Working Class*, which projected the image of the exploiting capitalist on the mind of the European proletariat, appeared in 1845: it was based on the English Blue Books. So was the legislation of 1847. History, which sometimes condescends to be ironic, had chosen her dates with meaning.

From 1832 to 1847 the student of Victorian history finds himself the bewildered spectator of a warfare between Radicals who upheld Factories and Workhouses, Tories and Chartists who abhorred them both, infidel Benthamites leagued with Conservative Anglicans against dissenting manufacturers, land owners denouncing the oppressions of Lancashire, and cotton masters yearning over the sorrows of Dorset. The movement for Factory Reform and against the New Poor Law, against Protection and for the Charter, are mixed in an inextricable confusion of agitation, of which, nevertheless, the main pattern is clear. The Factory Act of 1833 introduced, in all textile factories, the ten-hour day for young persons under eighteen and a forty-eight-hour week for children under thirteen, with the obligation to attend for two hours every day at a school which often did not exist. In this last provision, and in the four inspectors appointed to observe the operation of the law, we see the Radical hand. Otherwise the Act is a watering down of the demands made by the Evangelical Tories, Oastler, Sadler, and Lord Ashley, on the basis of the Ten Hour movement in the West Riding. To the workpeople it was a disappointment, and their resentment went to animate the growing body of Popular Radicalism. Thrown on themselves, they turned towards Direct Action, Trade Unions, and the Charter. To the employers it was a warning, since the reduction of children's hours of necessity brought with it a rearrangement of all working hours, which ultimately the State might generalize. Outside the factories, indeed, the seventy-two-hour week was becoming common in many trades.

But for the next few years the focus of agitation was not Factory reform, but the New Poor Law. The resources of the Poor Law Commissioners were limited; the Benthamite watchword – aggregate to segregate – remained a watchword only; and their comprehensive scheme for dealing separately with the young, the sick, the aged, the vagrant, and the destitute was never put into effect. In its place nothing was visible but the New Bastilles, and the proposal which the workhouse system seemed to involve of applying factory discipline – if not prison discipline – to the pauper, lashed the working classes to fury. It was at this time that The House acquired its sinister meaning, and the Poor Law first inspired that repulsion which has hobbled our administration ever since. The Forty-third of Elizabeth, which declared the Right to Work, had degenerated into the Right to Relief without working. But it was the Charter of the Poor. The New Poor Law was the charter of the ratepayer, and it was failing of its purpose. The formula which had worked in the rural south failed when it was applied to the industrial midlands and the north. Reluctantly the Commissioners surrendered their principles and set the people to task work, or road-making, as if they had been Tudor magistrates faced with a short harvest. And the poor rate rose again.

The failure of the New Poor Law to fulfil its promise, the inevitable harshness of a new administration suddenly applied to a people with no idea of administration at all, the brutality that went on in some workhouses and the gorging in others,[1] the petty tyranny of officials and the petty corruption of Guardians, discredited the scientific Radicals and brought the

[1] Against the oft-repeated tale of the Andover gristle set the dietary discovered in one workhouse: bread 72 oz., gruel $7\frac{1}{2}$ pints, meat 15 oz., potatoes $1\frac{1}{2}$ lb., soup $4\frac{1}{2}$ pints, pudding 14 oz., cheese 8 oz., broth $4\frac{1}{2}$ pints, and compare it with the tables, in Chapter II of *Early Victorian England*, of ordinary working-class food.

sentimental Radicals to the front. *The Pickwick Papers* is not a Victorian document: it belongs to a sunnier time, which perhaps had never existed. The group of novels that follow, *Oliver Twist, Nicholas Nickleby, The Old Curiosity Shop*, is charged with the atmosphere of the thirties. They have the Radical faith in progress, the Radical dislike of obstruction and privilege, the Radical indifference to the historic appeal. But they part from the Radicalism of the Benthamites in their equal indifference to the scientific appeal. Dickens's ideal England was not very far from Robert Owen's. But it was to be built by some magic of goodwill overriding the egoism of progress; not by law, and most emphatically not by logic.

The economists and the reformers had drawn the bow too tight: it almost snapped in their hands. But so, too, had the Evangelicals, and even goodwill was suspected if it came arrayed in religious guise. At the sight of Wilberforce, Cobbett put his head down and charged. Young Anglicans were prepared to defend black slavery only because the Evangelicals were against it. Sir Andrew Agnew's Sunday Observance Bill, the most rigorous piece of moral – and, indeed, class – legislation since the Long Parliament, supported by 128 members of the Commons, with Lord Ashley at their head, brought the two humorists of the age into the field together. Dickens riddled it in words; Cruikshank in pictures. But in all Dickens's work there is a confusion of mind which reflects the perplexity of his time; equally ready to denounce on the grounds of humanity all who left things alone, and on the grounds of liberty all who tried to make them better. England was shifting uneasily and convulsively from an old to a new discipline, and the early stages were painful.[1] To be numbered, to be visited, to be inspected, to be preached at, whether the visitors were furnished with a Poor Law Order or a religious mission, whether they came to feed the children or to save their souls, frayed tempers already on edge with mechanical toil, and hurt – often unreasonably, but still it hurt – that very sense of personal

---

[1] It has been suggested to me that the Railway Time-table did much to discipline the people at large. I think this is true.

dignity on which the scientific reformers, as strongly as the sentimentalists, relied for the humanization of the poor.

The one field in which they might have co-operated without reserve was the care of children. The Factory Act of 1833 was incidentally an Education Act as well, though a very imperfect one, since for the purposes of the Act any cellar might be returned as a school and any decayed pedlar as a schoolmaster. The year 1840 saw the chimney-sweeping children brought under public protection. The next advance was inspired by the revelations of the Employment of Children Enquiry of 1840 and registered in the Mines Act of 1842. In the following year Peel's Government tried to carry the Act of 1833 one step farther. They were beaten by a union of manufacturers and dissenters: 'worthy and conscientious men', Brougham wrote, 'who hate the Established Church more than they love education.' In 1844 Graham reintroduced his Bill, omitting the educational clauses which had given so much offence, but reducing the hours of children's labour to six and a half, of men's to twelve. Lord Ashley stood out for ten: the Government resisted. Peel pointed out that the Bill dealt only with textile factories and that notoriously the conditions in other workshops were worse. 'Will you legislate for all?' he asked. It was a rhetorical question. But it was answered with a solid shout of 'Yes'. Without meaning it, the House of Commons had undertaken to regulate the factory system throughout the land, and a few nights later they recalled their decision. But the tide was running fast and the conversion of Macaulay is symptomatic. As a young man he had dealt his blows impartially between paternal Toryism and deductive Radicalism, between Southey, Owen, and James Mill. His economics, like those of most Englishmen, were in descent not from Ricardo, but from Adam Smith and Burke.

'It is one of the finest problems in legislation, and what has often engaged my thoughts whilst I followed that profession, "what the State ought to take upon itself to direct by the public wisdom, and what it ought to leave, with as little interference as possible, to individual discretion". Nothing, certainly, can be laid down on the subject that will not admit of exceptions, many permanent, some occasional. But the clearest line of distinction which I could draw, while I had any chalk to draw it, was this: that the State ought to confine itself to what regards the State, or the creatures of the State, namely, the exterior establishment of its religion; its magistracy; its revenue; its military force by sea and land; the corporations that owe their existence to its fiat; in a word, to everything that is *truly and properly* public, to the public peace, to the public safety, to the public order, to the public prosperity. In its preventive police it ought to be sparing of its efforts, and to employ means, rather few, unfrequent, and strong, than many, and frequent, and, of course, as they multiply their puny politic race, and dwindle, small and feeble. Statesmen who know themselves will, with the dignity which belongs to wisdom, proceed only in this the superior orb, and first mover of their duty steadily, vigilantly, severely, courageously: whatever remains will, in a manner provide for itself. But as they descend from the State to a province, from a province to a parish, and from a parish to a private house, they go on accelerated in their fall. They *cannot* do the lower duty; and, in proportion as they try it, they will certainly fail in the higher. They ought to know the different department of things; what belongs to laws, and what manners alone can regulate. To these, great politicians may give a leaning, but they cannnot give a law.'[1]

A great body of principle, self-interest, and sentiment had to be shifted, before the public mind could pass this point. Of principle, because State intervention was still commonly pictured as that system of State regulation of industry which Adam Smith had confuted. Of self-interest, because it does undoubtedly mean a restriction of a man's right to do what he will with his own. Of sentiment, because the intense dislike of interference and domiciliary visits which history had bred in us, took into its field the workpeople and the factory; and the religious,

---

[1] Burke, *Thoughts on Scarcity*, 1795.

the economic, and the social codes all combined to emphasize the vital importance of individual effort, whether the prize was domestic comfort or heavenly joy. But experience tells, and by 1845 it was becoming evident that the line between what the State may do and what it must leave alone had been drawn in the wrong place, and that there was a whole world of things where the individual simply could not help himself at all. He could not build his own house, or even choose his own street. He could not dispose of his own sewage or educate his own children. In Macaulay's mind the sphere of State interest now includes not only public order and defence, but public health, education, and the hours of labour. It includes, what is most remarkable of all, that triumph of private enterprise – the railways.

'Trade considered merely as a trade, considered merely with regard to the pecuniary interest of the contracting parties, can hardly be too free. But there is a great deal of trade which cannot be considered merely as trade, and which affects higher than pecuniary interests. Fifteen years ago it became evident that railroads would soon, in every part of the kingdom, supersede to a great extent the old highways. The tracing of the new routes which were to join all the chief cities, ports and naval arsenals of the island was a matter of the highest national importance. But unfortunately those who should have acted refused to interfere. That the whole society was interested in having a good system of internal communications seemed to be forgotten. The speculator who wanted a large dividend on his shares, the landowner who wanted a large price for his acres, obtained a full hearing. But nobody applied to be heard on behalf of the community.'[1]

Was Hudson listening that night? For Hudson, 'Mammon and Belial in one', was nearing his apogee and his fall. The

---

[1] Speech on Fielden's Factory Bill, May 22, 1846. In the Government, the same view was strongly urged by Dalhousie, who was able to give effect to it in India.

Midland and North-Eastern systems were under his control: he
had carried the Sunderland election against Bright and Cobden
in 1845, when *The Times* chartered a special train to bring the
news of his return; his financial triumphs, his country houses, his
parties in Albert Gate, his friendship with Prince Albert, gave
him an almost legendary prestige.[1] But Hudson was one of
those not uncommon characters who persuade themselves that
an aptitude for business carries with it a genius for fraud. He
kept one block of shares in demand by paying the dividends out
of capital; with even greater simplicity he helped himself to
others which did not appear in the books and sold them at a
profit. Naturally he was the strenuous, and, no doubt, the
sincere, opponent of Government supervision; and naturally
when the bubble burst, with a loss to the investor, it was
reckoned, of nearly £80,000,000, the public attitude to Government supervision underwent some change.

In this atmosphere Fielden's Bill was finally carried. Those
who have read the debates may perhaps think that the
opponents had the best of the argument. The 58-hour week
(which, in effect, was what the Bill established) was a plunge,
and an opposition supported by Peel, Graham, and Herbert for
the Conservatives, by Brougham, Roebuck, and old Jo Hume
for the economists, and backed by the warnings of the most
experienced officials, is not to be ignored. But the debates mark
at once the waning of the economics of pure calculation and the
growth of that preoccupation with the quality of life which is
dominant in the next decade. There is a remarkable passage in
Peel's speech, in which he refers to the criticism of the Italian
economists that their English colleague concentrated on wealth
and overlooked welfare.[2] But he need not have gone to Italy
for it. He could have heard it from Sadler and Southey and
Young England; he could have read it as far back as 1832 in the

[1] Mrs Hudson hardly kept pace with her husband's elevation; once, on a visit to
Grosvenor House, she was shown a bust of Marcus Aurelius: 'It ain't the present
Markis, is it?' she inquired.
[2] Peel was probably thinking of Sismondi's *Nouveaux Principes*.

Quarterly Review. This alternative economic was not thought out; it remained instinctive, sentimental, feudal; and the natural alliance of the scientific Benthamite administrator and the authoritative Tory gentleman was never fully achieved, or achieved only in India. But it was creeping in and on. 'Of course, all legislative interference is an evil – but' runs like an apologetic refrain through the speeches of those who supported the Bill. And the 'but' grew larger as the conviction of evil grew less assured.[1]

9

'Railway companies may smash their passengers into mummy and the State may not interfere![2] Pestilence may sweep our streets and the state may not compel the municipalities to put their own powers in operation to check it! We have heard of the Curiosities of Literature and some day this book will be

[1] I may here refer to Mrs Tonna's *Perils of the Nation*, hurriedly compiled for the Christian Influence Society in the alarm following the Chartist Riots of 1842. It undoubtedly represents a great body of educated opinion of, broadly speaking, a Tory Evangelical cast, and furnishes a link between the Sadler-Ashley thought of the thirties and *Unto this Last* of 1860. Her analysis of the social trouble is (*a*) defective conceptions of national wealth; (*b*) exorbitant power of the employing class; (*c*) unwillingness to legislate between employer and workman; (*d*) competition, which had (i) destroyed the notion of fair wage, fair price, and fair profit, (ii) lowered the quality of goods. It will be seen how near all this comes to the Ruskin of twenty years later. Mrs Tonna's remedies are naturally somewhat vague: specifically, education, housing, and direct industrial legislation; generally, the organization of a better opinion among the upper and professional classes. Incidentally she believes the beautiful doctrine that when God sends mouths he sends meat, and regards contraception (and Harriet Martineau) as the 'most horrifying abomination of Socialism'. The book had a wide circulation, but I refer to it, not as an agent, but as a symptom, in the struggle to get away from the impersonality of Capital and Labour to the idea of a fair deal and a decent population. Directly, Carlyle contributed little: but the atmospheric effect of his insistence on personality, immaterial values, and leadership was immense.

[2] Railway travelling was much more dangerous in England than on the Continent. Fatal accidents were more than fifteen times as frequent as in Germany.

numbered among them.' So did *Eliza Cook's Journal* dispose of the already antiquated individualism of Herbert Spencer's *Social Statics* in 1851. Eliza Cook knew what the lower middle classes were thinking about. 'There have been at work among us', a Nonconformist preacher told his people, 'three great social agencies: the London City Mission; the novels of Mr Dickens; the cholera.' It had never been forgotten: it was always due to return. It came in 48/49 and again in 54.

The Health Legislation of the Victorian age is a blended product of Poor Law and Municipal Reform. By 1830 the old boroughs were falling into imbecility; they had for the most part ceased to perform any useful service; improvements in lighting, draining, gas, water, markets, streets, even in police, were carried out under special Acts by special commissioners, and the corporations were little more than corrupt electoral colleges. When the franchise was bestowed on the ten-pound household-ers at large, the corporations had lost their reason for existing unless some one could find something for them to do, and make them fit to do it. One article in the Benthamite code prescribed representative local bodies for all purposes – miniatures of Parliament and Cabinets, with trained officials selected by open competition. The Municipal Reform Act did not go so far as this: it created 178 elected corporations, but with limited powers and little supervision from above. London was reserved for separate treatment: even a Benthamite quailed before the magnitude of the metropolis, which was misgoverned by four counties, innumerable vestries and commissions, the Bailiff of Westminster, and the Corporation of the City of London. The field of the new municipalities was the police and good government of the towns. They were allowed, though not compelled, to take over the duties of the Special Commis-sioners, and it was by the gradual assumption of these activities that the great municipalities mastered the problems of town life.

That of all these problems health, in the widest sense, was the most important, had been realized at the time of the cholera visitation, and the lesson was constantly hammered home by Chadwick from the Poor Law Commission. All that the science of the day could discover or suggest – and the discoveries were as awful as the suggestions were drastic[1] – was embodied in his Report of 1842. In 1848 the results were brought together. In the early Poor Law administration, the Commissioners had no representative in Parliament, so that the Tyrants of Somerset House were without a Minister either to control or to defend their masterful proceedings: they really were bureaucrats, as Palmerston explained the new word to Queen Victoria, from *bureau* an office and *kratos* power. The defect was made good in 1847, and the Commission was provided with a Parliamentary President. The Act of 1848 created a parallel Board of Health in Whitehall with power to create Local Boards and compel them to discharge a great variety of duties, from the regulation of slaughter-houses to the supply of water and the management of cemeteries. It was a patchy and cumbrous piece of legislation: one municipality might adopt the Act and its neighbour not, and cholera might bear down on a district, while the average mortality of the last seven years had been too low to give the Board a ground for intervention. And when they were allowed to intervene, they must first inquire and then report, and then make a provisional order and then get the order confirmed, and then, most difficult of all, see that it was not evaded by local jobbers, backed by the Private Enterprise Society.[2] There was not enough staff to go round: the local doctors could not be got to report their wealthy patients for maintaining nuisances: it is not supposed that municipal affairs as a rule engage either the most intelligent or the most disinterested of mankind, and the impact of the irresistible Chadwick on the immovable incuriousness of the small municipal mind could only end in explosions.[3] The virtue of the Act of 1848 lay less in its immediate

---

[1] The principal were: municipal water supply, scientific drainage (land and town), an independent health service (with large summary powers for dealing with nuisances), and a national interment service. Why this last was regarded as important will be understood by any one who looks at Walker's *Gatherings from Graveyards*.

[2] Founded in 1849 to resist the operation of the Act. There is a good account of the working of the Act in *Two Years Ago*, which is drawn from the Mevagissey outbreak of '54.

[3] He was retired in '54. One of his last feats was a circular enjoining Local Authorities to consider 'insolvency, bankruptcy, and failure in previous pursuits as

results than in the large opportunities it gave for local initiative
and scientific intelligence to work together. Gradually, over the
country as a whole, rapidly in some aspiring boroughs, the filth
and horror which had crawled over the early Victorian towns
was penned back in its proper lairs, and perhaps the first step
towards dealing effectively with slums was to recognize them as
slums and not as normal phenomena of urban existence. In the
mid-fifties returning exiles were greeted by a novel sight. The
black wreath over London was thinning; the Thames was
fringed with smokeless chimneys. The Home Office had begun
to harry offenders under the Smoke Nuisance (Metropolis) Act
of 1853.

But the great development of municipal administration
belongs to the next generation. The advance of education was
much more rapid. In fact, by 1846 it had already passed out of
its first phase of mass production by monitors and private
initiative into the phase of trained teachers and public control.
Under the monitorial system, the more forward children
imparted the elements to the junior groups. As a device for
getting simple ideas into simple heads as fast as possible it was
successful.[1] Up to a certain point the Bell and Lancaster
children made astonishing progress; most children like playing
at school; and the system was not intended to carry them further
than the Three R's. The British and Foreign School Society
backed Lancaster and simple Bible reading; the National
Society for Promoting the Education of the Poor in the
Principles of the Established Church stood for Bell and the
Catechism. A fine class-distinction tended to keep them apart
through the Victorian age; the British Day scholar was not, as a
rule, of the poorest class. The success of the two societies in
diffusing elementary instruction was admitted, and the first
intervention of the State in the education of the people took the
shape of a grant in aid, in 1833, for school-building; of £11,000
to the National Society and £9,000 to the British and Foreign.
Six years later the distribution was entrusted to a Committee of

presumptive evidence of unfitness' for official employments.
[1] It was adopted for a time at Charterhouse.

Council, nominally: effectively, to their Secretary, Kay-Shuttleworth of the Manchester Report.

A survey of elementary education in the thirties revealed to thoughtful contemporaries a profoundly disquieting picture. School-buildings were rarely good, often indifferent, sometimes thoroughly bad. The same might be said of the teachers. The average school-life was perhaps two years, perhaps eighteen months. The Society Schools, which represented the best practice of the time, were helped out by Sunday Schools which also gave a little instruction in reading and writing, sometimes in arithmetic, and by a mob of private ventures, of which the one kept by Mr Wopsle's great aunt and attended by Pip was, if anything, a favourable specimen. At Salford it was found that of 1,800 children nominally at school, less than half were taught to read or write. In Liverpool less than half the child population under fifteen went to school at all, and the other half did not miss much. The fees were 6d. for readers, 9d. for writers, 1s. for counters. Masters made 17s. a week, Dames 6s. A curious difficulty occurred in the collection of these statistics. 'Catch me counting the brats,' one Dame replied. 'I mind what happened to David.' At Newcastle half the children escaped from schools which are briefly described as horrible. Bristol was rather better; more than half the children were at school, paying a penny or twopence a week. Leeds was worse, for there 15,000 went untaught altogether; Sunday schools provided for 11,000, and less than 7,000 were in such rudimentary secular establishments as existed. In Hull a close investigation revealed that of 5,000 children who had been to school, 800 could not read, 1,800 could not write, and just half could not do a sum. It was much if the victims could write their names. From the marriage registers it would appear that in the thirties about one-third of the men and two-thirds of the women could not. Nor was there much evidence of improvement in the past thirty years. In Manchester, about 1810, the Signers were 52, the Markers 48; by 1838 the proportion had only moved to 55 and 45.

Clearly no society could be left to rest on a substratum of ignorance so dense as these figures show, especially after the

Reform Bill had divulged the arcanum of party government, that the franchise might be extended. Of what use were cheap papers to a population which could not read them? The passion for an educated people, which united all reformers and gives a lasting nobility to the tortuous career of Broughham,[1] was frustrated by the absence of any foundation on which to build, and the Mechanics' Institute from which so much was hoped sank into play-centres for serious clerks. The Philosophical Radicals had their solution. As usual, it was entirely right, and as usual, it was entirely impracticable. In dealing with the difficulties of Victorian administration it is necessary to remember that hardly any one had yet thought of the county as an administrative unit, except for its ancient functions of justice and highways. Twice in the thirties a Radical Bill for the creation of elected County Boards fluttered for an evening in the unfriendly air and died. There was the Imperial Government: there were the boroughs. But between Whitehall and the people at large there were, except for the Poor Law Unions, no administrative links or gradations. Chadwick, who thought of everything, had meditated a system of local authorities for all purposes based on the Poor Law Unions, but he was darkly suspected of a design for abolishing the counties to begin with and cutting up the immemorial map of England into Benthamite rectangles. The Radicals proposed to divide the country into School Districts, levying an education rate, maintaining infant schools, elementary schools with a vocational bias, continuation classes, and training colleges. In process of time the schools would be wholly staffed by trained teachers; education should be compulsory from six to twelve, and it should include instruction, by means of Government text-books, in political economy. The Radicals had substituted the inspiration of Ricardo for the inspiration of Scripture. Otherwise, this project has a very modern air. Radical projects always have, after their origin has been forgotten.

It was far too modern for 1843. Parliamentary Government

[1] The appointment of Panizzi to the British Museum was one of Brougham's best jobs.

63

can only operate with the equipment and feelings of the current age. The Voluntary Schools were there. And any attempt at educational reform had to reckon with the most intense of Victorian emotions, sectarian animosity. It must be allowed for everywhere, and a few years later it flamed up with a vehemence which consumed the most promising experiment yet projected. Immediately on his appointment Kay-Shuttleworth produced, and the Committee of Council accepted, a plan for a Training College, complete with model school and practising school. It broke down on the question of religious instruction. The Dissenters would not stand the parson in a State school. The Establishment would not stand any one else. Even the Church of Scotland, which might have minded its own business, took a hand in the game. The plan was withdrawn. With an energy typical of himself and his age its author opened the College himself and for some years lived a double existence, as an official at Whitehall and the Principal of a Training College at Battersea. The example was decisive. Voluntary training colleges sprang up in quick succession, and the foundations of a teaching profession were laid. The system was consolidated by the Minute of 1846 – apprenticeship to a master, a course in a Training College, the Certificate, additional pay for the Trained Teacher, and the unkept promise of a pension at the end. Charley Hexam – surely the most detestable boy on record – was apprenticed to Bradley Headstone. Sue Bridehead was a Queen's scholar at Salisbury Training College when she made her disastrous expedition to Wardour with Jude. They are products, perhaps unusual products, of the Minute of 1846.

But the new grant system which the Minute established – £1 from the Treasury, in augmentation of salaries, for every £2 raised locally – brought up the whole issue of State intervention or State abstention. The Dissenters, who had wrecked Graham's Bill of 1843 for educating factory children in Church schools with a conscience clause, took the field against the Committee of Council. As of all the churches the Church of England was the richest and, in fairness it must be added, the most generous, it was foreseeable that the two pounds would be more readily forthcoming for Church schools than for any other. In effect, therefore, and in the circumstances inevitably, the Government grant would be a subsidy in aid of the education of little Churchmen, or the conversion of little Dissenters. That the bulk of the child population might better have been described as little heathen seems to have escaped the notice of the reverend opponents to the measure. But the onslaught of the Voluntarists was encountered with a conviction equal and an eloquence superior to their own, and probably the only speech on Education which has ever been read with pleasure by any one except the author is Macaulay's defence of the new grants against Mr Duncombe, Mr Baines, the Congressional Union, and John Bright. Henceforth the education of the people was admitted to be a primary function of the State. From this admission it is not far to the Radical position – education universal, compulsory, and secular – and the only question remaining was how slowly and by what devious routes and compromises it would be reached, and how much energy would be squandered by the way on the interminable rancours of Church and Dissent.

10

The Tory ascendancy under George III had modified the political colour of the Anglican body. In the earlier Hanoverian decades, the hierarchy, nominated by the Government, was, on the whole, Whig; the clergy, appointed by lay patrons, Tory. Then, gradually, the Sees came to be filled with men in closer sympathy with the mass of the clergy, men, too, for the most part, of a type superior in piety and learning to the bishops of the first two Georges, while, with the improvement of the land, Holy Orders became a more and more attractive profession for the sons of gentlemen. Thus the Church of England after its long lethargy was reconsolidated, with a distinctly aristocratic colouring, about the time when the Evangelical example was raising the moral level of its ministers. The result was that phase which Froude declared to be the golden age of the Church, when her princes were still princes,[1] and her pastors enforced the simple morality and administered the simple consolations, of village life, with the authority due rather to personal character, birth, and learning than to any pretensions as priests.

There was another side to the picture. The ministers of the Church were at once too rich and too poor. The Archbishopric of Canterbury and the Bishopric of Durham were each worth £19,000 a year; Rochester, £14,000; Llandaff less than £1,000. Of 10,000 benefices, the average value was £285. Less than 200 were worth £1,000 and upward, but among them were livings of £2,000, £5,000 and one of over £7,000 a year. The poor parson was therefore very poor, the curate poorer still, best off in Rochester on £109 a year, worst off in St David's on £55. The mischief was aggravated by pluralism, non-residence, and nepotism. A great Church family, taking sons, nephews, and sons-in-law together, might easily collect £10,000 a year among them and leave the greater part of their duties to be discharged by curates at £80. The best of parsons could not help being a little too much of a magistrate and landowner, and not enough of a pastor.[2] Into the gaps left in his spiritual ministrations crept dissent, with its opportunities for personal distinction,[3] close converse, and mutual inspection. At the beginning of our period it was estimated that the Church, the Dissenters, and the Romans were in the ratio of 120, 80, and 4. The figures of Church attendance taken in 1851 show the Establishment

[1] The last, I suppose, was Charles Sumner, Bishop of Winchester till 1869, whose hospitality was the most conspicuous of his many virtues.

[2] Whately of Cookham is the best example. 'A Whately in every parish' was a catchword of Poor Law reformers. Froude was thinking of his own father, the Archdeacon of Totnes.

[3] In 1860 H. F. Tozer wrote of Norway, 'The priest's residence is usually the nicest house in the neighbourhood, and the priest's daughters are the most eligible young ladies. It is surprising in these circumstances that dissent does not spring up.' The implication is as illuminating as P. G. Hamerton's remark that few educated people had ever seen a dissenter eat.

decidedly preponderating in the south and south-west, except in Cornwall; and holding its own, with varying majorities, everywhere, except in the old Puritan strongholds of Bedford, Huntingdon, and the West Riding, and in Northumberland. An absolute figure of effective membership it is impossible to give. Out of a population of 2,000,000 in the diocese of London it was reckoned that there were 70,000 communicants.[1] But a distinction must be drawn between the country and the old towns on one side of the new agglomerations on the other. In the one, everybody, except the free-thinking cobbler, would at least have called himself one thing or the other, and there were few families which were not sometimes represented at the Sunday service. In the other, great multitudes were as indifferent to the distinction as the inhabitants of Borrioboola-Gha. It was to these masses that the Churches, often in unfriendly rivalry, had next to address themselves.

In dogma there was little to choose between a worthy clergyman of an evangelical cast and a worthy dissenting minister. Socially, by their University education, and their relations with the gentry, the clergy as a body stood in a class apart and, with the preachers who collected little congregations about them in hamlets and the back streets of towns, who ministered in Zoar and Bethel and Mizpah and Shebaniah, they had little in common. But the ministers of the older bodies were often as learned as the clergy, and their congregations more exclusive than the mixed multitudes who, from habit as much as conviction, were gathered in the parish church. The Unitarians were, on the whole, the most intellectual of the dissenting bodies: they went to the theatre. The Independents represented traditional middle-class Puritanism: the more fervent, and more rhetorical, Baptists struck lower in society, among the tradesmen in small streets. With them and with the dissident

[1] Lord Robert Montagu's statistics in 1860 are at least amusing. He reckoned: Baptists, Congregationists, Jews, Mormons, &c., $16\frac{1}{2}$ per cent.; Wesleyans (seven sorts) and Roman Catholics, $16\frac{1}{2}$ per cent.; Church of England, 42 per cent.; Irreligious Poor, 25 per cent. I fancy they are pretty near the mark. Of the great underworld, Lord Shaftesbury said that only 2 per cent. went anywhere. The figures of 1851 are not very trustworthy, but it would appear that of 100 possibles 58 went somewhere.

Wesleyans we approach that brand of unattached Nonconformity with which Dickens was so familiar, and which is represented for us by Mr Stiggins and Mr Chadband.[1] The 4,000 Quaker families were a body, almost a race, apart.

But between them all there was, at the beginning of the nineteenth century, a state of stable equilibrium which the political advance of the middle classes, the Oxford Movement, and the growth of the Wesleyans destroyed. As it left the hands of its founder, the Wesleyan body was a society, autonomous in government and independent in action, but essentially supplementary to the Established Church. Under his successors, especially Jabez Bunting, it developed into a church itself. Active, zealous, and resourceful, it gave a personality to the somewhat formless individualism of earlier Dissent, and it satisfied, and steadied, thousands of men and women who, but for the Wesleyan church, would, in the break-up of the old society, have drifted without direction or restraint, into vice, or crime, or revolution. By providing a far larger sphere of action for the laity than the Church or the older denominations furnished, it brought romance and ambition into a class which, under the pressure of the new civilizations, was losing both purpose and aspiration; and the Wesleyan organization – the class meeting, the circuit, the conference, the Legal Hundred – has powerfully affected the constitution of political parties and Trade Unions. The activity of the Wesleyans radiated through the older denominations and was not without effect on the Church itself. By 1840 it was supposed that they numbered half a million members in England and Wales, and their attitude on any political question was anxiously calculated by the managers of both political parties. They were as a body not unfriendly to the Church: they were zealous upholders of the Constitution. 'Wesleyanism', Bunting said, 'is as much opposed to Democracy as it is to Sin'; and among the causes which led to the defeat of Chartism and the great pacification of the fifties must be

[1] See also Theodore Watts (Dunton's) account of Ebenezer Jones's childhood in Canonbury, and the 'tea-and-toast' ministers who terrified the children who waited on them (*Althenaeum*, 1878).

numbered the resolute opposition which the Wesleyans offered to subversion in society or the State.[1]

In the eighteenth century the ancient opposition of Rome and Oxford had died down; courteous gestures were exchanged across the frontiers; in the French wars the Pope became an almost attractive figure. Yet the growth of a new anti-Roman feeling was inevitable. Evangelicalism emphasized the points of difference and gave them alarming value for the individual soul; travellers reported the shocking condition of the Papal States. And there was always Ireland. To be misgoverned in this world and damned in the next seemed to many thousands of sober English families the necessary consequence of submission to Rome. Nor could it be comfortably pretended that the claims or activity of Rome were abating, and no Englishman could read the contemporary history of France without a running commentary in which Louis XVIII played the part of Charles II and Charles X stood for the fanatical James. If the Bishops had seen their way to vote for Reform in 1831, they would have made themselves as popular as the Blessed Seven in the Tower. It was the misfortune of the Church that her politics should be officially branded as illiberal just when her theology was about to come under suspicion of Romanticism. The combination, coinciding with the Radical drive against privilege, produced that Political Protestantism which waxed with the growth of the middle-class electorate and waned in our time with the spread of religious indifference and with the dilution of the middle-class vote by universal suffrage.

---

[1] The writings of Mark Rutherford show E. V. Nonconformity at its self-righteous worst. Of its other side, as a civilizing agency, credulous, conceited, but of heroic tenacity, one of the most sympathetic records I know is *Warminster Common* by W. Daniell. Daniell (who had gifts of healing, the nature of which he did not recognize) must have been very like an early Christian bishop up country. Incidentally, this little work enables me to determine one important question of social history – the origin of the chapel tea-fight. It was invented by Daniell, and the first was held on December 13, 1815. Tea was an expensive and select drink, and the tea-drinkings at Warminster were, as the following extract shows, almost Eleusinian in their rapture:

'Christmas 1829. Drank tea at Chapel with the Christian friends (a purely religious meeting). A holy unction attended and great was the joy. We could all say (we trust experimentally) "Unto us a child is born".'

The immediate occasion of the Oxford Movement was the suppression of ten Irish bishoprics by the Whig Government. The danger to the Church was exaggerated, but in 1833 much seemed possible that time proved imaginary. It was believed that Government emissaries had directed the attack on the Bishop of Bristol's palace in 1831. It was known that James Mill, an official man in the confidence of the ruling powers, had prepared a plan for the conversion of the Church into a Benthamite institution of public utility. Sunday services, without, of course, any form of prayer or worship, were to be preserved: the parish would attend, in its best clothes, to hear a lecture on botany or economics and receive prizes for virtuous behaviour. The day of rest and gladness would end with dances expressive of the social and fraternal emotions, but avoiding any approach to lasciviousness, and an agape at which, naturally, only soft drinks would be served. In principle there is no difference between amalgamating the see of Ossory with the see of Ferns, and applying the revenues of the Church to magic lanterns and muffins. In their alarm, certain divines, their imagination outstripping the practical difficulties in the way (and, in fact, the Whig Government having rearranged the revenues of the Irish Church split on the question what to do with the surplus) decided to act before it was too late. Seven thousand clergy assured the Archbishop of their attachment to the Church: a lay address, signed by 230,000 heads of families, followed. Eminent Nonconformists allowed it to be known that they could countenance no aggression against the Establishment, which was still the national bulwark against infidelity; and the storm blew over. In the peace that followed, the rulers of the Church showed that they had taken their lesson.[1] The vexatious question of tithes was equitably settled by the Commutation Act of 1836. Pluralities were regulated, the grosser inequalities of church livings levelled out. There the movement, having demonstrated, and stimulated, the vitality of the Church,

[1] The guiding hand was Blomfield of London, who also edited Aeschylus, and was a principal originator of the Sanitary Enquiry of 1839. But he would not allow ladies to attend Geological lectures at King's College, London.

might have been re-absorbed into the main stream of invigorated Churchmanship. But feelings had been too deeply stirred. In any case, it was inevitable that in a generation which had been enchanted by Scott and bemused by Coleridge,[1] the corporate and sacramental aspect of the Church should re-emerge, and that religion would have to find a place for feelings of beauty, antiquity, and mystery, which the ruling theology had dismissed or ignored as worldly or unprofitable or profane. Now, too, the question had been raised, on what foundation could the Church of England, disendowed and disestablished, take her stand, and it had to be answered even though the danger had passed. Hitherto, Churchmen had taken their Church for granted as the mode of Protestantism established by law. The Oxford Movement created an Anglican self-consciousness, parallel to the self-consciousness of the Protestant denominations, based on the assurance of apostolic descent, and inevitably, therefore, tending to sympathy, at least, with the one Church whose apostolic origin could not be denied.

Apart from these two processes, the crystalization of Anglicanism round the Tractarians and of Nonconformity round the Wesleyans, a larger and more fluid conception of the Church was gathering strength. The Oxford divines took little note of Nonconformity. Their object was to brace and fortify the Church against the coming onslaught of Liberalism and infidelity, and in the thirties, after the Oxford leaders, Newman and Pusey themselves, perhaps the most conspicuous, certainly the most influential, figure in the English Church was one who by his own profession was a Liberal and in the eye of his critics was not much better than an infidel.[2] But neither Anglicans nor Protestants had any real conception of the forces which

[1] One critic divided the rising generation into fluent Benthamites and muddled Coleridgians. S.T.C. once said to Miss Martineau: 'You seem to regard society as an aggregate of individuals.' 'Of course I do,' she replied. There is much history implicit in that encounter, and by 1850 Coleridge had won.

[2] 'But is Dr Arnold a Christian?' Newman once asked.

were gathering against that stronghold of their common faith, the inerrancy of Holy Scripture; they were only beginning to learn, when they went out of the University or the seminary, how little religion meant to the half-barbarized population of the great towns. The diffusion of scientific knowledge among the educated, the spread of old-fashioned rationalism downwards through the masses, had created a new problem for the religious teacher. Milman, walking through the City early one morning, was held up by a group of porters and made to deliver his opinion: did God really command the Israelites to massacre the people of Canaan? It was the test question. Macaulay, putting himself on Butler, wrote that in the Old Testament we read of actions performed by Divine command which without such authority would be atrocious crimes. Lyell – who could sometimes be led on, in a small company after dinner, to admit that the world was probably 50,000 years old – called on him and asked him to speak out. He refused. At the height of such a reputation as no other English man of letters has enjoyed, he could not face the storm that would have broken on the head of the infidel who questioned the humanity of Joshua or the veracity of Moses.[1]

Here, not in schism or disendowment, in the rabbling of bishops for their votes, or the burning of their palaces in a riot, lay the danger which only Arnold clearly apprehended. The union of the Churches was an incidental stage in his pro-gramme. The foundation was a new conception, in which, no doubt, we can detect something of Lessing, something of Coleridge, something of Carlyle, but which in purpose and direction was Arnold's own, of the significance of history as the revelation of God. The world, as he conceived it, needed new rulers, and the rulers needed a new faith, which was to be found in the historic record, in the Bible, doubtless, most of all, but in

[1] When Lyell, then aged 62, came forward in support of *The Origin of Species*, Darwin wrote: 'Considering his age, his former views, *and his position in society*, I think his conduct has been heroic.'

the Bible – and here he broke definitely with Oxford and current Protestantism alike – interpreted not by tradition, but by science, scholarship, and, above all, political insight. 'He made us think', a pupil wrote, 'of the politics of Israel, Greece and Rome.' In this sentence we come as near as we can hope to get to the secret of Arnold's power. He took the self-consciousness of the English gentry, benevolently authoritative, but uneasily aware that its authority was waning, and gave it religious and historic justification.[1]

I I

Of these three schools, united in their emphasis on personal conduct, the Protestant, on the whole, accepted the social philosophy of the age, the Anglican ignored it, the Arnoldian challenged it. The Nonconformist business man, like Bright, severe with himself and others, within reason generous and within reason honest, is one of the central Victorian types. So, and of the same ancestry, is the preaching politician, like the Corn Law rhetorician, Fox. Another, of which Mr Gladstone may serve as the representative, is the new High Churchman, instructed in his faith but submissive to his teachers, touched by the art and poetry of old religion, inclining to regard the Church as the one immovable thing in a changing and shifting world, and therefore less concerned with its future than with its past, less with the application of his faith to the circumstances of the world than with its integrity as transmitted from the fathers. As individuals, the High Churchmen worked as manfully as any: Walter Hook in Leeds created a new standard of duty for every parish priest who has come after him. But as a school, they shook off with well-bred impatience the humanitarian

[1] On the whole, William Arnold's *Oak field* seems to me to convey most completely the effect that Arnold made on those who came under his influence.

professions which had become associated with the Evangelical creed, and few Tractarian names will be found connected with the reforms which are the glory of the Early Victorian Age. This rather was to be the sphere of action of the third school. In the forties we are aware of a new type issuing from the Universities and public schools, somewhat arrogant and somewhat shy, very conscious of their standing as gentlemen but very conscious of their duties, too, men in tweeds who smoke in the streets, disciples of Maurice, willing hearers of Carlyle, passionate for drains and co-operative societies, disposed to bring everything in the state of England to the test of Isaiah and Thucydides, and to find the source of all its defects in what, with youthful violence, they would call the disgusting vice of shopkeeping. These are the Arnoldians.

In the meantime the Oxford Movement had gone into liquidation. Through the thirties it advanced, in the face of authority, with irresistible force. But the farther it went, the more certain appeared its ultimate objective, and with the publication of Tract XC it seemed to have unmaksed itself. The purpose of the Tract was to clear away the popular interpretations which had grown up round the formularies of the Church, to prove that the Articles rigidly construed were more susceptible of a Catholic than a Protestant meaning, or, as Macaulay put it, that a man might hold the worst doctrines of the Church of Rome and the best benefice in the Church of England. In this sense, at least, the Tract was received and condemned by the Heads of Houses, and the Tractarians stigmatized as Romanists without the courage of their convictions. And by 1843, when Newman left St Mary's, Protestantism was beginning to work almost hysterically even on sober English opinion, which, having accepted Catholic emancipation as the completion of the Union, was now challenged by O'Connell to regard it as the basis of disruption to be achieved, if need be, at the price of civil war. Deviations of doctrine, like novelties of observance, were watched by ten thousand critical eyes; the Hampden controversy and the Gorham controversy were followed as attentively as any debate in Parliament, and, far away in Borneo, Rajah

Brooke wrote home to his mother that he had not had much time for theology, but he had composed an answer to Tract XC. The decision of Pope Pious IX to revive the Roman Hierarchy in England was answered with an outburst of frenzy of which the Tractarian clergy were almost as much the objects as the Papists themselves.

But to the new Englishman of the late forties and fifties, a travelled man bred up on Carlyle and Tennyson and the romantic classics, the world was a far more interesting place than it had been to those late Augustans, imprisoned in their island, among whom Evangelicalism struck root, and his religion conformed to the awakening of his senses. The theology of Oxford he still viewed with distrust: at sisterhoods and processions he frowned with dark suspicion. Insensibly, however, the Tractarian influence was affecting his notions of public worship. The Hanoverian vulgarity of a Royal christening, with a sham altar loaded with the family plate and an opera singer warbling in the next room, shocked a taste which was insensibly forming for simplicity and reverence and the beauty of the sanctuary. Churches were swept; churchyards tidied; church windows cleaned. High pews behind which generations of the comfortable had dozed the sermon out, red velvet cushions on which the preacher had pounded the divisions of his text, the village band in the gallery, the clerk under the pulpit, gradually disappeared: very cautiously, crosses were introduced, and flowers and lights. Liturigcal science became a passion with the younger clergy, and the wave of restoration and church building brought with it a keen, sometimes a ludicrous, preoccupation with symbolism. Dickens was not far out when he observed that the High Churchman of 1850 was the dandy of 1820 in another form.[1]

The great ritualist controversy belongs to later years: its originating issue was the fashion of the preacher's garment.[2]

---

[1] Newman, in *Loss and Gain*, has put the same point with more dexterous satire.

[2] And the material, wood or stone, of the Holy Table. In the ruling case (Holy Sepulchre, Cambridge) a document was tendered under the title *Restoration of the Churches the Restoration of Popery*. Which, after all, was what Pugin wanted.

The custom at the end of the morning prayers had been for the minister to retire and reissue from the vestry in the black gown of a learned man. As the practice spread of reading the Ante-Communion service after the sermon, the double change from white to black and back into white again was felt to be unseemly. But preaching in his whites – his vestments as a minister – the parson might be thought to claim for his utterances an authority more than his own, the authority of a priest, and so surplice riots became a popular diversion of the forties. In 1850 the ritual of St Barnabas, Pimlico, was holding up the Sunday traffic, and we have a glimpse of Thackeray testifying in the crowd: 'O my friends of the nineteenth century, has it come to this?' Ten years later blaspheming mobs stormed St George's in the East in defence of the Reformation Settlement. But gradually new standards of dignity, reverence, and solemnity assimilated the worship in the ancient meeting-place of the village, the portentous assembly room of a London parish, and the Gothic churches which were rising by hundreds in the populous suburbs and industrial towns. Protestant vigilance was easily alarmed, but even an Ulsterman could hardly suspect that the hand of the Pope was at work when the Communion Table ceased to be a depository for hats, the font a receptacle for umbrellas.

Like the Philosophic Radicals, the Tractarians vanish as a party to work in widening circles out of sight, and when, years afterwards, their memory was recalled by Kingsley's tempestuous challenge and the genius wasted on Rome was at last recognized by England, it was in an age less concerned to know whether Newman's faith or some other faith was the right one, than whether in the modern world there was any room for faith at all. For all this vehemence of surface agitation, it had been growing every year plainer, on a deeper view, that neither Pauline nor Patristic Christianity, neither the justification theology nor the infallibility of the Church, could be maintained as a barrier against the 'wild, living intellect of man'. Religion had, somewhat hastily perhaps, made terms with the astronomers. The heavens declare the glory of God, and the better the

76

telescope the greater the glory. The geologists, attacking one of the prime documents of the faith, the Mosaic cosmogony, were more difficult to assimilate or evade. One of the earliest of them had taken the precaution of inviting his theological colleague to sit through his lectures, as censor and chaperone in one; and, on the whole, the religious world seems, in the forties, to have been divided into those who did not know what the geologists were saying and those who did not mind. A far more serious onslaught was preparing from two quarters, abroad and at home. English divinity was not equipped to meet – for its comfort, it was hardly capable of understanding – the new critical methods of the Germans: it is a singular fact that England could not, before Lightfoot, show one scholar in the field of Biblical learning able and willing to match the scholars of Germany. Thirlwall, whom good judges declared to be the ablest living Englishman, was silent, and what was passing in that marmoreal intellect remained a secret. The flock was left undefended against the ravages of David Strauss. On the other side, the English mind was particularly well equipped to grasp the arguments of the biologists. The natural sciences in all their branches – rocks, fossils, birds, beasts, fish, and flowers – were a national hobby; the *Vestiges of Creation*, issued with elaborate secrecy and attributed by a wild surmise to Prince Albert, was a national excitement; translated into golden verse by Tennyson, evolution almost became a national creed. *In Memoriam*, which is nine years older than the *Origin of Species*,[1] gathered up all the doubts of Christianity, of providence, of immortality, which the advance of science had implanted in anxious minds, and answered them, or seemed to answer them, with the assurance of a pantheistic and yet personal faith in progress.

In Memoriam is one of the cardinal documents of the mid-Victorian mind, its ardent curiosity, its exquisite sensitiveness to

---

[1] Some of the evolutionist parts of *In Memoriam* are actually older than *Vestiges*. Tennyson really understood the workings of the new scientific mind, as of the upper class political mind. He was the natural laureate of an age morally conservative and intellectually progressive. Party zeal has claimed Newman's *Essay on Development* as a forerunner. But have the partisans read Milman's rejoinder? Or the *Essay on Development* perhaps?

nature, and, not less, perhaps, its unwillingness to quit, and its incapacity to follow, any chain of reasoning which seems likely to result in an unpleasant conclusion. In his highest mood, Tennyson sometimes speaks like an archangel assuring the universe that it will muddle through. The age was learning, but it had not mastered, the lesson that truth lies not in the statement but in the process: it had a childlike craving for certitude, as if the natural end of every refuted dogma was to be replaced by another dogma. Raised in the dark and narrow framework of Evangelical and economic truth, it wilted in the sunlight and waved for support to something vaguely hopeful like the Platonism of Maurice, or loudly reassuring like the hero worship of Carlyle. New freedom is a painful thing, most painful to the finest minds, who are most sensitive to the breaking-up of faiths and traditions and most apprehensive of the outcome. The stress of the age is incarnate in Arthur Clough. Deeply influenced by Arnold in his boyhood, he had stayed long enough in Oxford to feel all the exhaustion and disillusionment which succeeded the excitement of the Tractarian movement. In the Church was no satisfaction. He had lost, as most educated men were losing, his hold on what had been the middle strand of all Christian creeds, faith in the divine person of Christ. The natural way of escape was into the open mockery to which Clough's temperament inclined him,[1] or into such a pagan equanimity in face of the unknown as the agnostics of the next age practised and proclaimed. But to his generation, so powerful still was the appeal of lost faith, so intricate the associations of right belief and right conduct, that that way was closed. Ruskin's final assurance, that it does not matter much to the universe what sort of person you are, was impossible to a generation impressed by its teachers with the infinite import- ance – and therefore self-importance – of the individual soul. The Tractarians by pointing to the Church, the Arnoldian school by their vivid realization of history, had relieved the

[1] His conjecture that the First Cause would turn out to be a 'smudgy person with a sub-intelligent look about the eyes' is very much in the manner of Butler, and therefore of Mr Shaw.

intense introversion of Evangelicalism.[1] But lacking faith, the individual was released from his own prison only to find himself alone in an indifferent universe.[2] Kingsley was relieving many souls of their burden by communicating his own delight in the body, in the ardours of exploration, sport, and sex. Unluckily the world is not entirely peopled by young country gentlemen, newly married to chastely passionate brides, and it is perhaps, rash to identify the self-contentment which comes of a vigorous body and an assured income, with the glorious liberty of the children of God. Nevertheless, the name of Kingsley, naturalist, health reformer, poet and preacher, on the one hand silenced as an advocate of socialism, on the other denounced as a propagator of impurity, may stand for the meeting-place of all the forces at work on the younger imagination of the years when, as it seemed to those who recalled the sordid and sullen past, England was renewing her youth, at Lucknow and Inkerman, with Livingstone in the African desert, with Burton on the road to Mecca, and speaking to the oppressors of Europe in the accents of Cromwell and Pitt. Of all decades in our history, a wise man would choose the eighteen-fifties to be young in.

---

[1] For Newman, see the profound diagnosis of Evangelicalism at the end of the Lectures on Justification, which, translated out of the technical terms of theology, is applicable to the whole age. Introspection within a closed circle of experience was the trouble. I cannot doubt that if Arnold had not been a schoolmaster, he would have been a fine historian. *Introverted* is, somewhat surprisingly, a word of the forties: Wilberforce used it of Peel.

[2] This mode of pessimism can be followed through *Dipsychus* and *Obermann* down to bedrock in the *City of Dreadful Night*.

Mr Gladstone, dwelling on the responsiveness of the people to good government, once said that every call from Parliament had been answered by a corresponding self-improvement of the masses. The years through which we have been passing afford some confirmation of this sanguine philosophy. The labouring Englishman in the fifties was much better governed than the labouring Englishman of 1830, and he was, taken in the mass, a much more respectable man. He was better governed, inasmuch as the State had definitely resolved to concern itself with the condition of his life and labour and the education of his children. He was more respectable because, with rising wages and cheaper food, with some leisure at home and the grosser kinds of insanitation put down, he was recovering his self-respect. More strictly, it might be said that the proletariat, which in the thirties seemed to be sinking into a dull uniformity of wretchedness, had been stratified. In this light, the contradictions which we encounter whenever we turn our eye to the condition of the people in mid-Victorian England are resolved. There was a vast, untouchable underworld. But the great industries were manned with families, often much better off than the neighbouring curate or schoolmaster, and not burdened by the middle class necessity of keeping up a position. This right wing, hopeful, comfortable, within sight of the franchise, the Respectable Poor, the Conservative working man, drew away. Crime, poverty, and drunkenness, which had reached their peak about 1842, were dropping year by year. The maypole had gone: the village feast and the club-walk were going; but the zoo, the panorama, the free-library, the fête, and the excursion ticket were bringing hundreds of thousands within the reach of orderly and good-humoured pleasure. It is a curious observation of the early fifties that the workmen were wearing the same clothes as the gentlemen. Still more oddly, the

French artist, Delacroix, noticed that the gentlemen were wearing the same clothes as the workmen.

One grey patch remained, growing drearier as the life ebbed out of the villages; but the brooding apprehension of thirty years had lifted. The testing time had come in 1848. The last Chartist demonstration was a demonstration only; for the artillery men who lined the Thames from Waterloo Bridge to Millbank, the shopkeepers who patrolled the streets, the Government clerks who laid in muskets and barricaded the windows with official files,[1] and the coal whippers who marched from Wapping with a general idea of standing by the Duke and a particular intention of breaking every Irishman's head, it was a demonstration and a festival. The storm which swept away half the Governments of Europe passed harmlessly over the islands, and the words which Macaulay wrote at the beginning of his history, that his checkered narrative would excite thankfulness in all religious minds and hope in the breast of all patriots, had a deep significance for his first readers, watching the nations of Europe sink one by one from convulsive anarchy back into despotism, and seeing, in the recovered unity, as much as in the prosperity of England, a triumphant vindication of the historic English way. The Great Exhibition was the pageant of domestic peace. Not for sixty years had the throne appeared so solidly based on the national goodwill as in that summer of hope and pride and reconciliation. After all the alarms and agitations of thirty years the State had swung back to its natural centre.[2]

Victoria was not in her girlhood a popular Sovereign.[3] She was tactless: she was partisan: the tragic story of Lady Flora Hastings showed her heartless as well. The figure that made its way into the hearts of the middle classes was not the gay, self-

[1] The Foreign Office consented to receive reinforcements from the Colonial Office 'if we lose any men'.

[2] In 1848 Thackeray declared himself 'a Republican but not a Chartist'. In 1851 he was writing odes to the Crystal Palace. But *Punch* was still Radical enough to resent the sight of Goldsticks walking backwards.

[3] But in Ireland, the young queen who was to rebuild the Church on the Rock of Cashel, was for a time an object of intense affection – partly, no doubt, because she was not her uncle, Ernest the Orangeman (and other things). Her failure to draw on this fund of loyalty was the gravest error of her life.

willed little Whig of 1837, but the young matron, tireless, submissive, dutiful. Her Court was dull, but the Royal nursery was irresistible. Prince Albert had seized the key positions – morality and industry[1] – behind which the Monarchy was safe. A revolt of the special constables would have been formidable: a virtuous and domestic Sovereign, interested in docks and railways, hospitals and tenements, self-help and mutual improvement, was impregnable. Such a Sovereign, and much more beside, Prince Albert would have been, and in this mild, beneficent light he displayed his Consort's crown to the world. As its power pursued its inevitable downward curve, its influence rose in equipoise.

In 1834 King William had strained prerogative to the breaking-point by putting the Tories into office before the country was quite ready for them. In 1839 the Queen had kept the Whigs in office when the country was heartily tired of them. But ten years later the Crown was called upon to exercise that power of helping the country to find the Government it wants, which makes monarchy so precious an adjunct to the party system. After repealing the Corn Laws, Sir Robert was defeated by a combination between his late allies, the Whigs, and his own rebels, the Protectionists. Lord John Russell came in, with Palmerston at the Foreign Office, Disraeli leading the Opposition. In 1850 Peel died, the only English statesman for whose death the poor have cried in the streets, and it soon appeared whose hand had kept the Whigs in power. In 1851 they were defeated; Stanley tried to form a Tory Government, failed, and the Whigs came back. Palmerston was dismissed for impertinence to his Queen, and Lord John groped about for a coalition. He was unsuccessful, and in 1852 Palmerston had the gratification of turning him out. Stanley (now Lord Derby) and Disraeli formed a Government, struggled through a few months against united Whigs, Peelites, and Radicals, and resigned. Old

[1] Again, like most things in Victorian England, this was a European episode. The English Court struck a mean between the pietism of Berlin and the bourgeois decorum of Louis-Philippe. The King of Prussia and Elizabeth Fry once knelt together in prayer in the Women's Ward at Newgate.

Lord Lansdowne was sent for, and dear Lord Aberdeen was commissioned, to form one coalition more. He succeeded, and went to war with Russia. Went is hardly the word. But the mismanagement of the opening campaign in '54 broke up the Cabinet, and with universal applause, superb assurance, and the recovered confidence of his Sovereign, Palmerston bounded into the vacant place. A brief eclipse in '58 hardly impaired his ascendancy, and till his death at eighty-one, with a half-finished dispatch on his table, in the eyes of the world and his country Palmerston was England and England was Palmerston. The political comedy has never been more brilliantly staged, and at every turn the Crown was in its proper place, selecting, reconciling, and listening, its dignity unimpaired by party conflicts and its impartiality surmounting individual distastes. 'I object to Lord Palmerston on personal grounds,' the Queen said. 'The Queen means,' Prince Albert explained, 'that she does not object to Lord Palmerston on account of his person.' In place of a definite but brittle prerogative it had acquired an indefinable but potent influence. The events of 1846 to 1854 affirmed for some generations to come the character of the new monarchy, just at the time when events abroad – Australian gold discoveries, India, and the Crimea – were giving the nation an aggressive, imperial self-consciousness.

From 1815 to the Revolution of '48 foreign affairs had engaged but a small share of the public atention. First came the depression after Waterloo and the slow recovery, with a terrible set-back in 1825. Then Ireland and Catholic emancipation took the stage, then Reform and the Poor Law, and Ireland again with O'Connell; then come the Oxford, the Chartist, and the Free Trade movements, the depression of the first years of Victoria, Ireland once more, and the Repeal of the Corn Laws. But from 1850 onwards the focus of interest is overseas; the soldier, the emigrant, and the explorer, the plots of Napoleon III and the red shirt of Garibaldi, take and fill the imagination. Domestic politics are languid. Once, if not twice, in twenty years, the franchise had brought England in sight of civil war: in the fifties a Franchise Bill was four times introduced

Quater ipso in limine portae
substitit, atque utero sonitum quater arma dedere,[1]

and was forgotten; the annual motion on the ballot became an annual joke. Ireland was prostrate, Old Chartists were lecturing on Christian evidences, or, more usefully, working quietly in the new trade unions; old republicans were shouting for war; old pacifists declaiming to empty halls. Nothing is so bloody-minded as a Radical turned patriot. Roebuck was all for bombarding Naples. Bentham's former secretary, Bowring, crowned his astonishingly various career by actually bombarding Canton. Only those whose memories went back fifteen years could understand the change of sentiment which made the arming of the volunteers in '59 possible, or how completely the confidence which inspired that gesture was vindicated by the patience of Lancashire in the cotton famine.

Adventurous and secure, the ruling class in the years of Palmerston was excellently qualified to found a commonwealth or reconquer an empire abroad, and, within the range of its ideas, to legislate wisely at home. Ireland, unhappily, lay outside that range. But University reform, divorce reform, the management of the metropolis, the resettlement of India, colonial self-government, the creation of the Public Accounts Committee, the Post Office Savings Bank, the Atlantic cable, that generation took in its stride, and the conversion of the vast and shapeless city which Dickens knew – fog-bound and fever-haunted, brooding over its dark, mysterious river – into the imperial capital, of Whitehall, the Thames Embankment and South Kensington, is the still visible symbol of the mid-Victorian transition.[2]

[1] Bob Lowe, Disraeli's 'inspired schoolboy'. I put this second among Virgilian quotations, the best being Gladstone's, when the Spanish Government unexpectedly met some bills and so stopped a hole in the budget.

'via prima salutis
Quod minime reris, Graia pandetur ab urbe.'

Pitt's 'Nos ubi primus equis', when the dawn came through the windows of St Stephen's, is not quotation, but inspiration.

[2] Modern hotel life begins with the Langham. The Prince of Wales, who attended the opening in 1865, remarked that it reminded him of the Astoria, New York.

Parties were changing; the strong and steady currents of Whig and Tory opinion were splitting into eddies. The friends of the late Sir Robert Peel, as they move to and fro across the stage, make Conservatism a little less Tory, and Liberalism a little less Whig. A new and popular Liberalism is forming of definite grievance and redress, Church rates and University tests, Army Purchase and Irish Disestablishment, and a humane and frugal distrust of Empire, aristocracy, adventure, and war. The re-education of the Conservatives, paralysed by the Free Trade schism, has begun, and the field is setting for the encounter of Gladstone and Disraeli when once Palmerston has departed. But the virulence of party conflicts is abating in a humorous, sporting tussle, where Palmerston keeps the ring against all comers, while Gladstone's budgets swing majestically down the tideway of an unexampled prosperity. In twelve years our trade was doubled, and the returns, indeed, of those years are a part of English literature because they furnished footnotes to Macaulay's third chapter. In four years from 1853 the profits of agriculture increased by a fifth. The whole debt left by the Russian war was less than one-half of a year's revenue and the revenue no more than a third, perhaps not more than a fifth, of the annual savings of the nation. But age and crabbed youth cannot live together; age is full of pleasure, youth is full of care; and the unfriendly and mistrustful union of Palmerston and Gladstone, a union almost breaking into open hostility over the French panic and the fortification of Portsmouth, and again over the Paper Duties, is typical of the poise of the age, looking back to the proud, exciting days of Canning and Pitt and another Bonaparte, and forward to a peaceful prosperity of which no end was in sight; an ignorant pride which forgot that Prussia had an army, a thoughtless prosperity which did not reckon with American wheat.

Parliament was changing, too. Till 1832 it was in effect and almost in form a single-chamber assembly, since a large part of the Commons were appointed by the Lords, and a man might easily have one vote – or one proxy – in the Upper House and half a dozen in the Lower. Separation implies the possibility at least of conflict. That it was avoided, that for all the hostility of the Radicals to the Peers, neither reform nor abolition of the Lords was seriously mooted, followed from the fact that socially the landed interest ascendant in the Commons had no hostility towards its chiefs in the Lords, and that politically the Duke could always induce the Tory Lords, in a crisis, to give way to the Whig Commons. They yielded in 1832; they yielded in 1846; and by neither surrender did the Lords as a House, or the aristocracy as a class, lose any particle of real power.

After the first shock of dismay they had rallied to the land, and the upward tilt of prices gave them the confidence they needed. Rents did not fall; they even began to rise; between '53 and '57, helped by the war, they rose by more than a tenth. The basis of mid-Victorian prosperity – and, indeed, of society – was a balance of land and industry, an ever enlarging market for English manufactures, and a still restricted market for foreign produce. The home harvest was dominant: a short crop meant high prices, low prices meant an abundant crop. If all other grounds were absent, the obstinate survival of aristocracy in Victorian England is capable of economic explanation. They were the capitalists and directors of the chief English industry: 3,500,000 acres under wheat, crops from 30 bushels upwards to the acre:[1] encircled by a prosperous and respectful tenantry, as proud in their own way as themselves, and a landless peasantry at the feet of both.

But their ascendancy rested hardly less on immaterials. If they had the one thing the plutocracy most respected in themselves, they had all the other things which the people missed in the plutocracy. In morals and intellect they were not disturbingly above or below the average of their countrymen, who regarded them, with some truth, as being in all bodily gifts the finest stock in Europe. By exercise, temperance, and plebeian alliance, the spindle-shanked lord of Fielding had become the ancestor of an invigorated race. They had shed

[1] All these statistics contain an element of guess-work. But the best opinion seems to be that, in the mid-fifties, England had rather more than $3\frac{1}{2}$ million acres, with crops running to 40 bushels. The yield over all was $26\frac{1}{2}$ bushels.

their brutality and extravagance; their eccentricities were of a harmless sporting kind; they were forward in good works; they habitually had family prayers.[1] Of two rich men, or two clever men, England was not ashamed to prefer the gentleman, and the preference operated for the benefit of many gentlemen who were both poor and stupid. Mr Podsnap is not a bad man: in the one crisis he has to face he acts with right decision. But Dickens's heart is with little Mr Twemlow, who never made a decision in his life and would probably have got it wrong if he had. If they had stood against each other for a borough constituency in the South it is not improbable that the ten-pound householders would have chosen Mr Twemlow. England is large, there is room, and a future, for Sir Leicester and the Iron-master, but Mr Podsnap is a belated and sterile type.

Mr Gladstone had two names for this peculiar habit of mind. Once he called it 'a sneaking kindness for a lord'; at another time, more characteristically, 'the shadow which the love of freedom casts or the echo of its voice in the halls of the constitution'. The philosophic historian may take his choice, and it is easier to frame a defence or an indictment of the Victorian attitude to aristocracy than to understand why, in a money-making age, opinion was, on the whole, more deferential to birth than to money, and why, in a mobile and progressive society, most regard was had to the element which represented immobility, tradition, and the past. Perhaps the statement will be found to include the solution. The English *bourgeoisie* had never been isolated long enough to frame, except in the spheres of comfort and carnal morality, ideals and standards of its own. It was imitative. A nation, hammered into unity by a strong crown, had ended by putting the power of the Crown into commission, and the great houses, in succeeding to the real authority, had acquired, and imparted to the lesser houses, something of the mysterious ascendancy of the royal symbol. For a hundred years they ruled, and almost reigned, over an England of villages and little towns. The new urban civilization

[1] Lord Hatherton used to say that in 1810 only two gentlemen in Staffordshire had family prayers: in 1850 only two did not.

was rapidly creating a tradition of civic benevolence and government, but it had no tradition of civic magnificence. To be anything, to be recognized as anything, to feel himself as anything in the State at large, the rich English townsman, unless he was a man of remarkable gifts and character, had still to escape from the seat and source of his wealth; to learn a new dialect and new interests; and he was more likely to magnify than to belittle the virtues of the life into which he and his wife yearned to be admitted, the life, beyond wealth, of power and consideration on the land. From time immemorial a place in the country had been the crown of a merchant's career, and from the first circle the impulse was communicated through all the spheres down to the solid centre of the ten-pound franchise and the suburban villa.

Within the limits thus marked out by instinctive deference, the electorate was free, and not, on the whole, ill qualified to make a general choice between parties and policies. Through its educated stratum, which was proportionately large as the electorate was still small, through the still costly newspapers written for that stratum, through the opportunities which the orders of the House still gave to private members,[1] it could maintain a fairly even pressure on Parliament, and the work of Parliament was correspondingly increased. Parliaments in the eighteenth century and in the French wars were not in the first instance legislative bodies: they met to ventilate grievances, vote

---

[1] This is of great importance for the character of Victorian Parliaments. After the disappearance of Speeches on Petitions in 1843, questions to Ministers steadily increased. The Government had only Mondays and Fridays, and on the motion for adjournment to Monday any member could raise any questions, the result being, as Disraeli said, a conversazione. (The present system of numbered questions goes back to a proposal for regulating the conversazione made in 1860.) Moreover, every Monday and Friday before Easter, on the motion for going into Committee of Supply, the same liberty existed. As a result, I find in one fortnight, besides several useful little Bills introduced or advanced, the following subjects reviewed by the Commons, often in great detail, on the initiative of private members (sometimes, of course, by arrangement with the Government): Corruption at Elections, Criminal Appeal, Civil Service Economy, Defective Anchors, the Shrubs in Hyde Park, Publication of Divorce Reports, Church Rates, Indian Finance, the Ballot, Naval Operations in China (by the Admiral Commanding, at great length), Flogging, Manning the Navy, competitive Examination, and the Export of Coal.

taxes, and control the executive. From about 1820 the age of
continual legislation begins, and, as it proceeds, the ascendancy
of the business end of Parliament over the debating end, of the
Cabinet over the back benches, is more and more strongly
affirmed. But between the two Reform Acts the executive and
deliberative elements in Parliament were still in reasonable
equipoise: Mr Gladstone's punctilious phrase, that the Government would seek the advice of the House, was not quite a
formality in an age when the Government commanded less
than half the time of the House; and the fact that a large
minority, sometimes a majority, of the Cabinet were Peers
relieved the congestion of debate by spreading it over two
Houses. As a branch of the legislature, the House of Lords is of
limited utility, and it could neither compel nor avert a change of
Ministry or a Dissolution; but it was an admirable theatre for
the exposition or criticism of policy, and Peel, a House of
Commons man through and through, came late in life to the
opinion that public business might be advantaged if the Prime
Minister were relieved of the management of the Commons and
set to direct operations from the security of the Upper House.

13

In the great peace of the fifties the lines of force released in the
earlier decades, lines best remembered by the names of Arnold,
Newman, and Carlyle, come round into pattern. It is about this
time that the word 'Victorian'[1] was coined to register a new
self-consciousness. 'Liverpool below, Oxford on top,' was said of
Mr Gladstone, and it might be said more generally of the
English intelligence of the fifties. Work shapes the mind, leisure
colours it; the grim discipline of the years of peril was relaxed:

[1] The first example I have noted is in E. P. Hood, *The Age and its Architects*, 1851.

life was richer, easier, and friendlier. To turn from the stark, forbidding dogmas of James Mill on Government to the humorous wisdom of Bagehot's *English Constitution*, with its large allowances for the idleness, stupidity, and good nature of mankind, is to enter another world of thought, at once less logical and more real, and the contrast not unfairly represents the change that had come over England in thirty years.

In the general movement of the English mind few episodes are so instructive as the revulsion which in the fifties reduced the Economic Evangelicalism of 1830 from dominant philosophy to middle-class point of view, and so prepared the way for the teaching of Pater and Arnold, the practice of Morris and Toynbee, the recognition, after years of derision or neglect, of Ruskin and Browning. 'Nothing', Bagehot once wrote, 'is more unpleasant than a virtuous person with a mean mind. A highly developed moral nature joined to an undeveloped intellectual nature, an undeveloped artistic nature, is of necessity repulsive,' and in the fifties England was becoming keenly aware of the narrowness and meagreness of her middle-class tradition. A process very like that which was stratifying the proletariate into the Respectable and the Low, was creating out of the upper levels of the middle class a new patriciate, mixed of birth, wealth, and education, which might be Liberal or Conservative in politics, Christian or nothing in religion, but was gradually shedding the old middle-class restraints on enjoyment and speculation. And of this readjustment of classes and values, if the basis was security and prosperity, the principal agents were the Universities and the public schools.

In 1831 Brougham had defined The People as 'the middle classes, the wealth and intelligence of the country, the glory of the British name'. In 1848 a pamphlet appeared under the title *A Plea for the Middle Classes*. It was concerned with their education. The Barbarians and the Populace were provided for. Strenuous work, and what seemed to economists a formidable expenditure, were giving popular education in England a dead lift to a level not much below Prussia, on paper, and, on paper, well above France and Holland, the three countries from which much of the inspiration had come. It was the education vote, indeed, which opened the eyes of the public to the cost of the social services, and there was a growing doubt, which the Newcastle Commission of '58–'60 confirmed, of the value received for the money spent. The leaving age had been forced up to eleven and the school life lengthened to four years. But the cellar and the pedlar still flourished, a substantial proportion of the children were still not taught to write and only a tiny fraction got very much beyond. Robert Lowe, introducing payment by results, with the catchword 'if dear efficient, if inefficient cheap', succeeded for the first and last time in interesting the English public in an education debate without the sectarian spice. Nor can it be doubted that his policy was right. If he levelled down the best schools, he levelled up the worst, and so made sure that, when compulsion came in the seventies, those who were compelled to go to school would learn something when they got there, to write a letter, to make out a bill and hem a shirt. It was not much, but in the thirties it would have seemed a visionary ideal. That the ideal had been so imperfectly realized, that the late Victorian democracy was not altogether unfit for its reponsibilities, was in the main the work of one man, and, if history judged men less by the noise than by the difference they make, it is hard to think of any name in the Victorian age which deserves to stand above or even beside Kay-Shuttleworth's.

In the early nineteenth century England had possessed in seven or eight hundred old grammar schools an apparatus for giving the middle classes an education as good as public opinion required for the class above and below, and by a disastrous miscalculation she let it run down. Not that it was wholly wasted. A good country grammar school, neither over-taught nor over-gamed, with a University connexion and a strong local backing, gave probably as sound an education as was to be had in England: such was Wordsworth's Hawkshead, and the King's School at Canterbury where Charles Dickens looked wistfully through the gates at the boyhood he had never known, and Tiverton and Ipswich and many more. They made good provision for the sons of the lower gentry, superior tradesmen, and farmers; a sound stock and fertile in capacity. When they were not available, the deficiency had to be made good by the private school of all grades, or the proprietary school. But beneath the level of schools which were in touch with the Universities all was chaos, where those which aimed lowest seem to have done best. The rest, the rank and file of the secondary schools, under-staffed by untaught ushers, were turning out, at fifteen or so, the boys who were to be the executive of the late Victorian industries and professions, and could be fairly described as the worst educated middle class in Europe.

The Taunton Commission, which in 1861 reviewed the whole system of secondary education, found that the girls were even worse off than the boys. In the better classes their education was still a domestic industry staffed in the first place by the mother, who might delegate the routine to a governess, and by visiting masters. Those families who could afford an annual stay in London added some intensive teaching by specialists in music, drawing, and the languages. The domestic system involved the employment of untrained gentlewomen as teachers, and the figure of the governess, snubbed, bullied, loving, and usually quite incompetent, is a standby of Victorian pathos. Lady Blessington first introduced it into literature, it reached its apotheosis in *East Lynne*. The silliness and shallowness of the boarding school is an equally constant topic of Victorian satire, but, like the boys' schools, they were of all degrees. Browning's aunts had an admirable establishment at Blackheath, and George Eliot was excellently taught at her Coventry boarding school. London was ringed with such institutions, through which the drawing-master and the music-master wearily circulated on foot from Battersea over the river to Chiswick and up by Acton to Hampstead and Highgate. Below the boarding-school class was that unfortunate stratum just too high to make use of the charity school, the National school or the British Day. For them there was rarely anything better than a superior dame's school in a parlour or a very inferior visiting governess.

That the education of girls, as codified by eighteenth-century manners and moralized by nineteenth-century respectability, tended to a certain repression of personality in the interests of a favourite sexual type, can hardly be denied. But in the Victorian age this type was moulded by the pressure of an uncompromising religion: if the convention was that eighteenth-century man preferred his women fragile, and nineteenth-century man liked them ignorant, there is no doubt at all that he expected them to be good; and goodness, in that age of universal charity, imported the service of others, and if service then training for service. Children and the sick had always been within the lawful scope of women's activities, and, in a generation not less scientific than benevolent, the evolution of the administering angel into the professional teacher, nurse, or doctor was inevitable. Often obscured by agitation for subordinate ends – the right to vote, to graduate, to dispose of her own property after marriage – the fundamental issue of feminism was growing clearer all through the century, as women, no longer isolated heroines but individuals bent on a career, drew out into the sexless sphere of distinterested intelligence, and the conception of autonomous personality took body; a process which may be truly named Victorian if only for the horror with which Victoria regarded it. 'I want', said Bella Rokesmith to her husband, 'to be something so much worthier than the doll in the doll's house.' In the profusion of Dickens, the phrase might pass unnoticed. But Ibsen remembered it.

The demand for a better sort of woman was not a new one: Swift had urged it vehemently in eighteenth-century England, Montesquieu in France. But the curriculum was still dominated by the economic uniformity of women's existence and the doctrine of the Two Spheres. Every girl was prospectively the wife of a gentleman, a workman, or something in between. For the few unmarried there was a small annuity, or dependence as companion, governess, or servant, in house or shop. Education, therefore, meant a grounding of morals and behaviour to last all through life, and a top dressing of accomplishments intended partly to occupy the girl's mind, partly to attract the men, and, in the last resort, to earn a living by if all else failed. For the intelligent girl in a sympathetic home there was a most stimulating provision of books, travel, and conversation. But this was no part of the curriculum at Chiswick or Cloisterham, and it would have been thrown away on Dora Spenlow. Economically the two spheres had hardly begun to intersect. Intellectually, the overlap was steadily increasing, and it was for this common province of taste, criticism, intelligence, and sympathy that wise mothers trained their daughters, sensible girls trained themselves, and the more fortunate husbands trained their brides.

Tennyson, always the most punctual exponent of contemporary feeling, published *The Princess* in 1847, a year in which many minds were converging on the problem. With the express approval of Queen Victoria, a Maid of Honour planned a College for Women, King's College undertook to train and examine governesses, and Bedford College started with classes in a private house. From these three movements all the higher education of women in England has proceeded, but by the sixties it had not proceeded very far. At Cheltenham and North London College, where those distinguished but unfortunately named ladies, Miss Beale and Miss Buss, held sway, the country had models capable of a rich development, and the age of development begins when, in 1865, Cambridge, with qualms, had just allowed girls to sit for Local examinations. London was still refusing to let them sit for matriculation. The collision of the Two Spheres is a Late-Victorian theme, almost a Late-Victorian revolution: in Mid-Victorian England only the first mutterings of the revolution can be heard.

14

Compared with the uncertain aims and methods of middle-class and female education, the growth of the Universities and public schools has all the appearance of a concerted evolution aiming at the production of a definite type.

The institution of serious examinations, at Cambridge in 1780, at Oxford in 1802, had created at the two Universities fields of keen intellectual emulation. The distinction of pass and honours not only set up an objective for the ambitious, but united them in an intellectual aristocracy where form was studied as eagerly as, in later days, athletic gifts.[1] By tradition Cambridge was mathematical and Oxford was classical, but Oxford had an honours school in mathematics before Cambridge established the classical tripos, and the awe-inspiring double first, whatever it may signify in feminine fiction, properly meant a first in the two final schools: it was correctly used of Peel and Gladstone. For men who took their reading seriously, the standard was high and the classical impression lasting. Except Brougham, who was educated at Edinburgh, it is not easy to recall any public man of eminence who could have talked science with Prince Albert; but many of them were competent scholars, several were excellent scholars, and the imprint of a thorough, if narrow, classical education is visible in Hansard whenever the speaker is Peel or Lord John Russell, Gladstone or Derby. It was equally diffused over Whigs and Tories, who could point back to the great examples of Fox and Windham; and the Radicals, who on principle might have been expected to be averse to a purely literary discipline, numbered by accident in their ranks the most illustrious classical scholar and the most exacting classical tutor of the age – George Grote and the elder Mill.

[1] Peel's translation of *suave mari magno: suave*, it is a source of melancholy satisfaction, was remembered all his life. Hogg and Shelley (in Hogg's *Life*) seem to me the first undergraduates, recognizable as such, on record.

THE
FALL OF DELHI.

(BY SUBMARINE AND BRITISH TELEGRAPH.)

We have received the following telegram from our own correspondent at Trieste :—

"TRIESTE, MONDAY, OCT. 26.

" The steamer Bombay arrived from Alexandria at half-past 10 a.m. to-day. She left Alexandria on the 20th inst.

" The Calcutta and China mails left Alexandria on the 19th per French steamer. The Bombay portion was to be despatched on the 21st, with intelligence from Bombay to the 3d inst.

" Delhi was assaulted on the 14th of September, and was in possession of our troops on the 20th. Full particulars not yet known. Our loss on the 14th was 600 killed and wounded.

" General Outram's force reached Cawnpore on the 14th, and General Havelock crossed the Ganges on or before the 19th.

" From Lucknow the accounts are favourable, and confident hopes are entertained that the garrison will be relieved.

" At Agra all was quiet up to the 19th.

" The dâks were stopped between Lahore and Mooltan. Cause unknown. The Punjab was otherwise tranquil.

" The intelligence from the Bombay Presidency is favourable, though a few cases of disaffection had occurred in the army in Scinde. At Kurrachee the 21st Bombay Native Infantry had been disarmed, and about 20 men of the regiment had been convicted and executed.

" At Hyderabad, in the same province, a company of native artillery had been disarmed.

" Portions of Her Majesty's 4th and 95th had arrived at Bombay.

" Prices of imports had generally advanced.

" Bank rates of interest unaltered.

" Government paper had rallied.

" Freights steady.

" Exchanges, 2s. 1⅝d."

From The Times, 27 *October* 1857

The nation has just sustained the greatest loss
that could possibly have fallen upon it. Prince
ALBERT, who a week ago gave every promise that
his valuable life would be lengthened to a period
long enough to enable him to enjoy, even in
this world, the fruit of a virtuous youth and
a well-spent manhood, the affection of a devoted wife and of a family of which any father
might well be proud,—this man, the very centre
of our social system, the pillar of our State, is
suddenly snatched from us, without even warning
sufficient to prepare us for a blow so abrupt and so
terrible. We shall need time fully to appreciate the
magnitude of the loss we have sustained. Every
day will make us more conscious of it. It is not
merely a prominent figure that will be missed on
all public occasions ; not merely a death that will
cast a permanent gloom over a reign hitherto so
joyous and so prosperous ;—it is the loss of a public
man whose services to this country, though rendered neither in the field of battle nor in the
arena of crowded assemblies, have yet been of
inestimable value to this nation,—a man to whom
more than any one else we owe the happy state
of our internal polity, and a degree of general
contentment to which neither we nor any other
nation we know of ever attained before.

Twenty-one years have just elapsed since Queen
VICTORIA gave her hand in marriage to Prince
ALBERT of Saxe-Gotha. It was an auspicious
event, and reality has more than surpassed all
prognostics, however favourable. The Royal marriage has been blessed with a numerous offspring.
So far as it is permitted to the public to know
the domestic lives of Sovereigns, the people of
these islands could set up no better model of the
performance of the duties of a wife and mother
than their QUEEN ; no more complete pattern of
a devoted husband and father than her CONSORT.
These are not mere words of course. We write in
an age and in a country in which the highest
position would not have availed to screen the most
elevated delinquent. They are simply the records
of a truth perfectly understood and recognized by
the English people.

From The Times, 16 *December* 1861

The Universities were definitely Anglican. At Cambridge a man could not graduate, at Oxford he could not matriculate, without signing the Thirty-Nine Articles.[1] The Commons in 1834 passed a Bill enabling dissenters to graduate. The Lords threw it out. Practically, it was not a matter of much consequence, as dissenters were not, as a rule, of the class whom Oxford and Cambridge served, and a new private venture called the London University was already at their disposal. It was strongly Radical in origin and affinity, it was entirely secular, and its curriculum was very much wider than that of the old Universities. The foundation of the University of London marks the entry of a new idea; the conception of a University as training for a specific profession, for medicine, law, engineering, or teaching, was in England a novelty to which the examples of Germany and Scotland both contributed. But as a seat of instruction University College rose at once to the first rank, and there are few pictures of the young Victorian mind so attractive as the pages in which Hutton set down his memories of Long and de Morgan, and their brother sophists, and of his walks with Bagehot up and down Regent Street in search of Oxford Street and truth. Liberal, accessible, and utilitarian, it might have been expected that the example of the Londoners would have been widely and speedily followed. That it was not, that the northern colleges emerged late and slowly from their original obscurity, shows how alien to the middle classes was the idea of higher education not connected with practical utility or social distinction, and how much was lost with the disappearance of the Nonconformist academies of the eighteenth century.[2] A feeble effort to provide the north with inexpensive culture was made by the Dean and Chapter of the richest of English cathedrals, but the historian of Victorian

---

[1] To which, incidentally, Wesleyans took no exception.

[2] Owens College, founded in 1815, begins to count from about 1860. Readers of *Endymion* will remember how the younger Thornbury was diverted from Mill Hill and Owens to Radley and Oxford. Of another Manchester father, Disraeli told the Queen that he sent his sons to Oxford to be made into gentlemen, 'but unfortunately they only became Roman Catholics'.

England will not often have occasion to mention the University of Durham.

Both at Oxford and at Cambridge the career of the pass-man was little more than the prolongation of his school days without the discipline. In fact, as Freeman put it, prospective parsons and prospective lawyers, young men of rank and fortune, were provided for; if they had any intellectual ambitions they were admirably provided for; if they had not, the Universities had little to give them, and outside the circle of the Church, the Bar, and the landed gentry, they had nothing to give at all. In their internal discipline they were overgrown with a picturesque tangle of privileges, distinctions, and exemptions; founders' kin and local fellowships, servitors and sizars, gentlemen commoners and fellow commoners: New College and King's took their degrees without examination,[1] and the tuft, the golden tassel on the cap, survived until 1870 at Oxford as a mark of noble birth. The governing oligarchy of heads of houses stood aloof from the general body of residents; and the fellows, except where personal influence drew together groups of disciples, stood aloof from the undergraduate. Compared with the eighteenth century, the intellectual life was intenser, manners and morals were more refined. Compared with the later nineteenth century, studies and sports were far less standardized, manners and morals were still barbaric. There was much unscientific cricket and rowing, a fair amount of riding and hunting, occasional street fighting, some wenching, and much drinking. But there is universal agreement that the state of the Universities was steadily improving as the juniors became less childish and the seniors less remote.

On the world outside their walls the ancient Universities exercised an exasperating fascination: they were clerical; they were idle; they were dissipated; they reflected those odious class distinctions by which merit is suppressed and insolence fostered; their studies were narrow, their teaching ineffective. And on every count of the indictment the reformers found themselves

[1] πάντων πλὴν ἵππων ἀδαήμονές ἐστε κυνῶν τε
καίτοι γ' οὐθ' ἵππων εἰδότες οὔτε κυνῶν.

supported by eminent friends within the gates, by Thirlwall at Cambridge and by Tait and Jowett at Oxford. The Commission of 1850–2 and the Acts of 1854 and 1856 only accelerated, and consolidated, a process of internal reform which had proceeded somewhat faster at Cambridge than at Oxford, partly because for ten years the activities of Oxford had been diverted to religious agitation, while Cambridge had had the good sense to profit by her Chancellor's experience as an undergraduate of Bonn.

The object of the Commission was to clear away the constitutional obstructions to internal development and to make the Universities more accessible to the middle classes, more useful to the pass-man, and more serviceable to pure learning. But in principle the Universities affirmed their essence, against Germany and Scotland, as places not of professional but of liberal education in a world which still acknowledged that public life, in the Church, in Parlaiment, or on the County Bench, was not only a more distinguished, but a better life than the pursuit of wealth by industrious competition. If we imagine Victorian England without Oxford and Cambridge, what barrier can we see against an all-encroaching materialism and professionalism? Even in their alliance, their too close alliance, with the aristocracy there were elements of advantage. The Clergyman was rarely an instructed theologian, but he was not a seminarist. The scholar growing up among men destined for a public career took some tincture of public interests; the Schoolmaster, the Barrister, the Politician, the Civil Servant, and the gentleman unclassified acquired the same double impress of culture and manners; and the Universities broke the fall of the aristocracy by civilizing the plutocracy.

The old Universities were fed by the public schools, and by the private tutor, commonly a clergyman; the preparatory schools for young boys were in existence, and one of them, Temple Grove at East Sheen, was famous. Some details have been preserved of the life lived by the boys: hands, face, 'and perhaps the neck', were washed daily; feet once a fortnight, heads as required; a vernal dose of brimstone and treacle purified their blood, a half-yearly dentist drew their teeth, it was the custom under flogging to bite the Latin Grammar. Not a bad preparation, one may think, for Long Chamber, where boys of all ages were locked up from eight to eight 'and cries of joy and pain were alike unheard'. But the system was not yet stereotyped, and much education was still received at home or in the study of the neighbouring rector. Apart from the ceremonial of Eton and Christ Church for the aristocracy, a public-school education was no necessary part of the social curriculum. Of Victorians born in good circumstances, neither Macaulay nor Tennyson, Newman, Disraeli, or Harcourt got their schooling that way, and at the University or in after-life it made no difference. The Old Giggleswickian was not yet a named variety.[1] Indeed, if the grammar schools had been equipped for their task, it is very probable that our higher education would, to our great advantage, have developed on a less expensive, less exclusive, basis. Practical parents disliked a purely classical curriculum; sensitive parents were dismayed by the tales of squalor, cruelty, and disorder which were told of almost every public school; and religious parents, warned by Cowper's *Tirocinium*, hesitated to entrust young boys to institutions which gave only a formal security for piety and morals.

Arnold reconciled the serious classes to the public school. He shared their faith in progress, goodness, and their own vocation; incidentally, he was convinced that, with some modest enlargement on the side of history, the classical curriculum was best fitted to produce the type of mind both he and they desired to see in authority. But for Arnold's influence, it is not at all improbable that out of the many experiments then being made in proprietary schools some more modern alternative might have struck root and become ascendant.[2] Arnold led us back

[1] The first Old —an I have noticed is, as might be expected, an old Rugboean in 1840. A man born in the fifties told me that until he was twelve he was intended for the local grammar school, as the family could only support one son at Eton. A discovery of coal on the estate altered the position. He had to begin by learning English in place of the N. Riding dialect which was his native speech.

[2] For example, in the schools run by that remarkable family, the Hills, from which Rowland Hill issued to reform the Post Office, or George Edmondson's

with firm hand to the unchangeable routine of the Renaissance; indeed, he could not have helped it if he had wished. To all complaints of the classical curriculum there was one convincing answer: there were hundreds of people who could teach it, there was hardly any one who could teach anything else. 'If you want science,' Faraday told a Royal Commission, 'you must begin by creating science teachers.'

In the eye of the law the public schools were nine in number, but in effect, in the sense of regularly preparing boys for the University, the list was continually enlarging. By 1860 they were not dominant, but they were ascendant in the Universities, and, as they grew, the private tutor fell away, leaving his ample rectory as a burden to his impoverished successor; the career and type of the public-school boy became standardized, and the preparatory schools rose in corresponding importance. The outlook of the newer schools was to some degree modernized by the demands of Woolwich and the Civil Service Commissioners for science and modern languages; but the Renaissance tradition was not seriously impaired, and when Lord Clarendon summed up all the charges against the public schools in a question to the Headmaster of Eton, 'We find modern languages, geography, chronology, history and everything else which a well-educated Englishman ought to know, given up in order that the whole time should be devoted to the classics, and at the same time we are told that the boys go up to Oxford not only not proficient, but in a lamentable deficiency in respect to the classics', the Headmaster could only answer, 'I am sorry for it'.[1] But public opinion did not want knowledge. It wanted the sort of man of whom Wellington had said that he could go straight from school with two N.C.Os. and fifteen privates and

Queenwood.

[1] The Headmaster of Westminster claimed that of his sixth form two-thirds could read Caesar and half could read Xenophon at sight. Perhaps the Queen was thinking of this when she told Mr Gladstone that education was ruining the health of the Upper Classes. But contrast the account we have of Sedbergh in the fifties. 'It was part of the tradition that every one should have read Homer, Thucydides and Sophocles before he went up.' Everything depended on the *genius loci*, which might vary from one decade to another.

get a shipload of convicts to Australia without trouble. With the reconquest of India and the reform of the Army after the Crimea, it needed them in increasing numbers; and it was satisfied that the best way to get them was to begin by producing public-school boys and overlooking their deficiencies in 'everything which a well-educated Englishman ought to know'. For the civil branches, indeed, something more was required which Oxford and Cambridge would supply. Macaulay annexed the Indian Civil Service to the Universities: Jowett and Trevelyan, beaten in '53, had their victory in 1870, when Gladstone annexed the administrative grades of the English Civil Service.

Isolated by history as much as by the sea, the English ruling class had bred true to the barbaric type from which absolutism and revolution had deflected the foreign aristocracies; round this type, with its canons of leadership – respect for the past, energy in the present, and no great thought for the future – Victorian England formed a new ideal, in which the insolent humanism of the eighteenth century was refined by religion, and the industrious puritanism of the early nineteenth century was mellowed by public spirit; and to disengage, to affirm, and to propagate the type, no better instrument could have been devised than the Universities and public schools, with their routine of authority and old books and their home background of country life and sport. That the ideal was in many ways defective is too obvious to be asserted or denied: it was the flower of a brief moment of equipoise, Protestant, northern, respectable. It omitted much that a Greek or Italian would have thought necessary to completeness: artistic sensibility, dialectic readiness, science, and the open mind – Aristophanes would have thought Sidney Herbert exceedingly superstitious:[1]

---

[1] But Aristophanes has given the best definition of the type that I know, 'an insider who enjoys his privileges and is regular in his duties to the outsiders'.

> μόνοις γὰρ ἡμῖν ἥλιος καὶ φέγγος ἱλαρόν ἐστιν,
> ὅσοι μεμυήμεθ᾽ εὐ-
> σεβῆ τε διήγομεν
> τρόπον περὶ τοὺς ξένους
> καὶ τοὺς ἰδιώτας.

Ariosto, one fears, would have set him down as a prig – and to its defects must be in large measure ascribed the imprecision of late Victorian thought and policy which contrasts so ominously with the rigorous deductions of the early Victorians. Yet in the far distance I can well conceive the world turning wistfully in imagination, as to the culminating achievement of European culture, to the life of the University-bred classes in England of the mid-nineteenth century, set against the English landscape as it was, as it can be no more, but of which, nevertheless, some memorials remain with us to-day, in the garden at Kelmscott, in the hidden valleys of the Cotswolds, in that walled close where all the pride and piety, and peace and beauty of a vanished world seem to have made their last home under the spire of St Mary of Salisbury.

15

In surveying a period of history it is sometimes useful to step outside and see what happened next. Of late Victorian England the most obvious characteristics are the Imperialism of Beaconsfield and Chamberlain and the counterthrust of Gladstonian Liberalism; the emergence of a Socialist and, in a lesser degree, of a Feminist movement as calculable forces; the decay of the religious interest and the suppression of the aristocracy by the plutocracy, a process masked by the severe and homely court of Victoria, but growing precipitate, after the agricultural depression, with the influx of South African money and American brides. Early Victorian had become a term of reproach when Victoria had still ten years to reign.

It was the good fortune of England in the years we have been surveying to confront a sudden access of power, prosperity, and knowledge, with a solidly grounded code of duty and self-restraint. In the fifties and sixties, the code still held good, but the philosophy on which it was based was visibly breaking up. It had rested on two assumptions which experience was showing to be untenable: that the production of wealth by the few, meant, somehow, and in the long run, welfare for the many; and that conventional behaviour grounded on a traditional creed was enough to satisfy all right demands of humanity. At our distance in time we can see the agnostic and feminist turn impending: we can understand the connexion, peculiar to England, between the socialist and aesthetic movements of the next age. But life was too leisurely and secure for agitation. The reforms of the forties satisfied the aspirations of the poor and the consciences of the rich, until a new tide set in and carried us forward again with the Education Act of 1870, and the legislation of Disraeli's Government, with which Young England, now grown grey, redeemed the promise of its far-off fantastic youth. In the fifties the main current of Utilitarianism was running in the channels which the great administration had dug for it: the springs of religious feeling opened by the Evangelicals had been led over the new fields which Newman, Arnold, and Carlyle – miraculous confederacy – had won or recovered for English thought; and Economic Evangelicalism was no more than a barren stock. The first Victorian generation had built with the sword in one hand and the trowel in the other: in the fifties the sword was laid aside and the trowel was wielded, quietly, unobtrusively, anonymously, by civil servants and journalists, engineers and doctors, the secretaries of Trade Unions and the aldermen of manufacturing towns. Early in the thirties, Nassau Senior had boldly declared, against the current Malthusianism, that if the influx of Irish labour could be checked and the outflow of English labour assisted the population question could be left to settle itself. Now his words seemed to be coming true. A race so tenacious of its immemorial village life that in 1830 a Sussex family could hardly be persuaded to seek its fortune in Staffordshire, or a Dorset family that Lancashire existed, was flocking by the hundred thousand in quest of the Golden Fleece, or the land where the gates of night and morning stand so close together that a good man can earn two days' wages in one. By 1860 the whole world was the Englishman's home and England was at peace.

Released from fear, the English mind was recovering its power to speculate, to wonder, and to enjoy. The dissolvent elements in Early Victorian thought, romance and humour and curiosity, the Catholicism of Oxford, the satire of Dickens, the passion of Carlyle, the large historic vision of Grote and Lyell and Arnold, were beginning to work. One of the last survivors of the mid-Victorian time spoke of those years as having the sustained excitement of a religious revival. Excitement was Lord Morley's word also, and all through the fifties we are aware of the increasing tension of thought. The Christian Socialists rose in ill-directed but fruitful revolt: the Pre-Raphaelites struck out for a freedom which they had not strength to reach. Tennyson, in *Maud*, Dickens in *Hard Times* turned savagely on the age that had bred them. We miss the precise objectives, the concentrated purpose of the earlier time. Science and poetry, business and adventure, religion and politics are not yet divided into separate, professional avocations; but they are thrown together in an irregular, massive synthesis, of which the keynotes still are competence and responsibility, a general competence not always distinguishable from a general amateurishness, a universal responsibility sometimes declining into a universal self-importance. Not for a long time had the English character seemed so upright, or English thought so formless, as in that happy half generation when the demand for organic change was quiescent, the religious foundations were perishing, and the balance of land and industry was slowly toppling.

We are nearing the years of division. In 1859 the last of the Augustans was laid by Johnson and Addison, and the Red House was begun at Bexley: in 1860 Ruskin issued as much of *Unto this Last* as Thackeray dared to print, and how great a part of late Victorian thought is implicit in five books of those same years, in the *Origin of Species*, Mill on *Liberty* and *Essays and*

Reviews: in FitzGerald's *Omar* and Meredith's *Richard Feverel* we can appreciate now better than their own age could have foreseen. We are approaching a frontier, and the voices that come to us from the other side, *Modern Love* and *Ecce Homo*, Swinburne's first poem and Pater's first essays, are the voices of a new world, of which the satirist is not Cruikshank but du Maurier, the laureate not Tennyson but Browning, the schoolmaster not Arnold but his son. The late Victorian age is opening.

16

But the Englishman, growing towards maturity in those years, felt himself no longer isolated, but involved in a world of accumulating and accelerating change. Swiftly, under the impulsion of Bismarck, the European pieces were setting to a new pattern. The North German lands ranged themselves with Prussia. To the south, Austria and Hungary had come together again over the body of their depressed and resentful Slavs. Italy, enriched by the cession of Venetia, had established her capital at Florence and her hands were closing on Papal Rome. The only barrier remaining between the old Europe – Congress Europe, the Europe of Canning and Palmerston – and the new, was the incalculable and untested stability of the French Empire.

Official incidents are rarely of much account in history, and the greater part of what passes for diplomatic history is little more than the record of what one clerk said to another clerk. But it is allowable to speculate on what might have happened if the Queen had had her way, and Robert Morier, who knew Germany as Palmerston knew Europe, had been kept in Berlin from 1866 to 1870. But Bismarck was an astute man: our Ambassador, a stupid man: Hammond, the Permanent Under-secretary, a jealous man. So Bismarck worked, unobserved, unsuspected; and in the June of 1870 Hammond could confidently assure Lord Granville that never had Europe been so profoundly at peace. War was declared on July 15. On August 6 the armies of France and Germany met at Saarbruck. Napoleon III surrendered at Sedan on September 2. On September 20 the Italian army entered Rome by the gate of Michelangelo. On December 18, in the Hall of Mirrors at Versailles, the King of Prussia was acknoweldged German Emperor. Europe had lost a mistress and found a master.[1] After the Siege, the Commune. 'Let us go to Montmartre,' an English visitor was overheard to say: 'It is the best place to watch Paris burning.'

The Prussian campaign against Austria in 1866 had imposed on the world a new standard, almost a new conception, of efficiency. But no one had ever taken Austria very seriously as a military power, and the swoop of the German armies on Paris came, to England at least, as a revelation. At the opening of the war, sympathies were on the whole with Germany: Englishmen had no great cause to trust Napoleon, they knew something of the corruption of government in France, and had seen more of the corruption of society in Paris. Feeling veered when the Empire had fallen, and France at bay began to show her natural bravery, the victorious Prussian his native brutality. Our public attitude, unruffled by the abuse discharged on us by both the combatants, remained entirely correct. But the Prussians had reached the Channel. There was no reason, yet, to suppose they would wish to cross it, but six months before there had been no reason to suppose they would fall on France. If the Almighty, with whose designs the new Emperor showed so intimate a familiarity, chose to direct a crusade on London, it was reasonably certain that the Army could not oppose him and not quite clear whether the Navy could stop him.[2] The prudence

[1] The phrase is Henry Bulwer's.
[2] The loss of the *Captain* in 1870 had raised grave doubts as to the efficiency of our naval administration. See the scathing inscription on the memorial in St Paul's, and Chesney's *Battle of Dorking*.

of Bismarck gave better assurance of the peace of Europe and the security of England.

Fortunately, at a time when the country might easily have run into panic, the War Office was in the hands of one of Peel's best pupils, Edward Cardwell. He had already to his record one of the useful codifications of the age, the Merchant Shipping Act of 1854[1] and the draft, at least, of one of its most memorable Statues, the British North America Act of 1867. Behind the convenient clamour over the abolition of Purchase, he worked steadily at the unification of the Line, Militia, and Volunteers, at the equipment and training of the Army for the new scientific warfare, the improvement of material, the formation of a Reserve. So steadily and so well, indeed, that England, which, when the Germans were before Paris was inclined to wonder whether she had an army at all, was, a few months later, when the Germans were back in Germany, ruefully considering the cost of an efficient one. To abolish Purchase the debt was increased by £7,000,000: to add 20,000 men to the Army and modernize its equipment the tax-payer had to find £3,000,000 in a year: a price well worth paying for the removal of those uneasy, fitful alarms which had been before, and were to be again, the parents of bad counsel and improvident administration.[2] The Army, as Cardwell left it, was a good machine: and it was not his fault if his successors, and the Duke of Cambridge, and public opinion always more and more concerned with naval defence, let the machine run down.

An island power needs an army as a defence against casual raiders, and as an expeditionary force. But its main strategy must be oceanic and its diplomacy will naturally aim at friendship with the chief military power of the Continent. Only when that power grows strong at sea must the island look for another friend. So in the sixteenth century we had swung from Burgundy to Valois: in the seventeenth from Bourbon to

---

[1] When 516 clauses went through Committee at one sitting. Is this a record?

[2] Field manœuvres were introduced by General Hope Grant in 1870. With the Volunteers' annual Field-day at Brighton, they did much to create that interest in the army and its doings which is characteristic of the later decades of the reign.

Hapsburg, and the time had come for a new variety of an old combination: England at sea, Germany by land, watching the Channel and the Rhine, the Polish frontier and the Indian passes, an equipoise which would hold until Germany looked seaward too. Russia, urged by that strange power of growth which had spread the Orthodox People from the Black Sea to the Arctic, and from the Baltic to the Pacific, was still moving forward. How near in truth she was to India was a question few could answer. But the completion of the Suez Canal in 1869 had opened a new route from India to England, and on its flank lay Constantinople, and behind Constantinople the Black Sea Fleet. The board was set, and the pieces in their place.

17

At home, the forces so long restrained by the genial ascendancy of Palmerston were seeking their traditional outlets, the abatement of privilege and the extension of the franchise. Mill was in for Westminster, and Gladstone out for Oxford. In 1866, Russell and Gladstone, unmuzzled at last and member for South Lancashire, introduced their Reform Bill. They were defeated, and for one bright summer evening London enjoyed the forgotten thrill of a battle between Reformers and Policemen. Derby and Disraeli succeeded and fell.[1] The Tenpound Householder imparted his privilege to the Householder at large, and the Lodger: the Forty Shilling Freeholder to the Twelvepound Householder. For another eighteen years the distinction of Borough and County persisted: and though, after 1867, the

---

[1] Having, incidentally, purchased the telegraph system for the Post Office. Proxies in the House of Lords, Church Rates, and public executions, came to an end in the same year, 1868.

social composition of Parliament began to alter rapidly to the advantage of the business man, the ascendancy of the rural gentry was not yet fatally impaired. Fortune was still on the side of her old favourites, and the Civil War in America postponed for half a generation the menace to the land. But the return of the Liberals in 1868 dealt a threefold blow to the Gentlemanly Interest. Purchase of Commissions was abolished, the Universities were thrown open to dissenters, the Civil Service to competition. Radicalism was making itself felt again, and two cycles of Benthamite reform were rounded off by the Ballot Act in 1872 and the fusion of Law and Equity in 1873. Never, it was said, had new members talked so much as they talked in 1868. Never had they had so much to talk about: never since 1832 had there been so many of them: the quiet time was over.

In its six years of office, this great but unfortunate administration contrived to offend, to disquiet, or to disappoint, almost every interest in the country. Of its three chief measures, Irish Disestablishment failed to placate the Irish and left English Churchmen uneasy. Forster's Education Act satisfied neither the Church nor the Dissenters. The Irish Land Act did not go to the root of the Irish land trouble and it planted a lasting anxiety in the mind of the English landowners. Lowe's fancy budget of 1871 ended in a squalid riot in Palace Yard, twopence on the income tax, and a lesson to the new electorate that they might be extravagant at other people's expense. The neutrality of the Black Sea, the prize of 1856, had to be surrendered: the Alabama indemnity had to be paid. After 1871 nothing went right. There were political jobs almost amounting to public scandals: there was a departmental scandal almost amounting to malversation of public money: Epping Forest was all but sold for building lots. Finally, Mr Gladstone, overrating both his ascendancy and his ingenuity, failed to reconcile the Catholic hierarchy and the Nonconformist Conscience to an Irish University which should teach neither modern history nor philosophy. England turned to the Tories, and in 1874 the Ballot sent Disraeli back with a majority that recalled the triumph of

1841.[1] Of the next thirty years, the Conservatives were in power for twenty-two.

But to any observant mind it was manifest that a revolution of far deeper and wider import than any shift of the balance of power in Europe, or the centre of electoral or social gravity in England, was impending. Such a change as had come over the human mind in the sixteenth century, when the earth expanded from Europe to a globe, was coming over it again. Now space was shrinking, time expanding. The earth had given up her most mysterious secret when in 1856 Speke stood on the shores of Victoria Nyanza and saw the Nile pouring northward. The Atlantic cable was laid at last in 1866. Even in domestic life the contraction was making itself felt: the Metropolis was becoming compact: its satelite villages, from Blackheath round to Chiswick, suburban. But as the home of mankind grew smaller to the imagination, so the history of the race was perceived to stretch in longer and longer perspective. Before the first ferment over the *Origin of Species* had subsided, a new window had been opened on to the past. In 1860 John Henslow, famous throughout Europe as a botanist, and to his neighbours better known as an exemplary parish priest, crossed the Channel to examine for himself the prehistoric discoveries claimed by Boucher de Perthes in the valley of the Somme. Convinced, his authority carried with it the consent of English science: a new age, not to be reckoned by the centuries of Europe or even the millennia of Egypt and Babylon, was thrown open to explorers, and close on the discovery of primitive man followed the discovery how much of man, not least his religion and his morality, was still primitive.

We are passing from the statistical to the historical age, where the ground and explanation of ideas, as of institutions, is looked for in their origins: their future calculated by observation of the historic curve. As Early Victorian thought is regulated by the conception of progress, so the late Victorian mind is overshadowed by the doctrine of evolution. But the idea of progress –

[1] I remarked to an old Gladstonian how quiet the Election of 1935 had been. 'Yes,' he said, 'like 1874. Very different from 1868. But then he had *driven* us so.'

achieved by experiment, consolidated by law or custom, registered by statistics – had, without much straining of logic or conscience, been made to engage with the dominant Protestant faith, and this, equally, in both its modes: in the individualism of the soul working out its own salvation, in the charity which sought above all things the welfare of others. Now, of the main articles of the common Protestant faith, the Inerrant Book was gone, and it had carried with it the chief assurance of an intervening Providence. To propose an infallible Church, in compensation for a Bible proved fallible, was a pretension which the Church of England had expressly, and in advance, disclaimed,[1] and which no Protestant sect could maintain. The only valid alternative was agnosticism, or a religion of experience. But in those very years when the historic impact was loosening the whole fabric of tradition, we can see, and it is one of the strangest paradoxes on record, historic speculation engaged in building an inerrant system of economics, and demonstrating, with inexorable scholastic rigour, the future evolution of society through class war into its final state of Communism. Disraeli about this time spoke of a 'craving credulity' as the note of the age. The human mind is still something of a troglodyte. Expelled from one falling cavern, its first thought is to find another.

Religion, conceived as a concerted system of ideas, aspirations, and practices to be imposed on society, was losing its place in the English world, and the Oxford scholars about Sanday who were to settle the documents of the faith with an exactness and integrity which Germany could not have out-matched, delivered their results to a generation which had ceased for the most part to be interested in the faith or the documents. The ethical trenchancy of the Evangelicals was passing over to the agnostic, who in their denunciation of the Sin of Faith, their exaltation of scientific integrity, could be as vehement, as dogmatic, and at times as narrow, as any of the creeds which they believed themselves to have supplanted.

[1] Articles XX and XXI.

He has left none like him—none who can rally round him so many followers of various opinions, none who can give us so happy a respite from the violence of party-warfare, none who can bring to the work of statesmanship so precious a store of recollections. It is impossible not to feel that Lord PALMERSTON's death marks an epoch in English politics. " The old order changeth, yield-" ing place to new." Other Ministers may carry into successful effect organic reforms from which he shrunk. Others may introduce a new spirit into our foreign relations, and abandon the system of secret diplomacy which he never failed to support. Others may advise HER MAJESTY with equal sagacity, and sway the House of Commons with equal or greater eloquence; but his place in the hearts of the people will not be filled so easily. The name of Lord PALMERSTON, once the terror of the Continent, will long be connected in the minds of Englishmen with an epoch of unbroken peace and unparalleled prosperity, and cherished together with the brightest memories of the reign of Queen VICTORIA,

From The Times, 19 *October* 1865

LATEST INTELLIGENCE.

[A portion of the following appeared in part only of our First and in our Second Editions of yesterday :—]

THE GERMAN TERMS OF PEACE.

(BY TELEGRAPH.)

(FROM OUR BERLIN CORRESPONDENT.)

BERLIN, JAN. 31.

The conditions of Peace, as announced by Count Bismarck to M. Favre, include the cession of Alsace and Lorraine, with Belfort and Metz, the payment of a pecuniary indemnity of 10 milliards of francs, the cession of Pondicherry, in the East Indies, and the transfer of 20 first-class men-of-war.

M. Favre has referred the decision to the National Assembly.

From The Times, 8 *February* 1871

Agnosticism had the temper of the age on its side, and the believers were hampered by the ancient ravelins and counter-scarps which they could not defend, and would not abandon. There are times when the reader of Victorian apologetic, whether the theme be miracles or inspiration or the authorship of the Gospels, whether the book before him be the *Speaker's Commentary*, or Drummond's *Natural Law in the Spiritual World*, or Pusey on Daniel or Gladstone on the Gadarene Swine, is nauseated by the taint of sophistry and false scholarship, and feels, as the better intelligence of the time did feel, that if men could force their intellects to think like that, it cannot matter much what they thought.[1] This was not the way, and nothing could come of it but a certain disdainful indifference to all such speculations, or a flight of perplexed unstable minds into the Confessional, into Spiritualism, into strange Eastern Cults.

A saner instinct counselled those who were not satisfied with the purely immanent order, physical or moral, propounded by science, to hold fast to the historic forms of devotion, and compel them to yield what they still promised and once had yielded: the certitude of experience as the reward of faith, insight into the nature of the transcendent, and the renewal, by the sacraments, of the saving impulse which Christ had through his Church imparted to the race. There, in the balanced emphasis on individual conduct and social coherence, on the personal origin and historic transmission of the faith, was the new Via Media. In this fusion of the Evangelical, the Arnoldine and the Tractarian teaching, this return to a faith more primitive than the creeds or the Bible, and shot with strands of Plato and Hegel, we can feel rather than discern the religious philosophy of Later Victorian England moving towards its next objective, while from *In Memoriam* to *The Woods of Westermain*, from *The Woods of Westermain* to the Choruses of *The Dynasts*, we can follow the secular intellect seeking its way to such an apprehension of Being as Process as might hereafter reconcile

---

[1] Or as an Edinburgh Reviewer (Bishop Wilberforce, I think) once said: 'Such intellects must be left to the merciful apologies of Him that created them.' But to whom is He to apologize?

the spiritual demands of humanity with the rapt and cosmic indifference of Evolution.

18

In the life of a nation, to dispose of one problem is to start another. To an observer of a benevolently Utilitarian disposition in 1865, it might well have appeared that the problem of progress had been solved. Few able-bodied men lacked employment, and indeed it seemed quite possible that at no distant date England would have to import foreign labour to adjust the balance of native emigration. That a great part of the population was under-nourished did, it is true, go to show that the distribution of wealth was less efficient than its production. But, even here, remedies were available within the accepted scheme of things: Trade Unions to keep wages in some correspondence with the earnings of industry: co-operation and profit sharing for the mechanic: free sale of land for the farmer, and small holdings for the labourer. Fawcett[1] was not following a flight of fancy, but a sober speculation, when he looked forward to a society of well-fed, well-educated citizens, with skilled artisans and peasant proprietors at the base, scavenged for and waited on by negroes and Chinese. It is the Early Victorian ideal of the Respectable Family, set upon the economic basis of free, but not uncontrolled, competition, and steady, but not unaided, self-help.

To the question: progress whither? the answer is agreed. But poetry and philosophy, the new history and the new science, had together posed a more fundamental question, evolving what? And the dominant minds of the seventies were those who had faced the question most boldly: who had, like Darwin

[1] *Economic Position of the British Labourer*, 1865.

himself, grown slowly to fame, and spoke with the equal authority of unquestioned genius and long meditation, who embodied in themselves the revolution in English thought, who were masters of the tradition and had found the tradition wanting. These are, beyond all others, Ruskin, Browning, and George Eliot. They had all been reared in the same atmosphere of middle-class industry and piety; they shared the same gifts of observation and analysis; and they were, one audaciously, the other dramatically, and George Eliot gravely and philosophically, in revolt.

Round them, growing up under their shadow, we see a younger group, marked with the same imprint, and bearers of the same ideas – the agnostics, Morley and Leslie Stephen: the romantics, Morris and Burne-Jones, Philip Webb and Swinburne: aesthetic Pater and disconcerting Meredith. They form no school, their derivation is various, and their allegiance divided. But there is a spiritual bond between them in the sense of personal value. A Socratic search for the good had begun again, to replace ideals which were toppling as their religious foundations cracked: we can count the schools that will come out of it, and name their manifestoes: *An Agnostic's Apology*, the *Renaissance*, the *Essay on Comedy*, *News from Nowhere*. And crowding into the picture are the pessimists and the pagans, the strenuous and the decadent, strong, silent men, and not so silent feminists, Celts and aesthetes, spiritualists and theosophists, Whistlers and Wildes and Beardsleys, all the fads and all the fancies into which the compact and domestic philosophy of Victorian England dissolved.

But if, again, we seek a clue to this phantasmagoria of a late afternoon, we shall find it best, I think, in Meredith. He had, in virtue of his birth-year, 1828, the strong decency, the vigour, gusto, and ebullience of the Early Victorians; but he charged them with a new spirit, the searching criticism of his maturer time. Browning and Ruskin had taken the same path. But Browning was preoccupied, as George Eliot was, with problems which could be stated, if not solved, in the terms of old theology and old ethics, God, Duty, and Immortality: righteousness and temperance and judgement to come; and the mind of Ruskin, endowed with every gift except the gift to organize the others, was more tumultuous than the tumult in which it was involved. The deceptive lucidity of his intoxicating style displayed, or concealed, an intellect as profound, penetrating, and subtle as any that England has seen; and as fanciful, as glancing, and as wayward as the mind of a child. But if Ruskin is all dogma and no system, Meredith's grotesque is the vehicle of a philosophy which is all system and no dogma.

What, we may ask – and it is the fundamental problem at once in Meredith's work and in all Late Victorian Ethic – what are the duties which the conception of Being as Process imposes on those to whom it has been revealed and who acknowledge no other revelation? It was not a new problem, and answers could be read in the ethereal verse of *Prometheus*, in the gritty prose of Harriet Martineau; more lucidly, and with an almost mystical clarity, in the closing stanzas of *In Memoriam*. Perfectibility was returning from the exile to which the reign of the economists had consigned her, enriched by the experience of two absorbing generations, and heartened by their victories, with a new objective and method, the gradual improvement of the race, by the transmission of a life more and more at harmony within itself, and more and more sovereign over circumstance. But whether the end was to be reached by the segregation of finer types, or the general elevation of the community at large; whether evolution had established competition as Nature's first law, or had indicated the emergence of a moral law above itself: heredity against environment, nature against nurture: the weakening of fibre by too much help, the degeneration of tissue by not help enough: the lessons to be drawn from the progress of fifty years, and to be drawn also from their failures; it is in such roving, ranging debates as these, that the thought of England is now involved; debates which, being grounded on no acknowledged premises, could issue in no accepted conclusion; explorations, rather; definings of problems, not solutions; the ideas of the future shaping themselves in the language of the past; and still set out with something of the romantic urgency of a more pious, a more confident, time. Some closeness of the northern fibre, the slow rising of the northern sap, keeps the years and the decades tight to each other. But the sap is rising: silently, inevitably the tissue is transformed.

It may well be thought that if England had been visited by such a calamity as befell Europe in 1848, America in 1861, and France in 1870, the urgency of reconstruction would have drawn the new conceptions into a new and revolutionary configuration which would have shaped new institutions to match. The Church of England would have followed the Church of Ireland, and the Throne the Church; and a rapid extension of the suffrage would have involved the fall of the aristocracy and the redistribution of their still rich lands. All the necessary ideas were in the air: whisperings against the Crown, more than whisperings against the Church and the Lords; against primogeniture and the aggregation of estates: and the ground-tone, always growing louder, is the discord of progress and poverty. But England, watching Paris burn, was in no mood to go too far or too fast, and a greater destiny was beginning to absorb her thought. Mistress of India and the seas, mother of nations, she might well see in her world-wide sovereignty the crown and demonstration of evolution in history.[1] The very contraction of the world was making the thought of Greater Britain[2] more intimate and familiar, and giving to Imperial hopes and aspirations an ascendancy over domestic doubts and fears.

---

[1] Ille populus qui cunctis athletizantibus pro imperio mundi praevaluit, de Divino iudicio praevaluit. Dante, *de Monarchia*, ii. 9.

It has always seemed to me (and I am speaking of what I remember) that, in its exaltation and in its almost Darwinian reasoning, this part of Dante's tract is a perfect rendering of the philosophic Imperialism of the end of the century; the distinction between the races, *apti nati ad principari*, and those *apti ad subiici*; the final cause of Empire, *subiiciendo sibiorgem, bonum publicum intendit*; natural disposition, *natura locum et gentem disposuit ad universaliter principandum*; and the survival of the fittest in *certamina* and *duella*. One might even deduce the Statute of Westminster from the principles laid down in i. 14.

[2] The phrase was Dilke's, then a Republican, and first used as the title of his travel book in 1868.

19

Doubts and fears there were. The roaring slapdash prosperity of a decade had worked itself out to its appointed end: overtrading, speculation, fraud and collapse; and the misery of East London in 1866 was a grim but timely comment on the complacency of Fawcett in 1865. In spite of a buoyant revenue and a record expansion of the export trade, there was already a chill in the air. The company promoter was beginning to take his toll of the surplus wealth accumulating from a decade past. After a century of immunity, the Cattle Plague returned. The advance guard of militant Fenianism reached Ireland from America, and that simmering cauldron began to bubble once more. In the spring of 1866 a catastrophe far beyond the mercantile panics of 1847 and 1857 fell on the City. The failure of Overend and Gurney, in its magnitude, and in its social consequences recalled rather the disasters of 1825. The new system of Limited Liability had brought into the area of speculative finance thousands of quiet-living families who had hitherto been satisfied with the Funds or a few well-established Railways or Foreign Loans. They were now the chief sufferers, and the contraction of their expenditure, and the loss of their confidence weighed on the country for years. It seemed as if the resiliency of old days had gone, as if we were moving from our apogee, yielding, as Cobden had foreseen, to the larger resources of America,[1] yielding, too, to the higher efficiency of the Germans.

'On the speedy provision of elementary education,' Forster warned the Commons in 1870, 'depends our industrial prosperity, the safe working of our constitutional system, and our national power. Civilized communities throughout the world are massing themselves together, each mass being measured by

[1] It is not always remembered that Cobden regarded Free Trade, not as a law of nature, but as a device for postponing the inevitable consequences of American competition. In his heart Cobden preferred the pre-industrial civilization in which he was born, and there is as much bitterness as belief in his economic creed.

its force: and if we are to hold our position among men of our own race or among the nations of the world, we must make up for the smallness of our numbers by increasing the intellectual force of the individual.' A movement long maturing was taking shape in action, and with it a controversy which of all Victorian controversies is perhaps the hardest to recall with patience.

It may be admitted, and by this time it was almost universally agreed, that simple instruction should be brought within the reach of all who needed it. Not universal, but still dominant, was the opinion that the instruction should include the Bible and the elements of relgion. No party would have dared to turn the Bible out of the schools, and no two parties could agree as to the terms upon which it should be admitted. Had the ground been unoccupied, or had it been completely occupied by the Church schools, the solution was obvious. In the one case, voluntary arrangements by all denominations:[1] in the other, a conscience clause for all dissenters, would have satisfied most reasonable men. But sectarians are not reasonable men: and it was plain that the vast deficiencies in elementary education could now only be made good by public effort; by schools tax-aided and rate-provided; and that the effort was bound either to enlarge or diminish the influence of the Church: enlarge it enormously if the parson was admitted into the new schools; diminish it, more slowly but as certainly, if he were excluded, and his own schools gradually sapped by the superior resources of the School Boards, and the superior efficiency of the Board Schools. So a debate was started which the compromise of 1870 – plain Bible teaching in one school and the Catechism in another; increased assistance to Church schools where they were efficient, and Board Schools to supplement them where they were not – did not end. Thirty years later the controversy flamed into life again over the Act of 1902, and even to-day a statesman who tampered with the settlement might find that the ashes were not quite cold.

But William Forster, a Dorset quaker, a Bradford manufacturer, and a Volunteer of 1859, had a sound eye for essentials. It

[1] This was the solution actually proposed by Walter Hook as early as 1838.

is not without its significance that, while Mr Gladstone found him 'an impracticable man', he was among the Queen's most trusted friends, for the Queen loved plainness as much as she hated Mr Gladstone: and in 1870 the essential was to get the children, somehow, into some sort of school. The incidental consequences of his great measure were of hardly less importance than its direct effects. The Education Act of 1870 was, for most English people, the first sensible impact of the administrative State on their private lives; the Beadle, vanishing figure of fun, underwent a strange rejuvenation into the School Board Man, the Attendance Officer; and how forcible and disturbing his appearance was we may divine from the consideration that in Birmingham, before the Act, forty children out of a hundred, in Manchester fifty, were running loose in the streets. Spiced with sect, moreover, the School Board Elections were, particularly in London, as hot as a parliamentary contest. To great numbers they gave a novel interest in local government: to a smaller circle, women as well as men, their first experience of administration. Nor, in any history of the Victorian age, should the school-builders be forgotten. Those solid, large-windowed blocks, which still rise everywhere above the slate roofs of mean suburbs, meant for hundreds of thousands their first glimpse of a life of cleanliness and order, light and air.

20

The Educational controversy points the sagacity of Disraeli's observation in 1868 that religion would give the new electorate something to take sides on. At no time since the seventeenth century had English society been so much preoccupied with problems of doctrine and Church order: at no time had the Establishment been so keenly assailed, or so angrily divided within itself. A misjudged appointment to a bishopric or deanery might influence a by-election, or provoke a Cabinet crisis. Church policy could shake a Government.

In the circumstances of nineteenth-century England, the argument for an Establishment must in fairness be pronounced to be convincing. The parochial system, worked by a married clergy, was unquestionably a civilizing influence which nothing else could have replaced. Whether it was in equal measure a religious influence may be doubted: the English Churchman was rarely so well informed in his faith as the Irish Catholic or the Scotch Presbyterian, and he was not called upon to be so active in his membership as the English Dissenter. The Church was on the defensive: Nonconformity had the strategic initiative. The Church was aristocratic: the Church was the greatest landed proprietor in the kingdom: and in the sixties even well-disposed men might wonder anxiously whether the Church was still the bulwark it had once been against Popery and Infidelity.

Viewed in perspective, the Anglo-Catholic movement is the emergence, in a prepared season, of the Caroline tradition, transmitted not only through the non-jurors but through many of the parochial clergy, unnamed, unknown, who had been bred in the writings of the Caroline divines. As both Newman and Pusey proved, it is possible to construct from those writings such a body of permitted belief as makes the barriers between England and Rome transcendible at all save two or three insuperable points. Perhaps at two only, because, if it be admitted with Hooker that transubstantiation is not matter for churches to part communion on, then all that remains is papal supremacy, and the veneration of the Virgin and saints. In other words, and to unspeculative English minds, the Anglo-Catholic had only to take one step more into idolatry, and the last step of all into Popery. Meanwhile, the movement which might by turns be labelled Latitudinarian or Rationalist,[1] or more simply and vaguely Broad Church, had been gaining steadily in force and authority. In the widest terms, it could be defined as the response to the challenge of science, as the effort to

[1] Add Arnoldine, Germanist, and Neologist, all terms of abuse rather than terms of art.

reformulate the Christian faith in language adapted to the outlook of the age, an age profoundly impressed with the unformity of nature, and increasingly critical in its acceptance of evidence. The question which the Zulu convert put to Bishop Colenso: Do you believe all that? could not be evaded for ever, and it would be difficult indeed to say with what inner acceptance the Gospels were read and the Creed recited by Thirlwall or Jowett or Stanley. The laity, not restrained even by the vague and liberal terms of subscription which the Act of 1865 imposed on the clergy, might speak more openly, and for a while, and to a certain number of serious souls, Seeley and Matthew Arnold seemed to offer a possible standing ground in a rising flood of doubt. But even the clergy, recruited, as they still for the most part were, from the families of clergymen and gentlemen, could not in the long run be bound to beliefs inconsistent with the views of the educated laity: and the intimate association of the professions, sacred and profane, from the Universities onwards; the social activity of the clergy from the bishops downwards; and together brought about the paradox which Mr Gladstone once set before the Queen – the tenacious vitality of a Church whose ministers, many of them, rejected both her authority and her creeds.

But proceedings for heresy being of a penal character, the law required an exact and circumstantial statement of the offence alleged, and the wise ambiguity with which the Church had formulated the mysteries of her faith, made it almost impossible to frame a charge which could, or a defence which could not, be sustained. In 1850 the Gorham judgement which allowed a clergyman to disbelieve in Baptismal Regeneration,[1] had produced a formidable secession to Rome. In 1860 a group of scholars put forth a volume of *Essays and Reviews*, not very remarkable in themselves, which was taken as a challenge to

---

[1] It was not uncommon for Low Church parents to have their children christened by Nonconformist ministers, so as to avoid the awful words 'seing now that this child is by baptism regenerate'. In 1864 Spurgeon preached a sermon calling on the Evangelicals to quit an establishment which admitted the doctrine. Over 200,000 copies were sold.

orthodoxy. After much agitation, not altogether creditable to the good sense or good faith of the orthodox, it was brought before the Judicial Committee of the Privy Council. An adverse judgement now would have forced many conscientious men to lay down their orders and would have checked the inflow of educated candidates, already shrinking as the Universities grew more secular. The privy Council held, however, that though Scripture contains the Word of God, it is not in itself the Word of God, leaving it to the individual judgement and conscience, it must be supposed, to determine which part is and which part is not. To any Christian minister convinced that the Word of God to mankind is conveyed in the person, the example, and the teaching of Christ, the liberty of interpretation thus accorded would seem to be enough.[1] By this decision the Philosophic party, the party of Free Speculation, were kept within the Church. The Sacramental school won their liberty in 1872 when the Privy Council acquitted Bennett, Rector of Frome Selwood, and authorized a view of the Real Presence as exalted as Pusey or his teachers had ever entertained. The Privy Council had rendered it so difficult for a Churchman to be a heretic that prosecutions for heresy almost ceased,[2] and the public mind turned with the greater avidity to the persecution of ritualism.

'I do profess *ex animo*,' Newman wrote in 1862, 'that the thought of the Anglican service makes me shiver,' and, indeed, abstracted from the gregarious joy of hymn-singing, the Anglican rite as he had known it did little to evoke the imagination, to gratify the senses or to stir any but the soberest emotions. But since then a combined movement, romantic,

---

[1] It is worth quoting one passage to show what passed for heresy in 1861: 'When the fierce ritual of Syria, with the awe of a Divine voice, bade Abraham slay his son, he . . . trusted that the Father, whose voice from heaven he heard at heart, was better pleased with mercy than with sacrifice, and his trust was his salvation.' Of all the anfractuoisites of the Victorian mind, none perplexes me more than Thirlwall's concurrence in the prosecution of the Essayists.

[2] The only one of consequence, the Voysey case in 1871, elicited from the Privy Council the opinion that a clergyman may follow 'any interpretations of the Articles, which, by any reasonable allowance for the variety of human opinion, can be reconciled with their language'. But in the matter of ritual, the Court is bound itself to determine the meaning of rubric and enforce it.

antiquarian, doctrinal, had transformed the worship which he found so dreary. In religion, as in poetry and art, the appeal of the Middle Ages was irresistible: and the whole tendency of the Tractarian movement was to exalt the priestly character, and to isolate the Eucharist as the chief act of worship. The law was obscure: the opinion and practice of the clergy were divided. But on the whole the laity were suspicious even of such modest and venerable symbols as altar lights and the mixed chalice: the attitude of the minister at the Communion Table might import doctrinal views of the deepest significance: and the younger clergy, going far beyond the practice or intention of the old Tractarians, were now bringing into the Anglican service vestments and gestures, which, as they had no ground in any living tradition, could only be interpreted as an accommodation to a foreign, and still suspect church. Indeed, set forth in the downright English of aggrieved Protestants, some of the new rites, such as rubbing black powder on the faces of people, sprinkling the candles with water, and giving the acolyte a decanter to hold, do not commend themselves as either seemly or sensible. To prepare the way for legislation a Royal Commission was issued in 1867. There were twenty-four minority reports. The Public Worship Regulation Act was passed in 1874. There were scenes: there were scandals: a few obstinate ministers retired to jail from which they were quickly, and with some embarrassment, released. In quiet times, their misdoings or their sufferings might have excited some popular commotion. But the times were not quiet and by 1880 the electorate had other things to take sides on.

It can hardly be maintained that these controversies engaged the better or deeper part of the public mind or that they were governed by any ardent desire for truth or the spiritual welfare of the people. When we have abstracted the condescension of middle-class Anglicanism and the social envy of middle-class dissent; the deep-bitten suspicion of Rome, recently enflamed by the Vatican decrees; timidity in face of new ideas, and pertness in face of old prejudices; we shall probably conclude that what remained might have been adjusted by a very moderate exercise of forbearance and common sense: by recognizing that the Church of England without ceasing to be Protestant had outgrown the formularies of the Protestant Reformation. But it was simpler then to say Mass in Masquerade and have done with it. And it is better now to remember that this distracted Establishment was still the home of men not inferior in life or learning to the greatest names in its history, of Westcott, and Lightfoot, and Dean Church.

21

There are moments when an English student of nineteenth-century history must wish that birth had given him for his central topic something less vast and incoherent than the growth of England from the compact, self-centred organism of 1830 to the loose and world embracing fabric of 1900. Not that the growth of the Empire is itself inexplicable or even intricate, because the orderly process of expansion and devolution was a natural function of geographical position and inherited self-government. But from about 1870 onwards we feel that the inner development of the race and its institutions is constantly interrupted, confused, and deflected, by urgent and exciting messages from its sensitive periphery, from the outposts and the seaways: messages which we must postpone for a while. Soon enough they will become insistently loud.

In 1867 a statutory commission sitting at Sheffield, long notorious as a disturbed area, elicited the fact that the Secretary of the Saw-grinders Union was responsible for one murder and twelve other serious assaults on unpopular employers and their workpeople. These outrages were isolated and irresponsible. But they called attention sharply to growing discord between the law and the economic system which it reflected on the one side, and on the other the necessary conditions of labour. Less reluctantly than ignorantly, Parliament had in 1825 conceded a modified recognition to the Trade Unions, but behind the Act of 1825 lay the whole body of law, going back to the days of villeinage, relating to Master and Servant. The status of the Unions was obscure: they could not protect their funds against embezzlement by their own officers: the rights and wrongs of persuasion and incitement, the definition of molesting and intimidating, were vexed topics to which, on the whole, magistrates were not disposed to apply the more lenient construction. The law was still dominated by the old apprehension of combinations in restraint of trade, and, in more personal relations, by the frank acceptance of the Master as a privileged person. On a breach of contract, the servant could only sue: the master could prosecute. The master could only be cast in damages, the servant could be imprisoned. For a time, after the Chartist collapse, the relations of capital and labour called for little public notice. But close on the commercial disorders, which followed the financial crisis of 1857, had come a long succession of strikes, to make it clear that whether Trade Unions were good or evil they had become a power in industry which must either be put under the ban, or brought within the scope, of ascertained law.

In 1875, Parliament recognized in its entirety the freedom of contract and the right of collective bargaining. The author of this wise and timely measure of pacification, which in our social history may rank with Fielden's Act of 1847, was a typical product of Early Victorian training. Of comfortable Lancashire stock: a Rugbeian of Arnold's time and a Trinity man; churchman, magistrate, and banker; Cross represents that combination of old sagacity and new intelligence which marks the blending of the traditional and authoritative element in public life with the exploratory and scientific. In history he does not rank as a great man: on the crowded canvas of Victorian politics he is barely an eminent man. Yet it might fairly be questioned whether any measures ever placed on the Statute book have done more for the real contentment of the people than the Employers and Workmen Act, and the Protection of

Property Act, both of 1875, and the consolidation of the Factory Acts in 1878. It was a singular chance, or an act of rare judgement, that gave Disraeli, rapt in the dreams of *Endymion*, a colleague to realize the aspirations of *Sybil*: 'Mr Secretary Cross, whom I always forget to call Sir Richard.'[1]

We are moving rapidly away from Cobdenism and the Joint Stock State. Both in Whitehall and in the municipalities, the wheels of administration, no longer a spasmodic intervention but part of the ordinary habit of life, are turning faster, and nowhere are they producing more remarkable results than in Birmingham. In many ways the change from Early to Late Victorian England is symbolized in the names of two great cities: Manchester, solid, uniform, pacific, the native home of the economic creed on which aristocratic England had always looked, and educated England at large was coming to look, with some aversion and some contempt: Birmingham, experimental, adventurous, diverse, where old Radicalism might in one decade flower into a lavish Socialism, in another into a pugnacious Imperialism.

> If the Devil has a son,
> It is surely Palmerston.

Hardly a generation had passed from Palmerston's death, before Europe had seen cause to suspect that the infernal dynasty had been continued in Chamberlain.

But in the seventies, Birmingham was best known as the seat, Chamberlain as the director, of an exceptionally vigorous experiment in political organization, and, more beneficially, in municipal order. Between 1831 and 1861 the population of the borough had almost doubled, and within the same years it had become, from one of the healthiest, one of the sickliest of English towns. In 1851 the physical welfare of nearly a quarter of a million people (less than 8,000 had the parliamentary vote) was supervised by one inspector of nuisances and one medical man, whose office, though unpaid, was on the grounds of

---

[1] And who, one fears, is now only remembered as the man who once heard a smile.

economy allowed to lapse. In the diseases which come from dirt and pollution the Borough as late as 1873 held the record against all England, a condition of affairs which is partly explained by the opinion strongly held in the Council that sanitary inspectors were unconstitutional, un-English, and a violation of the sanctity of the home: in short, cost more than the ratepayers of Birmingham were willing to spend. Indeed, any one who wishes to understand why the legislation of the forties and fifties was so ineffective, and what the invincible resistance was that frustrated the energy of reformers, will find the answer as clearly written in the proceedings of the Borough Council of Birmingham as in those of any corrupt and languid corporation left over from the reform of 1834. But it was in Birmingham that John Bright made his appeal to the boroughs to be 'more expensive'[1] and his younger colleague's municipal career was the answer. The purchase of a Gas Company in 1873, the adoption of the Public Health Act in 1874, the summoning of a Municipal Conference in 1875 are not things that show large in history. Yet if we put to ourselves the question – of all the doings of the mid-seventies, which in the long run mattered most? – we might find that our difficulty lay in deciding between the municipal administration of Chamberlain and the industrial legislation of Cross.

[1] 'I only hope that the Corporations generally will become very much more expensive than they have been – not expensive in the sense of wasting money, but that there will be such nobleness and liberality amongst the people of our towns and cities as will lead them to give their Corporations power to expend more money on those things which, as public opinion advances, are found to be essential to the health and comfort and improvement of our people.' Jan. 29, 1864. Note the Ruskinian touch in 'nobleness'.

22

The events of 1874 and 1880 lend some colour to the view that the electors never vote for a party but only against one. Disraeli came in because the country was tired of the Liberals, and the Liberals came back because the country distrusted Disraeli. The brief recovery of the early seventies had been followed by a long depression and a series of calamitous harvests; and the whole world was labouring under the disturbance of the French indemnity, and the wild speculation which had followed it in Germany. For four years, too, the country had lived under the costly excitement of Imperial politics, war, annexation, debt, and a contingent liability for fresh debts, fresh annexations, and fresh wars. It was time to call a halt.

The contraction of the world, which was bringing the army of every great power closer to its neighbours' frontiers, was bound, in the Near East, either to consolidate or to distrupt the Turkish Empire. It existed on sufferance, based on mutual jealousies and the well-grounded belief that the Turk was no despicable fighter. France was for the time being out of action: Germany was recovering from her victory in 1871, and its consequences, and was so far disinterested. Austria was easily satisfied. There remained the two half Asiatic powers: England, watching the Mediterranean, the Canal, and the Persian Gulf; and Russia, heir of Byzantium and protectress of the Orthodox people as far as the Adriatic. It was unfortunate that this natural antagonism cast England also for the part of protectress of the Turk, while leaving her without any power to make her protectorate effective. The Turk remained a foreign body in the European system, and the bad humours that generated about him necessarily infected our domestic politics as well.

All through 1875 the Conservatives were busy carrying their social and industrial legislation through the House, no difficult task with a leaderless opposition: and they crowned a successful year with the purchase of the Suez Canal Shares.[1] Meanwhile, a tithe revolt, not very unlike the agrarian agitation in Ireland, had broken out in Bosnia. The power addressed a homily to the Porte: the homily was followed by a memorandum: the Sultan was deposed by his Prime Minister, the memorandum withdrawn, and the homily ignored. By the summer of 1876, Serbia, Montenegro, and the province of Bulgaria were all involved, and rumours began to circulate that in Bulgaria the conduct of the Turk had been such as even his old protectress could hardly condone. At this moment, the Prime Minister, now past seventy, decided to seek the ease of the Upper Chamber, and Gladstone, issuing from his lettered retirement,[2] leapt into life as the leader of the Liberals, against the Turk and Disraeli. The clash of armies on Rhodope was echoed in a personal contest as hot as the encounter of Pitt and Fox.

> Like fabled gods, their mighty war
> Shook realms and nations in its jar:

and never perhaps have Englishmen contrived to find themselves so greatly excited over issues with which so few of them were concerned.

On the broadest view, it might be acknowledged that in maintaining the integrity of Turkey and negativing the Russian protectorate in 1855, England had assumed a certain responsibility towards those races whom it pleased Palmerston to

---

[1] Besides the two Trade Union Bills already mentioned, other measures of this fruitful session were the Food and Drugs Act, the Merchant Shipping Act (Plimsoll's line), a Public Health Act, and the Artisans' Dwellings Act. Disraeli suggested that the Queen should become Patroness of the Artisans' Dwellings Company. She declined on the ground that she knew nothing about its finances. Two years later, the chairman, who bore 'the inauspicious name of' Swindlehurst, after a life of good works, went to prison for embezzling its funds. Victoria was no fool.

Might one add the Public Entertainments Act, which legalized matinée concerts? The day-return ticket from the outer suburbs, the tea-shop, and the visit to the Grosvenor Gallery, count for something in the greater liveliness of Late Victorian England.

[2] He published *Homeric Synchronisms* in 1876 and was engaged on *Retribution* (the theme of the Bampton Lectures for 1875). It is pleasant to find Professor Shewan, in his last volume of Homeric Essays, adhering to views first put forward by Mr Gladstone, long before Minos was revealed.

describe as the Nonconformists of Turkey. In quiet times their position was probably not worse than that of the Irish Catholics in the eighteenth century, and Palmerston himself had drafted a plan of reform which would have given them such rights as Irish Catholics enjoyed after the Emancipation, or as had been promised to the people of India by the Queen's proclamation in 1857: toleration, equality before the law, access to all military and civil office. But twenty years had made it clear that the Turk would never of his own accord accept or execute any plan or reform whatever. Always a ruler, he meant always to rule: to the sentiments and civilization of Europe he was indifferent: in its jealousies and divisions he was deeply versed. He is also credited with a sense of humour, and it must have found exercise in contemplating the proposals put forward by his enemies in England: that the Ottoman should be bodily transferred from Europe elsewhere; that England should garrison the Balkans with 100,000 men; that the Balkans should be delivered to Austria and German Austria ceded to Prussia in compensation; or their sudden discovery that Russia was a liberating and civilizing power.

Those who kept their heads in this tornado of irresponsible altruism were right in thinking, first, that the English Government might have joined more heartily in the homily; second, that it should have taken the Bulgarian atrocities more seriously. Between the Turk and his Christian victims no Christian power could be neutral. Between the Turk and the Russian no English Government could be disinterested. When, therefore, in November 1876 the Tsar made a private gesture of friendship at Livadia and the overture was publicly declined at the Guildhall, the practical conclusion to be drawn was that the Government had subordinated its interest in the Christians to its suspicion of Russia: in a word, considerations of morality to considerations of Empire. This was the theme of the oratorical carnival held at St James's Hall on December 8, 1876, an occasion which would have been even more edifying if some of the historians, novelists, and divines, who met to settle the business of the world, had explained how England was to get 100,000 men into

Turkey, how much it would cost, and how many of them would come home again. Instead, Lord Salisbury went to Constantinople.

By this step the Government recovered its control of the situation. The Conference of the Powers did, indeed, fail of its immediate object, to enforce a settlement in Bosnia and Bulgaria. But it made clear to the Turk that he could expect no assistance against Russia, and to the public at home that no armed intervention on behalf of the Nonconformists was contemplated or was possible: in other words, that a policy of British Interests was to be pursued, that within the limits thus indicated Russia might do as she liked, and that the issue of peace or war turned, therefore, on Russia's willingness to recognize them. Fortunately they were plain to all men: Constantinople and the Straits, the Gulf and the Canal: and the history of the years 1877 and 1878 comes in brief to this, that Russia accepted the invitation and respected, or was forced to respect, its restrictions. In European Turkey 11,000,000 souls were transferred from Mohammedan to Christian rule, and the map of the Near East was settled for another generation. England emerged with a trifling addition to the National Debt, the Island of Cyprus, and an undefined protectorate over Asiatic Turkey and all its Christian inhabitants. That results so gratifying to the imagination and the moral sentiments should have had so little effect on the General Election of 1880 is one of the most instructive facts in the history of Victorian England. Instructive and intelligible: because the Conservative rout can be interpreted as the last effort of liberal, detached England, the England of Peace, Retrenchment, and Reform, which still brought to its politics something of the shrewdness of a Lancashire board meeting, and something of the fervour of Exeter Hall, to save itself from the complications and costs of world empire, to cut the glory and get on with the business. It was time to call a halt: it was time to look at Ireland.

But there is an epilogue to be disposed of first. We stayed in Cyprus. In 1882 the Navy was called upon to perform what Mr Gladstone called 'the great and solemn act' of bombarding

Alexandria, and the egg of a new Empire had been laid. In 1885 Canadians were sailing to the war in the Sudan and fleets and armies were gathering for war with Russia. A party which takes office with no programme except to reverse the course of history invites such ironies.

23

But Ireland will be kept waiting no longer, and if we endeavour to contemplate the Irish question as a problem of pure politics, we shall probably judge that it was capable of two solutions only. Either Ireland was an integral part of a really United Kingdom, under a sovereignty as much Irish as English, or it was a subject province. But in either case, a territory in which the Sovereign cannot protect loyal subjects from gross and continual outrage cannot be regarded as effectively part of his dominions, and it must either be recovered or abandoned. Between these two ideas, Reconquest and Separation, modified into Resolute Government and Home Rule, Late Victorian policy wavered. As early as 1865, John Bright had suggested that the Conservative and Liberal leaders should bring forward a joint scheme for the government of Ireland.[1] It is not easy to conceive the formula on which they could have come together, unless it was that, as the Irish would be content with nothing short of Home Rule, they had better have it at once, with the reservation that, as they would not long be content with Home Rule, they had better not have it at all.

But the formula would have had to provide for the facts that a certain part, whether large or small, of the Irish people was definitely hostile to the English connexion, that socially and

[1] It is a curious fact that the land system of the Free State rests on the Bright clauses (land purchase) of the Act of 1870, developed by three Conservative and one Liberal Act, of 1885, 1898, 1903, and 1909.

economically the structure of England and Ireland was fundamentally different, and that what England and the Scottish Lowlands, which had shared and in part directed her development, regarded as normal, was in fact a peculiarity of their own. Nowhere else in the world had the factory system of capitalist, manager, and labourer been so thoroughly applied to the land: nowhere else was the cultivator a precarious tenant of the soil he cultivated.[1] It was no doubt conceivable, and it was often argued, that a secure administration would attract capital to Ireland, that capital alone was required to create that balance of land and industry which in England provided a market for the farmer's produce, a demand for the labourer's work, and a steady revenue for the landlord, the merchant, and the investor: in short, that the missionary efforts of the Anglican Church having failed to make the Irish good Protestants, Ricardian economics might be applied to making them good tenants. But the precedent was not encouraging.

The Devon Commission, on the eve of the great famine, had diagnosed the malady; and the Land Act of 1870 was an attempt to apply the remedy they had indicated. The object of all agrarian legislation must be to keep the land and the people on it in a good heart, and, in the last analysis, the prosperity of Ireland depended on the contentment and energy, and therefore on the security, of the tenant cultivator. Here was no powerful class of resident, improving landlords, or rich and masterful farmers; and what history had not created, no law could provide. Instead, circumstance had produced, generally in Ulster and sporadically in the other provinces, a custom which made the tenant effectively part owner of the land. So definite was the custom that the Ulster tenant could sell his leasehold, his successor stepping into his rights without any new contract with the owner. In effect, where the Custom of Ulster held full sway, the landlord had a rent-charge on the land, the tenant had the rest. This was the formula now to be applied by Parliament to the whole soil of Ireland. Palmerston had

---

[1] The only man who thoroughly grasped this historic dissidence was John Mill.

characterized it in advance in the last, and not the least effective, of his popular phrases: Tenant's right is landlord's wrong. The Act of 1870 was an act of confiscation to redress a process of confiscation which had lasted for centuries, and it failed because it did not confiscate enough. The landlord was left with the right of eviction,[1] in a country where there is not enough land to go round. From the evictions after the Famine came the Migration, which gave the Irish a place of arms in America, and out of the evictions of the late seventies came the Land League, Home Rule, and in the far distance Civil War.

The phrases of a controversy which hung over public, and infected private, life for so many years, a controversy in which the two fixed elements are the steely resolution of Parnell and the serpentine persistence of Gladstone, can be briefly enumerated. The Land Act of 1881 recognized the Three Fs: Fair Rents, Fixity of Tenure, Free Sale. Parnell set out to test its efficacy, and was sent to Kilmainham Gaol. Six months later Parnell was released and Lord Frederick Cavendish murdered. Spencer, with a new Coercion Act, went to Dublin to save what seemed to be a society on the eve of dissolution. The fearful disorders of the preceding years somewhat abated, and, in the Cabinet, opinion so far matured that in May 1885 the Prime Minister was able to enumerate in a letter to the Queen almost as many Irish policies as he had colleagues. Except on one point they were not irreconcilable. But the creation of a Central Irish Board, 'a vestry striving to become a Parliament', was a reef in the fairway. At this point the Government was defeated on its Budget and the Conservative policy was announced. It began with the cessation of all special or coercive legislation, and it went on . . . how far? Parnell believed, or pretended to believe, as far as Home Rule, and in this faith the Irish voters throughout Great Britain were ordered to vote for Lord Salisbury.

But what little the Conservatives got from the Irish alliance in the boroughs they more than lost by the labourer's vote in the

---

[1] Either by raising rents in good times, or not lowering them in bad, and 1879 was as bad a year in Ireland as it was in England.

counties, where their old Protectionism was still remembered against them. Ulster went Conservative and the rest of Ireland followed Parnell. Together, Conservatives and Nationalists almost exactly matched the Liberals. But, once in office, the Conservatives gave no ground for supposing that any Irish hopes would be realized, and they were dispatched. The Liberals returned. Hartington and the Whigs held aloof: John Bright had called the Nationalists rebels, and when he said rebels he meant rebels, like those whom his idolized North had crushed to preserve another Union. The first Home Rule Bill was laid before the Cabinet and Chamberlain resigned. It was introduced into Parliament, together with a Land Purchase Act, and it was defeated. Ninety Liberals followed Bright, or Chamberlain, or Hartington, and at the General Election of 1886 the Unionist parties were in a majority of 110: Mr Gladstone's attempt to reverse the decision in 1893 brought them back with a majority of 152 and a policy of Land Purchase and Resolute Government. Ireland receded from the foreground of politics. The Irish party broke up, but the issue of reconquest or separation remained.

'It will lumber along,' Melbourne used to assure his agitated young mistress. But how much longer Parliament could lumber along if it was not relieved of some part of its burden, had by 1880, if not earlier, become a matter of serious consideration. Its efficiency depended very largely on mutual forbearance and the recognition of certain unwritten rules; and when, in 1877, Parnell kept the Commons sitting for twenty-six hours on a Bill in which he was not in the least interested, the House as a body was quick to scent danger. But how to guard against it was a puzzle to which no obvious answer was forthcoming. Four years later, on the introduction of Forster's Coercion Bill – the fifty-eighth, some one calculated, since the Union – a forty-hours sitting was brought to an end by the intervention of the Speaker, acting on his own responsibility and from a sense of duty to the House. Parnell had paralysed the law in Ireland, and the legislature of Westminster. The legislature could protect itself by new rules for the conduct of debate. But the framing of those rules with due regard to freedom of speech and the rights of minorities was not easy, and it was not of good omen that the oldest and most august of Parliaments should have to borrow from the youngest and most uproarious, the device of *clôture*, to preserve its dignity and efficiency. And, that nothing might be wanting to impair the repute of the House, night after night, and session after session, it found itself employed in extruding Brandlaugh, whose only difference with many of those who voted against him was that they did not believe in God and he said he did not.

Devolution was one remedy for congestion, and one of the most tempting arguments for Home Rule was that it would get rid of the Irish, and Irish legislation, together. Shorter and less frequent speeches were recommended rather than tried. More relief was promised by the creation of two Standing Committees, on Law and Trade. But the physical fact remained that there were not hours enough in the day for the House to get through its work, if half the hours were spent in the repetition of exhausted arguments and motions to adjourn. The New Rules of 1882 were designed to strengthen the hands of the Speaker or Chairman in controlling the course of debate: to reduce the opportunities of talking at large: to deliver the House from the habitual offender, while leaving it still at the mercy of the habitual bore. On the whole they produced their intended results: an occasional Irish night wasted less time than a constant blockade: they are the basis of modern Parliamentary procedure. But by the older hands they were accepted as a humiliating necessity; another melancholy proof that the days of government by gentlemen were over. Those who knew their precedents were not slow to remark that the Irish had learnt their tactics from the phalanx of Tory Colonels in 1870, bent on opposing the abolition of Army Purchase.

It was one of Lord Salisbury's paradoxes that only uncontentious legislation should be brought before Parliament: if it were contentious, then public opinion was not ripe for it. The notion that a party should enter office with a ready-made list of things it meant to do, begins to take hold in the years just after

Palmerston's death, when the press rang with policies and predictions of what the returning spring of Liberalism would bring forth. This legislative ardour was somewhat checked by the experiences of 1868 to 1874, and not legislation, but relief from legislation, was the promise held out by Disraeli. Gladstone was in closer touch with the spirit of his time when, in 1880, he included neglect of legislation among the sins of his predecessor's Government. The charge was no truer than most of his statements about Disraeli, but it told. The age of programmes is on us, and of programmes Chamberlain was a master-maker.

To raise, by agitation, a powerful head of opinion; through the Caucus, to embody it in a solid well-drilled party; to cast it into legislative form, and then by means of the closure to force it swiftly through the Commons; these, to certain masterful and aggressive spirits, were the tactics proper to modern politics. Two difficulties indeed there were. One was the House of Lords and its incurable Conservatism, which sooner or later, and sometimes very soon indeed, assimilated even the Liberals who entered it. The other was the absence of any clear and definite object on which opinion could be excited. Between the Repeal of the Corn Laws and Home Rule, no domestic issue came before the public on which a powerful agitation could be founded and sustained: and the aspiring agitator was baffled not by any apathy of the public so much as by the distraction of its interests. Orators might thunder, processions might stream along the Embankment to testify against the insolence of the Lords in holding up the Franchise Bill in 1884, knowing all the while that the minds of the people were set not on the Lords or the Franchise, but on a lonely and heroic figure far away in Khartoum. Between Ireland and the Empire there was not room enough to plant an agitation or time enough for it to grow. The great Free Trade leaders were neither in office nor candidates for office, and could devote themselves for years wholly to one cause. The new Radicals had half a dozen causes on their hands, and the responsibilities, actual or future, of office as well. The Unauthorized Programme of 1885 was, to some serious minds, a portent of revolution. But a great deal of it was carried out by Conservatives who hardly remembered that it had ever been a programme at all.

If Lord Salisbury was right, or serious, it would follow that public discussion is of greater consequence than Parliamentary discussion. In this respect, the England of his prime was better served than it had ever been before. In argument, information, and style the higher journalism of the seventies and eighties had reached a remarkable level. First, in order of dignity, were the Liberal *Edinburgh* and the Conservative *Quarterly*, and the three new monthlies, the *Fortnightly*, the *Contemporary*, and the *Nineteenth Century*: the squibs and arrows of the *Saturday*; for Sunday reading the mellow gravity of the *Spectator*. In London there were eight dailies of the first political importance, in the provinces perhaps as many more. Salisbury himself, Gladstone, Harcourt, Dilke, Morley, Chamberlain, were constant contributors to the press. If the public was not well informed, it was not for want of instructors; and if the political leaders could not always commend their views, they could at least count on having them known and understood. Disraeli found that, in office, he could not write; and, out of office, he preferred to express himself in works of imagination. This reticence may have been designed, as it certainly assisted, to sustain the note of mystery which was so grateful to his inward ear. But it also kept him at a distance from the public, and it is probably true to say that the most famous scenes in his career were acted before an audience, of which the majority was hostile and the minority puzzled. He took no pains to stand well with educated opinion: the others did, and the Reviews were their forum.

To the people they spoke from another stage. Earlier Victorian history is punctuated with famous platform feats. From the later seventies the noise is continuous, the reverberations in the press incessant. The newspapers had begun to notice that the public was less interested in parliamentary debates than of old, but its appetite for oratory was insatiable. Whether it was an inherited craving for the spoken word, or the pleasure of making the great ones feel the approval or the censure of the people, whether speeches satisfied an intellectual or a dramatic taste, to hundreds of thousands speech-going was a delight as keen as a Puritan's joy in sermons. But on whichever side the orator takes his stand, what an ancient would have called the Common Places are the same: justice and freedom, welfare and security, the greatness of the Empire, its dangers, its moral obligations; from which might be deduced, as occasion served, the duty of giving votes to all men over twenty-one, and of not giving votes to women at all; of staying in Egypt and abandoning the Sudan; the capitulation to the Boers in 1881 and the defiance of Russia in 1885; Establishment in England and Disestablishment in Wales. In issuing from the Curia to the Forum, eloquence did not at once put off her senatorial robes, and the speakers of the eighties, though none could recapture the enchantment of Midlothian, could always rise, were expected by their tense and patient audiences to rise above the sentiment and invective[1] which is the staple of party speaking, to the reasoned articulation of great principles, which is the essence of political oratory. A sound body of political philosophy might still be extracted from the rich information of Dilke and the fine reasoning of Courtney, the robust indiscretions of Salisbury, the close argument of Goschen, and Hartington's grand good sense. We are far from Limehouse still. But Lord Randolph had pointed the way.

By 1886 every argument on either side of the Irish case had been stated, confuted, reiterated, and shredded to the last syllable. But still Mr Gladstone was there, aways ready to fan the tiring ardour of his followers with a moral emotion which may seem to us to be strangely in excess of the occasion. Surely it is possible to be a religious man and an intelligent man, and yet not deem it necessary to enter into the chamber of the soul, the recesses of the heart, yea, the presence of Almighty God, when the question at issue is whether in the last Irish tussle, the policeman or the Ribbonman hit the other first; be it in politics or in poetry, few English optics are fine enough to determine

---

[1] In 1905 an old woman in Warwickshire warned a young candidate: 'We don't like to hear the gentlemen becalling one another.'

whether a pale light in the western sky is the birth of a star or the dust above a Dublin street fight. Released from power, the old man employed the most wonderful resources of voice, presence, experience, fame, of scholarly and religious accomplishment, ever given to an English statesman, to keep Ireland before the eyes of a people already stirring away from Liberalism towards an Imperialism or a collectivism of which he understood nothing. But in those same years, the West Britons were gathering material for a new statement of Irish nationality, a new assault on the impermeable arrogance of the conqueror, and imparting to English thought not a little of their own resentment, impatience, and disaffection. To a foreigner, the age through which we ourselves have been living is the age of Galsworthy, Wells, and Shaw; before them of Wilde. Something, doubtless, beside literary enjoyment guides his taste, and in his malicious preference for what is most critical and most subversive, we catch an echo of that passionate jealousy of England which for a generation was the most widely diffused emotion in Europe, a generation when it seemed at times not wholly out of reckoning that a second League of Cambrai might be formed for the spoliation of a greater Venice. But two Irishmen in a list of four. It is to be thought of.

24

The Reform Movement of 1830 resulted in ten years of Whig government, and a sharp Conservative reaction. The Reform of 1867 gave the Liberals six years of office, and the Tories another six. The last extension of the suffrage in 1885 eclipsed them for six months and then put them in power for seventeen years. Disraeli's forecast that the enlarged electorate would be preponderantly Conservative was justified, but by accident perhaps as much as by any inner necessity.

The election of 1868 was fought, partly on a general, abstract Liberalism, and partly on the personality of Gladstone: and 1874 was far more a defeat for the Liberals than a victory for Conservatism. The country wanted not a programme but peace. The results of 1880 were equally astonishing to both parties, neither of whom had expected or feared much more than a slight majority either way. What the country hoped for, beyond the cessation of Imperialist adventure, it is not so easy to determine. Few of the myriads who waited in the snow for hours to hear Mr Gladstone speak, held up their babies to see him pass, and decorated their tables with Sweet Williams, could have guessed that in five years they would be called upon to make their choice between the abandonment of a lifelong loyalty, and surrender to the Irish party.

Practical men, without underrating the other elements in the catastrophe of 1880, were disposed to assign no small part of the results to the working of the Caucus, or as it was often called, the Birmingham System, the organization on a democratic basis of the whole party in the boroughs. But in 1880 the borough for electoral purposes was still the borough for municipal purposes: burgesses and voters could be organized on parallel lines, and rewarded for their political constancy by municipal honours, appointments, and contracts. The Act of 1885 which broke up the boroughs into single-member constituencies made it less easy to drill or corrupt the constituents. The Caucus had not time to take root, and the course of events was against it. In 1886 the Birmingham Caucus stayed Liberal. Chamberlain went Unionist and carried Birmingham with him.

The Liberal split had other consequences. Hitherto, the historical parties had not been unevenly represented at all levels of society, and of the two, the Whig houses were more conspicuous than the Tory. But as they crossed the floor, the balance altered. There was a concentration of wealth, titled and untitled, on the Unionist side, and there ought to have been a corresponding concentration of Radicalism – or Socialism – on the Liberal side. But the chief Radical crossed the floor too. History seemed to have decided once more, as in the thirties, that while there was room for Whigs and Tories, or Liberals and Conservatives, there was no room for any one else. The debates of two centuries had channelled the political landscape down to bedrock, and into one of the two great streams all the minor affluents must find their way, or be wasted in the desert.

But meanwhile, partly from the natural operation of time, and partly, no doubt, from the delicate impulsions which Disraeli gave to that operation, the relations of the Crown with Ministers and people had been subtly transformed. Between them, the Queen and the Prince Consort had created a position which the Queen alone could not fill. For a while the Albertine practice had kept its sway; vigilant, impartial, imperturbable. Then a character, long suppressed, gradually lifted its head: vigilant indeed, laborious, fearlessly truthful: but excitable, impassioned and self-willed: Melbourne's Victorian, grown middle-aged; respected for her virtues and pitied for her sorrows, rather than loved, as she was hereafter to be loved by a people to whom her Consort had become a dim figure of their fathers' time: who had long forgiven, if ever they remembered, the acerbity of her warfare with one Minister, the too compliant ear she turned to the Imperial wiles of another. In 1870 perhaps the most general, though secret, opinions among thoughtful observers was that the virtues of its wearer would preserve the Crown for one successor, hardly for more than one. Professed or active republicans were few, and the spectacle of Paris had diminished their numbers: but the scandalized horror with which the Commons howled down Auberon Herbert's avowal of his principles in 1872 may have masked a certain misgiving. Republican simplicity is appropriate to a Republic: but a Court which does not allure the intelligent, attract the smart, or dazzle the many, makes the worst of both worlds if it is not frugal as well: and Victoria's demands for dowries and allowances were unconscionable. Fifty-three members voted to reduce the grant to Prince Arthur, Duke of Connaught, and the invective with which Gladstone met Dilke's request for light upon the Civil List was heard in a glum silence on the Liberal benches. It is worth reflecting – it is a pity Victoria did not reflect – what a turn our history might have taken if the greatest Liberal of all time had not been to the innermost fibre penetrated with a veneration for all ancient, all established things: for the Church, the Universities, the Aristocracy, the Crown.

The lengthening experience of the Queen, laid up in in a most retentive and faithful memory, was making her an excellent person to talk things over with; if she had mastered the nervous horror of London which drove her to Balmoral and Osborne, and had kept her Ministers under the charm at Buckingham Palace, her influence would have grown with her experience; if she had been a woman on the intellectual level of her Consort, her influence might have become very great. On three occasions after the Prince's death she intervened with decisive effect: in checking the hysterical fussiness with which Palmerston and Russell were behaving over Schleswig-Holstein under the grim contempuous eyes of Bismarck; in promoting the passage of the Reform Bill of 1867; in releasing the deadlock of the Houses over Reform and Redistribution in 1884. But Disraeli made her a partisan: the hoarded experience which might have been freely at the disposal of all her Ministers was reserved for such favourites as Salisbury and Rosebery, and the influence was dissipated in reprimands and injunctions, often shrewd, always vigorous, but sometimes petulant and sometimes petty.

But on the people the figure of the Queen was growing in power and fascination. Her Conservatism did her no harm with a nation which was beginning to think, and dream, and shout Imperially, and which, politically, was outgrowing certain of the limitations of its fathers. Early Victorian England, with some of the defects, had the one great merit at least of oligarchic government: a clear and rational political philosophy. Certain men, whose rank and wealth gives influence and standing, are appointed by the respectable classes to consult for the people, to the end that they may be well ordered. Of these, the most influential and capable are in turn selected to administer the finances and the chief offices of State. They are Ministers of the Crown, but like Pitt in Johnson's famous distinction, they are

LORD BEACONSFIELD has been re-
moved at a time when he was still the foremost
statesman of the Conservative party, and while he
attracted the attention of the country only in a
less degree than MR. GLADSTONE himself. This is
not the occasion for a cold and critical examination
of LORD BEACONSFIELD's course in politics during
half a century. Few leaders of parties have been
the objects of so much denunciation and suspicion,
and scarcely one can be named who, in the face of
many and great obstacles, so steadily advanced
to a commanding place in the State. But to-day
censure will be generously silent. There was much
that was dignified and still more that was brilliant
in LORD BEACONSFIELD's career, and on those parts
of it even his enemies, not always chivalrous in
their attacks upon him, will prefer to dwell at the
hour of his death. The doubts which sometimes
tried the allegiance of his followers—though when
the time for action came no leader was ever more
loyally obeyed by a proud and powerful party—will
be forgotten in regret for the loss of a chief who,
whatever his faults, added many remarkable pages
to the history of English Conservatism. No dis-
sentient voice will break in upon the tribute of
admiration, in which foes, we are sure, will
cordially join with friends, that must be paid to
LORD BEACONSFIELD's high courage, his unswerv-
ing purpose, his imperturbable temper, and his
versatile mastery of Parliamentary tactics. His
oratorical gifts, though not comparable for artistic
effect and passionate power with those of MR.
BRIGHT, or even with the accomplished fluency and
skilful command of facts in which MR. GLADSTONE
is unrivalled, were, perhaps, rarer than either, and
will not soon be matched again in the House of
Commons.

From The Times, 20 *April* 1881

148

THE FALL OF KHARTOUM.

(FROM OUR CORRESPONDENTS.)

(BY EASTERN COMPANY'S CABLES.)

ALEXANDRIA, FEB. 5.

The following telegram has reached Sir Evelyn Baring from Lord Wolseley :—

"Korti, Feb. 5.

"Khartoum fell on the 26th

"Sir C. Wilson arrived at Khartoum on the 28th, and found the place in the hands of the enemy. He retired, under a heavy fire from the river bank.

"The steamers in which he returned were wrecked some miles below the Shabluka Cataract, but the whole party were saved, and landed on an island, where they are in safety. A steamer had gone to fetch them.

"The fate of General Gordon is uncertain.

"General Stewart is doing well. Nearly all the wounded from Metammeh are being brought to Gakdul."

I forward the above message, though it was probably known in London before it was published in Cairo.

It is impossible to add any comment to such news, or to describe the disgust and consternation manifested at Cairo and Alexandria.

From The Times, 6 *February* 1885

149

ministers given to the Crown by the people; that is by the limited and stable body of householders and freeholders, by whom in turn they are judged, upheld or removed. The mere existence of a Crown in such a system imparts an element of mystery and make-believe not very easy to reconcile with its philosophy. Rationally considered, the Monarchy was only an accident, a legal fiction or an historical survival; and if Victoria and her young husband had chosen to devote themselves entirely to the other avocations and accomplishments of their class, to travel, society, and good works, the machinery of Government could with very little difficulty have been adjusted to gratify their wishes; the wheels would have revolved without any loss of power from their abstention.

Walter Bagehot's restatement of the philosophy of the Constitution in 1867, turns on two points for which the stricter theory, Whig or Radical, had not provided. One is, the presence in every community of an irrational appetite, call it emotional or imaginative, which Monarchy satisfies, and also stimulates; a desire for dignity, serenity, and grandeur. The other is the advantage, even the necessity, of having somewhere in the state a person beyond the competition for office, who is entitled to be heard in any matter on which he may think it his duty to speak; who has the right to warn, to encourage, and, therefore, to be consulted by, the agents of authority.

Of Victoria it must be said that she did associate herself in too lively a manner with the competition for office, she did speak too often on matters which were not within her competence; her distribution of warning and encouragement was far from impartial; and her facility in reproof exposed her to snubs which her wiser consort would never have allowed her to incur. Now that her relations with her ministers are known with some degree of intimacy, it is permissible to say that if she never overstepped the limits of her admitted powers, she did not always behave well within them: she did her duty, but often with a reluctance and temper which in a more critical age might have been even dangerously resented. In so doing, she undoubtedly weakened the political authority of the Crown.

But, more and more fully with advancing years, she was able to satisfy the imgination of her people: such resentment as the followers of Mr Gladstone not unjustly felt – and feel still – could do nothing against a Queen so august, so homely, so doubly armed with the reverence and affection of her people: and rational criticism of the Monarchy was as powerless, because as irrelevant, as it always is when applied to any creation of affection, reverence, and imagination.

To go below the respectable class for voters, and to oust the gentlemen from government, is Democracy: and, as the Queen once said 'a democratic monarchy is what she never will belong to'. The elections of 1868 showed a voting strength, in England, of a little over 2,000,000; in Scotland, about 150,000; in Ireland, less than 100,000. The redistribution of seats had left England, south of the Thames, and apart from London, with 119 members, against 101 for the six Northern counties. Eighty peers had sons in the Lower House. Democracy, it was plain, was advancing at no formidable pace: and the elections of 1874 showed an equally well marked fondness for old ways and old families. Even 1880, though it planted two advanced Radicals, if not Republicans, Fawcett and Dilke, in office, and Chamberlain in the Cabinet, did not make any violent alteration in the general composition of Governments and Parliaments. In Beaconsfield's Cabinet of thirteen, there were six peers: in Gladstone's of fourteen there were five.

For the measure which was to change completely the old political landscape of England, the two parties made themselves jointly responsible. The Franchise Bill of 1884, by extending the household and lodger franchise to the countries, added some 2,000,000 voters to an electorate of 3,000,000. The Conservatives insisted that a Redistribution Bill should be produced as well, and by their majority in the Lords they were able to suspend the Franchise Bill until their demand was satisfied. To the other alarms of an anxious year was added the prospect of a conflict between the Houses, and a concerted attack on the Lords by Chamberlain and the Radicals. But, privately asked to say what they wanted, the Conservative leaders produced a plan even more drastic than the Cabinet had contemplated. No less than 107 boroughs, with a Parliamentary history often going back to the origins of the Constitution, where to be swept away, and 166 seats released for redistribution, Yorkshire getting 18, Lancashire 24, London and its suburbs 37. It is impossible not to share some at least of the regrets with which contemporaries regarded the disappearance of the little boroughs, and the variegated representation of interests which their existence had endured. The independent member may have been correctly defined as the member whom no one could depend on, but his presence saved Parliament from becoming merely the register of party opinions. The success of the Birmingham Caucus had given party managers a new idea of their importance and power; and there were plenty of candidates ready to pay for their admission to a political career by bargains which the traditions of the political class had hitherto discountenanced. 'The old type of judicial member,' Salisbury told the Queen, 'who sat loose to party, and could be trusted to be fair, has disappeared. They are all partisans:' delegates, bound by the contract that if the electors vote as the candidate asks them, the member shall think as the organization bids them: 'greedy place-seekers', the Queen sobbed, 'who do not care a straw for what their old sovereign suffers,' bearers of such unhistoric names as Asquith and Morley and Bryce.

25

But if we survey this landscape in another light, we are aware of a certain fading of one familiar tint. An observer from a distant planet, able to watch the seasonal changes on the earth's surface, would have noticed that everywhere the golden area was growing, except in England, where the green was winning against the gold. He would rightly have concluded that a change of cultivation was in progress. He would not have known that he was witnessing the end of a social order.

That English farming was the best in the world, all the world acknowledged. It had to be, because, as the saying went, with wheat at fifty shillings it only began to pay after a crop of twenty-eight bushels to the acre had been got. One might, perhaps, say further, that a wealthy landowner, understanding the economics of agriculture, a farmer master of its practice, a village not over populated, with pure water, decent houses, allotments, and a school, made up the most successful experiment in social organization that England had so far seen. There were, it is true, many points at which the experiment might go wrong. The landlord might be encumbered: the rain unseasonable. 'Is there anything about the weather in your rules?' a farmer once asked his Union men. But so long as prices kept up, a new landlord or a good harvest might put all right again. In the war year, 1855, wheat was at 74s. After 1877 it never touched 50s. again;[1] in 1884 it dipped below 40s.; in 1894 it was at 22s., and the harvest of that year of panic sold at 19s. The grazing counties stood the storm best. But the corn counties were stricken, it seemed, beyond recovery. Great wars have been less destructive of wealth than the calamity which stretched from 1879 the wettest,[2] to 1894 the driest, year in memory.

Never again was the landed proprietor to dominate the social fabric. Indeed, if the broad acres of the gentry had been acres of wheat and grassland only, there would soon have been a cry for a Land Purchase Act in England as well as in Ireland. But they were acres of coal and acres of dock: they included the most fashionable streets in London, the most popular watering places, miles of suburban villa and wastes of urban slum. For two generations, moreover, the surplus profits of the land had passed into industry or commerce or foreign bonds. The agricultural depression completed the evolution from a rural to an industrial

[1] I am referring to the yearly average.
[2] This is the year of Tennyson's lines:

> The cuckoo of a joyless June
> Is calling through the dark.

state which the application of steam to machinery had begun, and it accelerated the further evolution from an industrial to a financial state.

Great figures, Derby, Shaftesbury, Salisbury, Hartington, Spencer, still kept the aristocratic idea alive and forcible. But gradually the deference which had been directed to birth, when birth meant commonly land and wealth, moved, as the land grew poorer, towards wealth itself. And not only the landed man, but the merchant and manufacturer also were coming to be overshadowed by the financier, the swiftness of his winnings, the riot of his display.[1] When in 1890 it was revealed that the old and sober house of Baring had lost its foothold in the torrent of foreign speculation, it was revealed also that hardly one English name figured any longer among the leaders of high finance. As the historic associations of wealth grew fainter, the imaginative or sentimental defence of inequality grew less assured: the world which had taken it as a natural thing that a Duke of Devonshire should grow the Victoria Regia in a glass-house like an Arabian palace, grew restive when Whittaker Wright began to display his ill-gotten glory in a subaqueous billiard room on the Surrey Heaths. It would have been hard to find even a Conservative who felt for a rich man, or a titled man, as such, the respect which Early Victorians had, not wrongly, paid to the founders of great industries or the heads of historic houses, on whose capacity they depended for good government and progress. There is a taint in the air recalling the corruption of the Second Empire, and the leanings of the Prince of Wales gave the new plutocracy a standing which cast some shadow over the whole world of rank and splendour.

Men spoke still of the land, but more and more the land was coming to mean house property or industrial sites. If it be truer

[1] There had been bursts of company promoting before, in the twenties, forties, and sixties. But the first man to appreciate the unlimited possibilities of limited liability was Albert Gottheim, otherwise Baron Grant, towards whose great house on the outskirts of Kensington Palace, a trustful public had contributed, it was reckoned, some twenty million pounds.

Honours a King can give, honour he can't:
And Grant without honour is a Baron Grant.

that in the long run every country gets the land law that its soil and circumstances require, history seemed to have determined that England was made for landlord and tenant, Ireland for the Peasant Proprietor. But no owner of rural property expected to make a trading profit, and an old rule laid it down that no gentleman should try to get more from his land than he would have got from its value in Government Stock. Urban property, on the other hand, might at any moment owe a sudden and enormous increment of value to some shift of population; to a new industry, a new railway station, a new municipal tramline; and the public was equitably entitled to a share in the wealth which it had created.[1] In this way, the nebulous project of land nationalization came to be condensed about one topic, the principle of betterment and the taxation of site values. In 1889 the new London County Council projected a Bill to secure for the ratepayer the whole of the increment due to public improvement. So far and so fast are we moving. So necessary is it for us to recall from time to time that we are in an age of transition: to remember, for example, that a boy who had heard Arnold say that railways had given the death blow to feudalism, might have lived to hear Bernard Shaw say that dynamite had given the death blow to capitalism, or Bramwell at the British Association in 1881 prophesy that within the lifetime of his audience steam would have made way for internal combustion. In that audience, doubtless, there were gentlemen whose lands were still ploughed with oxen.

But along with this dipping of the balance from country to town, we can discern another process at work, which, if the word had not been taken for other purposes, might most compactly have been described as the socialization of wealth. Economists may talk of the manufacturer or the labourer. But on a closer view, one is rather the symbol of a ramifying organization, the ownership of which rests in innumerable

---

[1] Which follows strictly from Ricardian doctrine. Because, if rent is the price of all differential advantages, any advantage bestowed by the community properly belongs to it.

shareholding hands;[1] the other, a unit in a disciplined force, which, if it supports him when he cannot work, may compel him to remain idle when he could. One becomes aware, too, when projects of expenditure are under discussion, of a subtle shift of speech. The older generation tends to speak of the taxpayer, the younger of the State. With reason, because the electorate of 1832 to 1867 had to pay its own way. After 1867, much more after 1885, there is a feeling abroad that the electors have only to give their orders; some one else will meet the bill.[2] The control of industry is more searching and regular; the volume of departmental legislation grows yearly. Free Trade is no longer an unquestioned dogma; even compulsory military service can be debated. In Forster's phrase, the nations are massing themselves; the temperature is rising under the interpressure of competition; and the rocky core of old individualism is being metamorphosed into something new. We may think of English history in the years, let us say between the Jubilee, the years of the great London strikes and the first Colonial Conference, as the epilogue to one age, or the prehistory of another. One picture is dissolving fast. Into what pattern the emergent lines and colours will fall, we cannot tell. But the proud and sober confidence which irradiates the mid-Victorian landscape, that will not be seen again.

[1] Of the scale on which trade was now thinking, Sir Henry Eliot's project for amalgamating the whole coal industry into a single trust is the most grandiose example.

[2] In the common discourse of the seventies and eighties, this is the meaning of Socialism; so that a Radical capitalist who was in favour of Disendownment and expropriation of the landowner might call himself a Socialist, as Chamberlain sometimes did.

26

When I think of old people I remember, people whose first memories were rich with stories of how Nelson stood and how Nelson fell; who saw the prentices marching with marrow-bones and cleavers through the streets of the City in 1821,[1] and heard the great bell of St Paul's tolling in 1901; of the next generation, whose span covered the last stage-coach and the first aeroplane, who had sat waiting for news from Lucknow and Sebastopol, and lived to listen for the guns defending London; when I consider their assured morality, their confident acceptance of the social order, their ready undertaking of its obligations; I have a sense of solidity, tenacity, and uniformity, which all the time I know to be in large part an illusion of distance, and I shall have failed of my purpose if I have not made it clear that the very word 'Victorian' may be used to mask a fallacy and a misconception.

I was born when the Queen had still nearly nineteen years to reign; I saw her twice, Gladstone once; I well remember the death of Newman and Tennyson, and my earliest recollection of the Abbey brings back the flowers fresh on Browning's grave. But if I place myself in 1900, and then look forward for thirty-six years, and backward for as many, I feel doubtful whether the changes made in the earlier time were not greater than anything I have seen since. I am speaking of changes in men's minds, and I cannot in my own time obsreve anything of greater consequence than the dethronement of ancient faith by natural science and historical criticism, and the transition from oligarchic to democratic representation. Yet the generation whose

---

[1] As I have never seen their song in print, I may as well set it down, as it was told me by one who had heard it:

> May Scotland's thistle never grow,
> May Ireland's shamrock never blow,
> May the Rose of England still decay,
> Till the Queen of England's gained the day.

memories went back yet another thirty-six years had seen and felt changes surely as great: the political revolution of 1830, the economic and social revolution produced by the railway and the steamship, the founding of the great Dominions. I read constantly that the Victorians did this and the Victorians believed that; as if they had all lived within the sound of the town-crier's bell, and at all times behaved, and thought, and worshipped with the disciplined unanimity of a city state on a holy day. I ask myself, Who are these Victorians? By what mark are we to know them? What creed, what doctrine, what institution was there among them which was not at some time or other debated or assailed?

I can think of two only: Representative Institutions and the Family.[1] I am speaking of sincere debate and earnest assault, of doubts widely felt, and grounded on the belief that there is a better way: and for the ordering of public and private life that age could imagine none better. I know that at time its fancy, flushed perhaps by Carlyle, would stray towards some simpler, more heroic mode of government; and that it was not very willing, could readily find reasons for not being willing, to extend the best mode of government to lesser breeds without the law. But, within the pale of civilized humanity, it had no doubts that Representative Institutions, if they were safeguarded from corruption, and if they were dominated by men with a high sense of the common good, afforded the only sure guarantee of public improvement or even stability. They were preservative, they were educative; they reconciled rulers and ruled, the cohesion of society with the rights and aspirations of its members; and the natural shortcomings of all representative bodies, vacillation, short views, slowness in action, were a price worth paying for their inestimable advantages. If, indeed, upon these there were induced faction and deliberate obstruction, then the future took a greyer colour. An age of great cities, Bagehot once said, requires strong Government. An age of great armaments and swift decisive movements by land and sea,

---

[1] If any one chooses to substitute 'monogamic idealism about sex', he may.

required a corresponding rapidity and certainty of authority. Eyes turned anxiously and admiringly towards Germany, her precision and thoroughness, the intelligence with which she was mapping out her future, the energy with which her government provided for the health and good order of her towns.

Really, the elements of strong government were here all the time, if we knew how to use them. The Benthamites had seen, long ago, where the secret lay; and if, as we are told, the ghost of Bentham sometimes walks in Gower Street, it must have danced on the night when Ritchie's Local Government Bill was carried in 1888. That measure might be quoted in proof of Lord Salisbury's paradox. No one had agitated for it; few were greatly interested in it; it was brought out of the departmental pigeon-hole where Dilke had left it, was accepted with almost universal approval, and may, without much exaggeration, be said to have transformed the tissue of English existence. Ritchie left the School Boards and the Guardians to be absorbed later. When the transfer of power was complete, the entire range of ordinary life, from birth, or even before birth, to burial, had been brought within the ambit of public interest and observation. In the middle, like a Tudor gateway worked into a modern building, remains the joint control of the Justices and the County Council over the constabulary. Otherwise, the whole system, now so comprehensive and searching, is nothing but the logical revolution of the Benthamite formula – local representation controlled by central experience, public zeal guided by professional knowledge.

The other vital article of the common Victorian faith is less easy to analyse. The Family may be regarded as of Divine institution, as a Divine appointment for the comfort and education of mankind. Or it may be thought of as a mode of social organization, based on certain primary facts, the natural attraction of the sexes and the long infancy of the human creature, and affording on the whole, with all its defects, the most satisfactory provision for that education and comfort. A very cursory observation of human affairs is, indeed enough to show that the attraction may be as transient as it is powerful; that relations within the family may be both painful and oppressive; and that, while the cessation of affection between the spouses is likely to make itself quickly felt, disaffection between parents and children may smoulder unseen to the mischief of both. To the religious man or woman, boy or girl, the trouble will appear as a cross to be borne, an infirmity or even a sin to be overcome: to others, as a misfortune to be endured as long as possible and then, if possible, thrown off.

The increasing secularism of English thought might have been expected to compel a more critical attitude to the family than in fact we find. Sexual ethic had attracted to itself so great a body of romantic sentiment: it was so closely associated, and even identified, with virtue in general, with the elevated, the praiseworthy, the respectable life, that the faintest note of dissidence might attract a disproportionate volume of suspicion and censure. Examples crowd on one's memory. I will mention only one. In 1873, on the death of Mill, a public memorial was proposed. The story of his youthful Malthusian activities was revived, and Mr Gladstone ostentatiously withdrew his support.

I do not believe that we are at a sufficient distance from the Victorian age to judge with perfect fairness its prevalent philosophy in a matter where only the utmost vigilance can prevent our thought from being at once clouded and coloured with, often unconscious, emotion. I have already indicated what I believe to be two vital elements in the analysis; physical recoil, exaggerating the ordinary asceticism of religion, and the necessary dependence of the women as a body in society, on the men. To these must be added the tighter domestic discipline that came from the management of large families: a discipline not yet enlightened – or distracted – by the psychological explorations which may perhaps, in the long run, prove to be the decisive achievement of our age. To go further would, in an Essay of this brevity, be to go too far. I will only record my belief – and I think I remember enough, and have read and thought enough to give my belief some weight – that the preoccupation, social or personal, with one emotion and its manifestations was mischievous; that it produced much false-hood and much injustice, much suffering and much cruelty; but that, on the other hand, in the circumstances of the age, the instinct of the age was sound in regarding romantic love as the right starting-point for the family, and family life, administered with sympathy and intelligence, as the right training ground for the generations in their succession:

> sic fortis Etruria crevit,
> scilicet et facta est rerum pulcherrima Roma.

The incidents and circumstances, too, of this life: its durable furniture and stated hours; its evening reading and weekly church-going; its long-prepared and long-remembered holidays; its appointed visits from and to the hierarchy of grandparents, uncles, aunts, and cousins; a life which did not differ in essentials whether the holiday was spent at Balmoral or Broadstairs; gave to those who were within it a certain standing with themselves, and cheerful confidence in the face of novelty, which is perhaps the clue to the Victorian paradox – the rushing swiftness of its intellectual advance, and the tranquil evolution of its social and moral ideals. The advance was in all directions outwards, from a stable and fortified centre. Of certain reformers of his own day, Morris tartly remarked that their aim was to turn the working classes into middle classes. Of Victorian reform as a whole the aim was the steady diffusion of culture and comfort downwards and outwards in widening circles. This was the ideal which Mill bequeathed to his disciples, and the better mind of the later nineteenth century was still guided, if no longer dominated, by the thought of Mill; and it could best be pictured to the imagination as such a way of life as the middle classes had fashioned for themselves in their families.[1]

[1] The books which, taken together, seem to me to give the truest idea of family life, its standards and morals, in the Victorian age, are the first volume of *Praeterita*, *David Copperfield*, Mrs Ewing's *Six to Sixteen*, the (anonymous) *Book with Seven Seals*, and

27

In an age of swift transition we constantly need some mark by which to register the rate of change. Especially is this true in a time, and in a country, where change proceeded, as perhaps it always will proceed, rather by massive internal transformation than by any outward or forcible readjustments. The seventies grow out of the sixties, with a slight acceleration after the death of Palmerston, the eighties grow out of the seventies, as the fifties out of the forties. But then; take any test that comes to hand; take, for example, the new, unpietistic handling of childhood by Lewis Carroll, Mrs Ewing, Mrs Molesworth; or in the drawings of du Maurier. A whole world of pious, homiletic convention has passed away, and who can say for certain how and when and why?[1] The stirring and good-humoured fifties had left a grace and lightness behind them, which we can feel in the dress and decoration of the time; in the layout of dinner tables, no longer burdened with gargantuan tureens and processional silver camels: in the freer fancy and franker manners of fiction. We can hear it in the urbane ironic prose which came natural to a generation whose wisest head was Walter Bagehot; and which, when wielded by Matthew Arnold, keep old Nonconformity in a state of hissing, bubbling wrath. The truculent, the pompous, the gushing, in literature or manners, are still there, but they are not the mode. It is a time of relaxation, and yet with the old undertone of gravity and responsibility. It is the time of George Eliot. Looked at from the Early Victorian years it is a time of licence, of an unrestrained and dangerous scepticism, a perilous trifling with the essential decencies of society and sex. Looking back, we may see it as a time of excessive caution and reserve. Both pictures would be true. Let any one think, for example, of *Middlemarch*, exactly

Mrs Hughes's *London Child of the Seventies*.

[1] It is amusing to find the *British Quarterly* (a Nonconformist organ) standing up in 1868 for *Tom Brown* and *Alice* against *Eric* and goody books in general.

poised between *Esmond* and *Tess of the D'Urbervilles*: and compare
the earnest and searching psychology with which the conscience
of Bulstrode is explored, and the strange reticence which veils
the life of Dorothea with Casaubon.

Or, consider more generally the position of women in 1850
and a generation later; their attitude to themselves and society;
of society to them. At the base, no doubt, we shall find
unchanged a solid block of what some may call convention,
some instinct, and some prejudice; a dislike of disturbance, a
real care for the finer qualities of women, and a genuine fear of
the consequences if they are led out of their proper sphere into a
world where, if they are unsuited to it, they will be wasted; if
suited, they may undersell the men. But at a higher level we
encounter the philosophic man, like Mill and Fawcett, who will
admit no inequality of status unless some utilitarian cause can
be shown: an attitude shared by many plain men who cannot
see why Miss Nightingale should not have a vote, and secretly
hold that even in the House of Commons a Women's party
could not possibly be a greater nuisance than an Irish party.
There are the professional men, like Henry Sidgwick,[1] scholars
and physicians, for whom sex is irrelevant to the work in hand.
And there are, most effective perhaps of all, the social observers,
of whom Meredith is the type, to whom a society with women
on the secondary plane, without, therefore, the collisions from
which the purifying spark of comedy flies, is a society half
finished.

Women's suffrage is not at any time in the nineteenth century
an obtrusive or even a prominent issue in public affairs. It could
not be until there was a sufficient number of women able to
conduct a political movement. But those who were able had
already tested their strength and shown that it could be

[1] Asked to name his favourite heroine, he wrote Rose Jocelyn. This was when
Evan Harrington (1861) was new. No one in the company had ever heard of her.
Swinburne's favourite was Violet North – and who has ever heard of her? But, put
the two together and you get a fair idea of what intelligent men were attracted by in
1860–80. Back to Sophia Western, and to Beatrice! Saintsbury's selection, Diana
Vernon, Argemone Lavington, and Elizabeth Bennet, shows the same leaning
towards the 'frank, young merchant'.

formidable. Between 1864 and 1868 Parliament, alarmed for the health of soldiers and sailors, had sanctioned a system for controlling prostitution, which might be, and in some instances, undoubtedly was, most gravely misused. Encouraged by Mill and guided by Fawcett, a group of educated women set out to repeal the obnoxious Act. By their exertions, a government candidate was defeated at one by-election, and a Cabinet Minister nearly defeated at another.[1] From this success it might safely have been deduced that the enfranchisement of women was in the long run inevitable, if only for the reason that no party could afford to lose such efficient allies. But it was never a party question. Strong advocates could be found in both camps; John Bright changed sides,[2] and the most virile and persistent opponent of women's rights was a Liberal whose experience of life, though he remained unmarried, was generally known to be in all other respects of an exceptional breadth. As early as 1884, ninety-eight Conservatives voted for an enfranchising amendment. In spite of James, as many Liberals would no doubt have voted with them, had not their leader intimated that the question of Women's Franchise was too sacred to be discussed on a Franchise Bill.[3]

It is not here that we must look for the ground of the social transformation that our own time has seen, but in the rapid improvement and extension of women's education, and their increasing activity in the professions and Universities, in local administration, in philanthropic work, in the Inspectorates. 'Women', wrote one of the wisest of them, 'are certainly great fools'; and if she could have heard some of the cruder feminist utterances of the later Victorian time, she might have doubted whether a hundred years had made much difference. But she would have seen, too, over the whole range of criticism and intelligence, women becoming an effective element in the

[1] Childers at Pontefract, the first election by ballot.

[2] His reasons are interesting. One was that women had not much to complain of. The other, that they were unduly susceptible to clerical influence.

[3] The cross-voting in 1897 is curious:

> Aye: Balfour, Dilke, Haldane.
> No: Asquith, Chamberlain, Bryce.

In truth, religion was for MR. GLADSTONE the first and the most permanent interest, as personal piety lay at the root of his character ; but whereas he began his career by publishing a book to prove that Church and State must be united, he honestly passed to the belief that in many cases they both flourish better apart. If it were necessary to prove his ever-present interest in religion, we might refer to a multitude of books not long published, such as the lives of MANNING, HOPE-SCOTT, and LORD BLACHFORD, and any of the countless volumes that describe the Oxford Movement. It is obvious that, in a country where seriousness is a great force, this must have proved to MR. GLADSTONE a source of strength, if of weakness also. Given beliefs as intense as those of MR. GLADSTONE, together with his gifts of mind ; and the history of his life, of his influence, and of the passionate antagonisms which he aroused, becomes intelligible. For to a profound persuasion of the essential rightness of his aims and methods he added gifts which have never in English history been found in combination—extraordinary physical strength and endurance, an absolutely unrivalled memory, dialectic of the highest order, and a copiousness of speech which on occasions could rise to eloquence of the most impressive kind. To these add a boundless capacity for work, a power of rapid acquisition beyond anything of which his colleagues had had experience, a personal magnetism which, when he chose to exercise it, was irresistible, and that rare combination, an equal grasp of principles and of details. At last, at eighty-four years of age, he laid down the burden of power, and after four years more he has died in that beautiful home at Hawarden which he loved so well and which, thanks to him, has become a familiar name wherever our language is spoken.

From The Times, 20 *May* 1898

There is much in what we see around us that we may easily and rightly wish to see improved. The *laudator temporis acti* may even contend that we have lost some things that had better have been preserved. But no permissible deductions can obscure the fact that the period in question has been one of intellectual upheaval, of enormous social and economic progress, and, upon the whole, of moral and spiritual improvement. It is also true, unfortunately, that the impetus has to some extent spent itself. At the close of the reign we are finding ourselves somewhat less secure of our position than we could desire, and somewhat less abreast of the problems of the age than we ought to be, considering the initial advantages we secured. The " condition of England question " does not present itself in so formidable a shape as at the beginning of the reign, but it does arouse the attention of those who try to look a little ahead of current business. Others have learned our lessons and bettered our instructions while we have been too easily content to rely upon the methods which were effective a generation or two ago. In this way the Victorian age is defined at its end as well as at its beginning. The command of natural forces that made us great and rich has been superseded by newer discoveries and methods, and we have to open what may be called a new chapter. But " the first of the new " in our race's story beats the last of the old." If we now enter upon our work in the spirit embodied in the untiring vigilance and the perpetual openness of mind that distinguished the QUEEN, if, like her, we reverence knowledge and hold duty imperfectly discharged until we have brought all attainable knowledge to bear upon its performance, her descendants will witness advance not less important than that of her long and glorious reign.

From The Times, 23 *January* 1901

articulation of the social mind. She would have seen the weight of accomplishments and attractiveness lifting, and the number of things a woman can do or think, without discredit or censure, increasing yearly. She would have seen another burden lifting too.[1] About 1875 the birth-rate in the provident and educated classes begins to fall. The Respectable Family is shrinking: and it is, though very faintly yet, beginning to lose its old patriarchal cohesion. It is a strange world we look out on when we stand on the slope of the Victorian age and watch the great lights setting: a world which would have startled and dismayed many of those who had helped to make it. But two of them could have faced it with a high confidence. One is Bentham. The other is Mary Wollstonecraft.

28

The great lights are sinking fast. Darwin has gone, Carlyle and George Eliot. Browning, Newman and Tennyson are nearing their term. So long and steadily had they shone that it was not easy to think of the world under other constellations. We are in such a twilight, such a pause again, as we observed sixty years before. But what meteor is this proceeding with as much noise as light across the sky? Once it was Bulwer: now it is Kipling. In their sudden and world-wide popularity they stand together, and the contrast between the sentimental exuberance of the one, and the aggressive ebullience of the other, does not go very deep. The introversion of the early time, its mournful and Byronic self-contemplation, had been relaxed, and turned outward on the world until it was ready to explode into a muscular and masterful self-expression.

When Er the Pamphylian in Plato's *Republic* watched the souls

[1] The earliest public discussion of this topic I have noted is in the *Fortnightly Review*, 1872.

choosing their destiny, he saw one who chose power, having lived its last life in a well-ordered state, practising virtue without philosophy. It is no bad account of the ideal which the mid-Victorian patriciate, the Arnoldians, the Christian Socialists, the believers in God's earth and the healthy mind, transmitted to their successors of the age of iron and empire. More faithfully than any of the sister nations, England had cherished the Renaissance figure of the Courtier, the man of bodily and social accomplishment and learning subdued to an accomplishment, a man of authority but a ready servant of the State. The success of the old public schools for their own purposes, the downward and outward extension of their notions and observances, had given this ideal a wide diffusion throughout English society. But the public schools were designed rather for a governing than an administrative class, for an aristocracy than for a clerisy, and while an aristocracy can live a long while on its conventions, it is the business of a clerisy to keep all conventions under review, to maintain an informed and critical resistance against the propagandist, the advertiser and all other agents of the mass-mind. The charge against the higher education of the Late Victorian age is that it surrendered the freedom it was meant to guard. In a world of exact progressive knowledge, where the foundations not of belief only but of daily habit were perishing, the public schools over-stressed and standardized ideals which were becoming inadequate to the conduct of modern life, and they did not adjust the balance of breadth of observation or fineness of reasoning. They preserved, indeed, some of the most precious things of the past: not untruly can the spirit of Sidney say, over some who were born in the last Victorian years, *Agnosco discipulos scholae meae.* But the larger and freer upbringing of the earlier Victorians made them a more receptive and independent audience for literature and science, for philosophic or political controversy; and for this closing of the general intelligence, this replacement of the fresh and vigorous curiosity of the former generation by a vaguely social, vaguely moral, vaguely intellectual convention, the public schools must take their share of blame.

Their share only, in a process of greater sweep. It would not be difficult to draw a parallel between the political, economic, and intellectual development of England from the middle to the end of the nineteenth century, a parallel which would be in some ways, no doubt, fanciful, but in many ways instructive. The rounded and solid culture of the mid-Victorians corresponds to the golden age of the staple industries. In a limited electorate, the educated classes, like the manufacturing and mercantile classes, still counted as a body; and science, fast as it was growing, was not yet either so extensive or minute that its achievements could not be followed and borne in mind. The public which bought 100,000 copies of the *Cornhill* when Thackeray was editor, supported the stout quarterlies, and paid toll to the proprietor of the *Athenaeum* at the rate of £7,000 a year clear profit, was, if not a well-informed public, at least a public that desired to take care of its mind, a public trained in the keen debates of the Oxford and Free Trade movements, and ready to act as jury if not judge in any controversy that might arise in future. But by successive stages, in 1867 and 1885, the educated class was disfranchised, while the advance of the arts and sciences was withdrawing them from the observation and practice of the individual educated man. Simultaneously the lead of the great industries was shortening: and, in compensation, capital, labour, and intelligence were flowing away to light industry, distribution, salesmanship.[1] After the age of the great producers: Armstrong, Whitworth, Brassey, comes the age of great shops and great advertisers. Famous names still kept our station in a world which had no naturalist to equal Darwin, and no physicist to surpass Clerk Maxwell, but the springs of invention are failing, and, for the successors of the Arkwrights and Stephensons we must look to America, to

---

[1] It was this readjustment that produced the *malaise* of the eighties. There is an admirable study of the process by Giffen (British Association, 1887) though I do not think he allows enough for the destruction of agricultural values. On this, the best work known to me is *Lage der Englischen Landwirthschaft*, 1896, by König, a thoroughly competent and sympathetic observer. The troubles of London in the eighties might be read as a local Malthusian tension – the result of an influx of disbanded labour from the country, and the stoppage of expenditure following on falling rents.

France, even to Italy. And where shall we look for the successors of the Mills and Ruskins and Tennysons? Or of the public for which they wrote? The common residual intelligence is becoming impoverished for the benefit of the specialist, the technician, and the aesthete: we leave behind us the world of historical ironmasters and banker historians, geological divines and scholar tobacconists, with its genial watchword: to know something of everything and everything of something: and through the gateway of the Competitive Examination we go out into the Waste Land of Experts, each knowing so much about so little that he can neither be contradicted nor is worth contradicting.

The shrinkage of native genius, or the cooling of native ardour, or the dying down, perhaps, of the old austerer impulses: Protestantism, Self-improvement, Respectability: had left the English mind open to fresh stimulation from without, from France in one way, Germany in another, from Russia, even from Norway. The first Romantic generation had fed, with equal zest, on German fantasy and German philosophy. The next was less susceptible to foreign influences; and the poetry and fiction, the history, art, and economics of mid-Victorian England have all a racy home-made flavour. Some lines of contact were, of course, kept open: through the Austins, for example, with Germany; through Mill and the Grotes with France; and the influence of Mazzini might repay some study. But, later, we become aware of a more general, deflecting, pressure from the Continent, and even a certain dominance of continental ideas.

There had always been those who urged a closer acquaintance with French ways, to whom the clarity of the French mind and the social ease of French life were as attractive as the loose, provincial heaviness of English thought, style, and manners was repellent. From Matthew Arnold's early time in the fifties, this French influence steadily increases, repaying the inspiration which had regenerated French poetry and painting in the days of Constable and Scott. It reawakened our art, which to foreign eyes had been asleep for two generations; to our literature it gave fresh standards of accomplishment. A living critic has described the shock of embarrassment and pain with which a generation, toiling after Flaubert in pursuit of the Right Word, read how Trollope did his daily stint of writing before setting out to hunt, or organize the country mails. The quest which led to *Treasure Island* was not on a false trail.

But, as the Elizabethan knew, an addiction to foreign ways is a powerful dissolvent of English propriety, and the impact of French Naturalism, in particular, was certain, sooner or later, to call for the intervention of the police. To bards and painters a certain limited eccentricity had always been permitted, but the notion of art as an enclosed world, obedient to its own laws only, did not come easily to a race which took its pictures much as it took its tunes, less for the excellence of the work than the pleasure of the response; and thought of the painter as an upper-class decorator, a recorder of domestic incident, winning landscapes, and right sentiments. On this level the Victorian enjoyment of art was sincere, and curiously uniform. On the whole, what Lord Landsdowne liked, the people liked, much as Penny Readings preferred the authors whom Queen Victoria read. How often one has seen this old community of tastes on the bookshelf of a cottage parlour or a country inn: the Works of Tennyson, the Works of Longfellow; some Bulwer, some Macaulay, some Victor Hugo; Dickens, and Motley's *Dutch Republic*: surmounted by a print of the *Shepherd's Mourner* or the *Meetings of Wellington and Blucher*. But who ever saw the *Poems* of Rossetti or a Whistler *Nocturne*?

Lord Morley, wishing to make clear some social stratification, once divided the public into those who had a Tennyson at home and those who had not. With *Enoch Arden* in 1863 the Laureate had captured the widest popularity that any great English poet has ever enjoyed. Only an Historical Index to his works could make clear at how many points he touched the passing interests of the day. It might be Evolution or Personal Immortality or the Nebular Hypothesis. It might be Chancery Procedure, or Company Promoting, or Industrial Insurance, or the Provision

of Coaling Stations.[1] On all he had spoken with the oracular
and mannered perfection to which his contemporaries submit-
ted and which drove the next generation to ribaldry and revolt.
In his own lifetime men spoke of him with Virgil as the
authentic voice of his race, an Imperial race in its golden prime.
The new writers and artists might fancy that they formed an
Estate: it was not an Estate of the Realm. Down to Lord
Morley's line and perhaps somewhat lower, poetry meant
Tennyson, fiction meant Dickens and George Eliot, art meant
Landseer, Millais, Leighton, and Watts.

To this native uniformity of taste and enjoyment, there
succeeds in the later decades a deliberate self-conscious
culture, of which some elements, and those the most elaborately
displayed, are exotic. The Pre-Raphaelites had forced their
world to look at pictures, and their originals, with a new eye:
Swinburne had set the English muse dancing to a new, and in
the end an intolerably wearisome, tune: Pater had furnished the
necessary philosophy with his doctrine of the aesthetic moment
and the gem-like flame. Greece, Rome, the Middle Ages; the
Renaissance, recovering somewhat from its moral condemna-
tion by Ruskin; the Catholic Church; Iceland, Paris, Japan; all
were made to contribute something to the new ritualism or the
new dandyism, of villanelles and peacock's feathers, Utamaro
and Cellini, strange odours, strange sorrows, strange sins. What
rapture to repeat, in a French accent more strange than all,
some sonnet of José-Maria de Heredia: what ecstasy in the very
syllables – Narcisse Virgilio Diaz.

Under its iridescent froth, the aesthetic movement, like the
Fourth Party in Parliament, was an earnest challenge to that
grey respectability which was thinning indeed but had not quite
lifted: with all their exotic postures, the aesthetes were the lawful

[1] It seems I broke a close with force and arms:
There came a mystic token from the King . . .
And the flying gold of the ruined woodlands drove thro' the air . . .
A Mammonite mother kills her babe for a burial fee . . . ,
Her dauntless army scattered and so small:
Her teeming millions fed from alien hands.

successors of exponents of Ruskin, Arnold, and Browning,[1] much as Balfour and Lord Randolph were the true inheritors of Disraeli and Young England. They brought, or brought back, into English life much that we should be poorer without: they recovered for us something of a European standing, and something of a European outlook: refining form and opening new sources of delight. The mischief lay in the addiction to what was less excellent so long as it was less known, to mere paradox and mere perversity. But the movement furnished its own corrective in the comedy which it created or provoked. We may easily forget how deeply our picture of the Victorian age is coloured by its satire, and how much that we call Victorian is known to us only because the Victorians laughed at it; how persistently, in the classes accessible to comedy, defective types and false postures were ridiculed into a sulky self-suppression; worn-out fashions blown away, and new attitudes approved. And, whether for censure or encouragement, few of the Victorian satirists were so timely or so effective as Wilde, du Maurier, and the Gilbert of *Patience*.

But while in art, and now in literature, we were becoming a suburb of Paris, in other ways we were falling into an unexpected dependence on Germany, a dependence resulting in part from the sincere respect of the educated classes, in part from the equally sincere alarm of the business classes. The establishment of the German Empire in 1870 had stripped off a film of insular self-confidence which was very imperfectly replaced by the glittering panoply of Imperialism. It is not only in the light of later events that we are constantly impelled to measure England against Germany: the compact, authoritative

---

[1] One might go further back to Pugin and the Ecclesiologists. And who wrote 'The report of their deeds and sufferings comes to us musical and low over the broad sea'? Wilde? No. Pater? No. John Henry himself (*Lives of the English Saints*). The grandfather of aestheticism is James Garbett of B.N.C., Professor of Poetry, 1842–52, of whom I should like to know more than I have been able to discover. His remark at a viva: 'Not read Dante? Cruel Man! Take him, Williams', sounds like the parent of more than one Pater anecdote. I have been assured by those who were in a position to know that the ripostes with which Wilde took the town were the current backchat of clever undergraduates, 1870–80. One of the most famous has an even homelier origin: it will be found in *Guy Livingstone*, 1853, as 'an old Irish story'.

structure of the one, with the indolent fabric of custom and make-believe here called a Constitution and an Empire. There, across the North Sea, not in the armies only, but in the factories, schools, and universities of Germany, Late Victorian England instinctively apprehended its rival or its successor. Germany was abreast of the time, England was falling behind.

Thus, before Rosebery had put the word into circulation, the conception of efficiency as the Germans understood and practised it; of technical, professional competence in every sphere of life; was gaining ground, to overshadow and, in the end, dislodge, the old faith in experience, in practical, instinctive capacity. The Later Victorian was not so sure as his father that a stout heart and a cool head would do more to make a soldier than all the diagrams of Jomini. Indeed, the South African war was to prove that, even without diagrams, hearts were not always so stout or heads so cool as a public school education might have been expected to ensure. It was becoming doubtful how long the personal energy of the manufacturer, even the high quality of his wares, would make up for an ignorance of chemistry and the metric system, and a lordly indifference to the tastes and requirements of his customers. The age of the pioneers was over, and for an age of close cultivation we were imperfectly equipped. It was once the boast of Manchester that if a railway were open to Jupiter, Lancashire could provide all the Jovians with shirts in a year. Fifty years later it seemed more probable that the first traveller would find a German already established and doing good business.

But the German secret was an open secret. There was no reason to suppose that they were individually or in the mass more intelligent or determined than their neighbours. They were simply, and for the particular need of the time, better educated. Thus in the widest sense the Later Victorian age became an age of technical instruction. The men who understood their time best, now put their benevolence less into charity than into education, and especially scientific education, or research. City companies and borough councils catch the movement and pass it on through schools and colleges. In 1887 we are by our own confession outclassed.[1] By 1897 the handicap is shortening. But no real or solid progress could be made until the great Victorian omission had been made good, and the executive class educated up to the level of the demands now making on it in a trained and scientific world. Over all those late Victorian years hovers the airy and graceful spirit of the School Inspector, ingeminating *Porro unum est necessarium*: organize your secondary education; and in the background, at the end of every avenue, stands the lonely and uncomprehended figure of the Prince Consort, surrounded by the Commissioners of the Great Exhibition of 1851.

29

A sense of vagueness, of incoherence and indirection, grows on us as we watch the eighties struggling for a foothold in the swirl and wreckage of new ideas and old beliefs. We must allow, it is true, for the distraction of interest by external affairs. But if we could, in imagination, first neutralize the Irish deflexion, and then remove the preoccupation with questions of Empire and defence, thus studying the England of 1890 as a direct outgrowth of the England of 1860, we should notice as the chief symptoms of internal change, first a greater care for the amenities of life, natural and domestic; and, behind this, a far more critical attitude towards the structure of society which few could any longer think of as divinely ordered, or logically irrefutable. The mind of 1890 would have startled the mind of 1860 by its frank secularism, not less than by its aesthetic and Socialistic tone.

[1] 'As a result of this stirring of the national pulse we see schools, colleges, and universities, now rising in our midst, which promise by-and-by to rival those of Germany'. – Tyndall's farewell speech in Jubilee week. When Abney became Inspector of Science Schools in 1873, they had six laboratories between them. In 1903 there were more than a thousand.

More particularly and concretely, especially if our eye falls on the winters of 1889 and 1890, we should observe a new, and grave, attention to the problem of poverty as exemplified by London. The Union Chargeability Act of 1865 had finally detached the labourer from his place of settlement, which in the country was usually his place of birth, and created that mobility of labour which the economist had desired or sometimes assumed.[1] Those who stayed on the land profited: of the three partners in agriculture, it seems certain that the labourer, relatively to his condition, lost less than the landlord and the farmer in the years of depression. From the time of Joseph Arch and the Labourers' Union in 1870 the standard of rural welfare ceases to fall: after the Reform of 1885 it begins to rise. But those who could not stay on the land, and could not emigrate, joined the reserve of labour in the towns; in that town above all which had always provided the largest market for casual and unskilled labour; and thus London in the eighties was for the first time confronted with troubles of a kind which hitherto had been associated mainly with the distant midlands or the north.

Of all the great capitals, London was the most orderly, and the good tradition was hardly interrupted by the comedy of 1848, or the Sunday Trading riots of 1857 and the Hyde Park riots of 1866, neither of which in truth was much more than a procession which got out of hand. In the eighties Trafalgar Square became the scene, and, in a way, the symbol, of Metropolitan disaffection, and in 1886 the police and the nerves of the capital were put to the test and found wanting. A demonstration, or two demonstrations,[2] met in the Square on a Sunday in February, and before the police recovered control of the situation the attendant roughs had helped themselves, it was rumoured, to some £50,000 of shopkeeper's goods. A second performance in 1887 was more vigorously encountered;

---

[1] Hardy and Rider Haggard, observers of unquestioned competence, agreed that village tradition came to an end about 1865.

[2] One to discuss, of all depressing topics, the Sugar Bounties.

for the rest of the reign London maintained its habitual good-humoured tranquillity; and the Dock Strike of 1889 showed the world that patience and self-discipline under suffering were not the virtues of Lancashire alone.

The alarm had been intensified by the magnitude of the London underworld, and the unknown efficacy of dynamite. Assassination was the rarest of crimes in England, and the indiscriminating violence of the time fuse and the bomb had always been associated with foreigners. Now, in quick succession, there were attempts on Westminster Hall, on the House of Commons, three great railway stations, the Tower, London Bridge, and the Nelson column. But whether Fenians or foreigners were behind them, the absurdity of some of the objectives, and the futility of most of the enterprises, suggests less a concerted attack on order than the exasperated exhibitionism which afterwards characterized the militant Suffragists. With the insane attack on the Royal Observatory in 1895, this spasmodic terror came to an end. Like the Fenian movement, of which it was an outlier, it had hardened rather than terrified the public; and, like all unsuccessful insurgents, the Trafalgar Square Socialists had alienated more than they had converted, and in the end perhaps amused more than they shocked. This was not the way. But the disturbance of London in the eighties had effected a concentration of interest upon poverty, its grounds, and incidents and consequences, which could not again be relaxed. That there was something wrong, whether it was remediable or not, every one had always known. But now they had seen it, and the sight left many of them asking whether it was remediable without organic changes, not in the political but in the economic sysem. They asked: and we have not yet heard the answer.

That they could ask, and at least project an answer, shows how profoundly the attitude of the thoughtful classes to the State and its problems had changed. And yet the change was natural, and explicable. To use a word which does not very well go with English conditions, the bourgeois ascendency which the thirties seemed to promise was never fully achieved. The resistance of the gentry, entrenched in Parliament, the Church, the Universities, and the land, was too strong: their wealth too great, their way of life too attractive. In the course of a generation or little more, the productive *bourgeoisie* had evolved, was tending at least to evolve, into a financial plutocracy, with a subordinate executive class: and the natural line of development for the gentry was to become the administrators of a State and Empire which they could no longer claim to govern as of right, advisers and leaders of a people whom they could no longer hope to rule. The impulse was much the same, whether it sent young men, in the footsteps of Edward Denison, to Whitechapel, or to Egypt and South Africa on Milner's staff.

A second age of inquiry, recalling the investigations of the thirties, is setting in, and, as of old, literature begins to consult the Blue Books. A forgotten but remarkable novel, Gilbert's *De Profundis*, is the link between *Sybil* and *Alton Locke*, and the literature of the Social Deposits so much in vogue in the Late Victorian years, of which in its day *All Sorts and Conditions of Men* was the most influential, *Esther Waters* is the classic, example. The bleak logic of the Philosophic Radicals, that indeed we shall not find. Instead, we have a very much wider psychology, of the individual and of the community, than they had possessed; a greater range of observation; a saving doubt of the imposing generality. The air is charged with a subtle potency, the product of the same ferment, which bred by turn the Christian Socialists and the Pre-Raphaelites, and took body in the republicanism of Swinburne, the economics of Ruskin, the workshops and romances of Morris. But this potency is controlled now by the exacter methods, the more rigorous scrutiny of evidence, which science was imposing upon all inquiry, and the ferment is charged with foreign elements; a strong infusion of Henry George, a dash of Mazzini, a dash of Tolstoi, not much Anarchism, rather more Internationalism, and a gradually solidifying contribution from Engels and Marx. In that hospitable, lightly-policed London, among whose most

respectable citizens were Russian Nihilists and Paris Commu-
nards, all theories might be propounded, and all would have to
run into the English mould or else evaporate in air.

Politically old Radicalism was not far from its goal of
universal suffrage, and the final identification of rulers and
ruled. So near was it indeed that the rest might be taken for
granted, and the younger Radical mind was thinking of another
course and another objective. In politics there is no Utilitarian
stopping place short of pure democracy. In economic life is the
identification of rulers and ruled conceivable at any point short
of pure collectivism? Are not the organs, in outline, there, in
Whitehall, in the Counties and County Boroughs? Of the two
lions in the way, one was dead, the other stricken. The
determinism of the classical economists got its death-blow when
Thornton exploded, and Mill recanted, the doctrine of the
Wage Fund. The administrative Nihilism of the Manchester
school had been confuted by experience, the example of the
School boards, the example of Birmingham. The old Radical
passion for logic and improvement, the old Tory confidence in
leadership and authority, were again moving towards their
natural alliance. But whether the inscription on the Union flag
should be read Tory Democracy or Socialism depended mainly
on the point of view of the beholder, who might perhaps in
some lights read it as Birmingham, in others Fabianism.

Any one who set himself to collect all occurrences of the word
Socialism in the Victorian age would probably conclude that it
might be taken, or made to mean everything which a
respectable man saw reason to disapprove of or to fear:
Macaulay detected Socialism in Wordsworth's *Prelude*. From
France it had brought with it associations alarming and
unsavoury, with subversion, plunder, and sex, which were
strengthened by the spectacle of 1848, the National Workshops
and the swift revulsion to despotism; and, though the Commune
of 1871 had no more necessary affinity with Communism than it
had with the Book of Common Prayer, the desolation of Paris,
the massacres and the reprisals, gave both names a terrifying
significance, which was not unfelt by the electors who returned

the Conservatives in 1874. The industrial legislation of 1875, the
extension of the franchise in 1885, and the Local Government
Act of 1888, made it certain that, whatever the driving force
might be, the channels within which English Socialism would
run would be insular and traditional: the Trade Union, the
Municipality, the Parliamentary Committee.

It was certain also that in the circumstances of that time the
driving force would be in large degree religious: not only
because the officials of the Trade Unions were often religious
men, chapel leaders, and preachers, trained in the administrative habits of Methodism, equally accustomed to declamation
and conference, but because the higher intelligence of the
movement was impregnated with all those ideas, which
descending from Coleridge, Arnold, and the Tractarians, had
enriched the humanitarianism of the eighteenth century and the
Evangelicals with a reverence for historical and social relations
in themselves. Even an anxious mind in the eighties might, on a
fair review of person and possibilities, have consoled itself that a
revolution led by Morris and Cunninghame Graham, would
certainly be picturesque: looking towards Gore and Dolling and
the Christian Social Union, that it would very likely be High
Church.

That it would be Utilitarian, both in scope and method might
also safely be assumed, because the Philosophic Radicals had
created a way of thought to which every administrator
instinctively conformed; a body of practice so extensive and
solid that it left little room for any invasion of Utopian concepts.
True, the central idea of their administrative philosophy, the
Local Authority for all purposes, had been blurred by special
legislation, the creation of sleepy rural School Boards and
obstructive urban Health Boards. But time was enforcing its
wisdom. Alexander Macdonald said in 1880 that the Conservatives had done more for the working classes in five years, than
the Liberals in fifty. A modern Tory might add that his party
did more for Socialism in 1888 than the Socialists themselves
did in another fifty. The permeation of local government by
Fabian ideas is the Late Victorian counterpart of the assault and

capture of the Poor Law administration by Philosophic Radicalism in the fighting person of Chadwick.

But we should be out in our analysis if we failed to give its
due place also to the tidal surge of a movement which had been
gathering momentum from the fifties onward. Right from the
beginning, from Robert Owen and the Christian Socialists, the
notions of industry and the good life had been kept together:
from Pugin onwards, the Gothic Revival had presented the
strangest blend of ethics and aesthetics, where it was of equal
importance that the mason and the carver should present
eternal truth in symbols and that they should not drink or swear.
We must think, too, that never perhaps had the natural world
appeared so beautiful as it did to a generation whose senses had
been trained to the last fineness by the art and literature of a
century, by Constable and the water-colourists, by Tennyson,
Ruskin, Kingsley, and all the school of word painters. But
against this world, so intimately seen and cherished, what way
of life for modern man to live by could be devised by minds
enchanted with the vision of some lightly populated, machine-
less time of guilds and craftsmen, villages and their Common
Halls, and white towns, if towns there must be, mirrored in the
streams, and walled and gated towards the forests of old
romance? Along that line there was no future. The machine, the
tenement, the multiple shops were there. Yet it was something
that over the heads of philosophic administrators and humanitarian reformers there should have hovered the belief,[1] or even
the fancy, that for the satisfaction of human needs, one thing
more was wanted than the equitable and scientific distribution
of material resources among the community of Respectable
Families.

But we must observe, as we saw before about 1870, that there
is no overt or general failure on which disaffection can seize to

---

[1] It was not absent from Chartism. In 1849 Gerald Massey's poem on the *Chivalry
of Labour* has the refrain: Come, let us worship Beauty. Massey made his name by
reciting, at Chartist meetings, George Smythe's Ode to the Jacobins. Smythe is
Coningsby, and Massey ended with Imperialist Odes of his own, which are a forecast
of Kipling's *Seven Seas*. So the web is woven.

confute the ruling order. Judged by the standards of 1840, the state of England in 1890, when the dark shadow of the eighties was lifting, was most enviable: and that, whether the eye rested on the imposing stability of the whole, or the steadily growing comfort and freedom of its component parts. In that year two veterans spoke their last word. In the Reichstag, Moltke rose to warn his countrymen against seeking by violence what could only be won by patience. In Parliament, Bradlaugh, round whom so fierce a storm had once raged, denounced the revolutionaries as men who would apply caustic to a cancer, and were impeding, not advancing, the progress to which he himself could bear testimony, and of which the land might be proud. But the standards had themselves changed, and the conceptions both of freedom and comfort were at once more exalted, more spacious, and less precise than those which had satisfied an earlier, more tight-lipped time. To attend a place of worship, to abstain from spirits, to read a serious newspaper and put money in the savings bank, was in 1840 as good an ideal as could be set before a man. To pursue it gave him rank as a citizen, the promise of a vote, and a share in a solid civilization. If thereto the State added a safe and healthy workshop, a decent house, and a good school, what more was there left to think of? By Early Victorian conceptions, little or nothing. By Late Victorian, much. Security remained; and leisure; the defence of the standard against the inrush of underpaid labour, casual or unskilled: protection against contingencies, support in old age. These are the ideas of the new age; and they embody themselves in a series of measures which pick up the thread of social legislation, dropped in the political convulsions of the Russian years and the Irish years, and culminate in what, though out of time, are in spirit the last of the great Victorian statutes, the Education Act of 1902 and the Insurance Act of 1911.[1]

---

[1] An expert was explaining its provisions to a journalist. 'I think I understand', he said: 'we have got to find a lot of money to set a crowd of Early Victorian benefit

30

If we range the forces operating on society at any moment into the Conformist and the Dissident, or the Stabilizing and the Exploratory, and apply this canon to the development of Victorian England, we shall remark how singularly detached they are from the traditional alignment of parties. There is one pattern of ideas, and another of parties, and of ideas neither party seems to be more or less receptive than the other. The most we can say is that on the whole for a generation after 1830, Liberalism suited England best, for a generation before 1900, Conservatism; while the dominant tendency is checked and deflected by a strong reaction towards Conservatism in 1840, and towards Liberalism in 1880, a reaction demanding in the one case greater efficiency in government, in the other greater moderation in policy. But of all those who shared on whichever side the impassioned expectations of 1868, how many would have ventured to prophesy that within twenty years the old Whig name would be heard no more?

Broken by the disaster of 1885, the Liberal party was nearing exhaustion. Traditionally reluctant to face the responsibilities or to yield to the excitements of Empire, it was reduced to peddling reforms for which there was no general or hearty demand: Welsh Disestablishment, Scotch Disestablishment, registration, drink, one man one vote:[1] or else evading argument on the eight-hour day, and anxiously reckoning the gain of the workman's vote against the loss of the employer's subscription. Yet there was a Liberal, a man equally conversant with problems of labour and defence: an Imperialist, a Radical, a Home Ruler: a man to whom in 1866 opinion would almost unanimously have pointed as the leader of future Liberalism. The long Conservative ascendancy was something of a mystery

clubs on their legs.'
[1] Thus making up the Newcastle Programme of 1891, ambiguously described by an adherent as a Blooming Plant.

to Conservatives themselves. How long would it have lasted if, besides the fame of Gladstone, the Liberals could have opposed to the weight and fire of Salisbury, Hartington, and Chamberlain, the capacity of Dilke? Lord Acton used to say that the course of history in the nineteenth century had been altered twenty-five times by assassination. In ten years Victorian history was twice deflected by a divorce. The fall of Parnell left Ireland with a dead god instead of a leader, and the fall of Dilke left Liberalism without a brain.

But the history of great nations is not written in the minuscule of personal incident, and if we could set against each other, in a Melian[1] debate, the spirit of Conservative and Liberal England, we should hear an argument proceeding thus. 'We still demand, as we always have demanded, that wherever privilege exists, it shall be abated, in such degree and measure as the welfare of the State requires. It was we who delivered industry and the Middle Classes from the domination of the landed interest, the Dissenter from the ascendancy of one Church; who opened the Army, the public service, the Universities, to merit; who gave the people their schools and the labourer his vote; who forced you to emancipate the Catholic and to repeal the Corn Laws.' And on the other: 'But who is to decide what the welfare of the State allows? And when you have admitted every man to vote, delivered the Welsh tithepayer from his parson, unsettled your own settlement of 1870, and destroyed whatever faint preponderance our constitution gives to education and property at the polls, what is there left for you to do? Will you deliver the poor man from the rich man, or will you be satisfied with watering his beer? And are you so sure that we are not nearer the heart of the matter than you? If you gave the labouring man his vote, who first stood up on behalf of the labouring children? Who made their schooling free? If you took the people at large into partnership in government – and we

---

[1] Not used at random. Many young men felt that the South African War was our Syracusan expedition. A friend of mine told me that nothing ever affected him so painfully as the change of Orange Free State into Orange River Colony. The evolution of Euripides from a pro-Boer into a League of Nations lecturer began about the same time.

could say something about your disfranchisement in 1832 and our re-enfranchisement in 1867 – who gave them the administrative organs by which their welfare is assured? If you emancipated the Jews, who emancipated the Trade Unions?'

'We own that we were behind you in some matters, as you were behind us in others. But we are ready to learn the lesson of our times. We have ceased to be Whigs. We no longer hold by the pre-eminent sanctity of property. And we think that your own forwardness in well doing is neither so philosophic nor so disinterested as you would have people believe. We seem to see that it has been sensibly quickened since you took Birmingham into your councils, and the rural labourer got his vote. But are there not dangers ahead for both of us? When there is no more political privilege to impart – and the women are waiting their turn – do you mean to outbid us with offers of public money, called Social Reform? Is it Protection you mean, or only Old Age Pensions? Do not forget you brought the Income Tax into existence. Can you set limits to the leverage of that instrument for the subversion of property? And are not our Estate Duties a more potent engine still?'

'We agree with you that the public corruption of great masses is the worst mischief that can befall a people. But we think that your practice in the abatement of privilege has given you a taste for innovation in itself, and a habit of setting class against class which we both fear and deplore. Both of us doubtless hold that a contented people will be a united people, and that unity is the only sure pledge whether of progress in peace or victory in war. But when we look abroad we see ourselves in a more dangerous world than you conceive. Our lead is shortening: our markets closing: and still our numbers are increasing. How many of the nations acknowledge your Free Trade? How far does your call for Peace and Retrenchment carry? Blame Nature, if we are Imperialists; or blame Fate, which set these islands at the meeting of the great sea-ways on the verge of an armed Continent. Hereafter, in a less perilous age than this, there will be room for you again. But unless you are Imperialists also, you will not be there to fill it.'

To an Englishman of 1870, Imperialism meant, in the first instance, the mode of government associated with Napoleon III, or more vaguely with Austria or the Tsar, and the association made the title of Empress[1] distasteful to many devoted subjects of the Queen. Its application under other conditions was defined by Lord Carnarvon, who, as a young Under-Secretary, had presided over the federation of Canada; who afterwards tried to federate South Africa, and nursed the fancy, at least, of federating Great Britain and Ireland; and who, in 1878, had broken with the Imperialism of Disraeli.[2] The age of indifference, he told an audience in Edinburgh, was over; we were at the parting of the ways. One led to a mere material aggrandizement of territory and armaments, of restless intrigue and reckless expenditure. The true Imperialism was a flexible and considerate policy of guidance, of justice between natives and settlers, of reconciliation, emancipation, and training for self-government.

Just twenty years later the *Oxford Dictionary* wrote:

> In recent British politics Imperialism means the principle or policy (1) of seeking, or at least not refusing, an extension of the British Empire in directions where trading interests and investments require the protection of the flag; and (2) of so uniting the different parts of the Empire having separate Governments, as to secure that for certain purposes, such as warlike defence, internal commerce, copyright, and postal communication, they shall be practically a single state.

Between these three there is room for many half tones, and for all the emotions, from an almost religious fervour to an almost religious horror, with which the name and idea of imperialism afected Late Victorian minds, according as it was regarded as the Mission of an Elect People, or Exploitation by Superior Power.

[1] Martin Tupper claimed to have thought of it first.

[2] This Disraelian Imperialism of ascendancy in Europe was an episode of no lasting importance. For the popular view of Disraeli as 'founder of modern Imperialism' I can see little evidence. In any case, these things are not 'founded': they come about. But the first man to state the new ideas clearly was Dilke.

The notion of Mission, adapted from the religious conception of the duty laid by the Lord upon his prophets, was popularized by Carlyle. Poet, novelist, statesman, journalist, every one who wished to give his doings the importance which in his own secret judgement, perhaps, they did not possess, put them down to the credit of his Mission. Nations have their Mission too, and by 1870 the conception had taken body in the Indian Civil Service. The purification of that service from the time of Clive onwards; its arrogant detachment from native life; its self-devotion and efficiency; its close association with the English Universities and Public Schools: all these things had combined to create, and to diffuse, such an ideal of a disinterested ruling class as could be accepted by the national pride and not disowned by the national conscience.

But the mention of India is enough to remind us that not for many generations to come can the contribution of Victorian England to history be assessed, because no one can yet say which of the ideas or which of the institutions generated in an age so fertile and constructive will in the end be found to have taken root and to be bearing. In the India of to-day, who will undertake to determine what elements come from the East India Company, what from Macaulay's Education Minute, what from the Queen's Proclamation of 1857? The Company, in a dispatch which shows the hand of the elder Mill, had laid it down that in compensation for the authority they had ceded to their conquerors, young Indians of rank should be trained for the administration of India: a policy of which an education in the arts and sciences of the West was the necessary outcome and agency, and which the Proclamation might be thought to have converted into a promise. Was the Queen's promise kept? The Queen did not always think so. The Mutiny could not be forgotten; and the colour bar, of which the earlier invaders were hardly conscious, grew firmer as easier communications brought women in increasing numbers to India. The material framework of the Peninsula, its language, its communications, its administrative order, are the creation of the Indian Civil Service. But whence will come the ideas with which they will be charged? Go through the list of great names in the Indian service and then consider: to an Indian a hundred years hence will any of them be so familiar as the name of Herbert Spencer, or will he be forgotten too?

But in India there was no body of white settlers: in Australia the aboriginal element was unimportant: in Canada, the West Indies, and New Zealand, relations had been stabilized by experience and time. The new Empire, in the Pacific, and above all in Africa, was being built by such enterprises and encounters, raids, martyrdoms, murders, and reprisals, as are inevitable when frontiers are shifting momentarily, a stronger race is bearing down upon a weaker, and trader, hunter, pioneer, and missionary are all upon the trail at once, and they are not all of one race: Arab slave dealers, French priests, Portuguese majors; remittance men, beachcombers, and determined colonists; seekers after rubber, seekers after ivory, seekers after souls; all the world in search of gold or diamonds, and fifty thousand Dutchmen in possession of the land where the gold and the diamonds were to be had.

Of this Imperialism, where much was exalted and much corrupt, much, and perhaps the greatest part, was no more adventurous. We must consider the influence of the telegraph and the war-correspondent, in vivifying messages which had once trailed through, months after the event, in official dispatches borne by sail; of the newer, livelier press, rapidly surrendering the make-believe that newspapers were the instructors of the people or that the Board-school population desired to be instructed;[1] of the ever-growing literature of travel and adventure, always pushing farther into the unknown and always leaving something for the next pioneer. Still armies might march into the mountains and be lost for weeks, as Roberts marched on Kandahar: into the desert and be lost for ever, as Hicks was lost at El Obeid. Still false prophets might arise in the wastes beyond Wady Halfa, still Lhassa was

---

[1] One old Chartist of '48 lived long enough to rebuke, in the reign of Edward VII, a professor turned journalist for the American vulgarity of his headlines. I fear the object of this censure was the philosophic L. T. Hobhouse.

unvisited, and a man might make himself as famous by ridings to Khiva in fact, as by discovering King Solomon's Mines in fiction. The ways of adventure stood wide open, and in Stanley the world had seen the last of the great adventurers. Those who measured him against Livingstone might qualify their admiration with no little distaste.

Thus to the slowly gathering, powerfully discharging emotions of an earlier day, when the grounds and preliminaries of war might be debated for a year, there succeeds a quick and clamorous sensibility: easily started, easily diverted, from Khartoum to Afghanistan, from Fashoda to the Transvaal; always there to be inflamed, one day by messages, pert or menacing, from the Kaiser or President Cleveland: another by truculent exchanges between Chamberlain and Caprivi. All the world is alike, whether it be Pan-Slavs trumpeting their designs on Trieste, Pan-Germans on Denmark, or Mr Olney informing the Queen's Majesty that her sovereignty in Canada is unnatural and transitory. We can observe the areas of special tension: there is the Far East, there is the North-West Frontier; there are always the Balkans; and in any one the discharging spark may suddenly flash. The service vote for 1890 was £31,000,000 showing an increase of no more than £6,000,000 since the death of Palmerston twenty-five years before. But by 1895 it was close on £37,000,000 and in 1899, the last year of Victorian peace, it had reached £47,000,000. These figures are evidence of the same preoccupation which discloses itself in the immense contemporary literature devoted to problems of Empire and defence,[1] a nervous and ranging preoccupation which seems at times to be reflected in a nervous and bewildered diplomacy, conforming to circumstances which no man could control.

But we may easily censure the diplomacy of the Imperialist age too harshly if we forget in what Titanic chaos it was

---

[1] Add a prodigious growth of popular, feuilleton stuff, about the Next War, with which is mixed up the Apocalypse, Daniel, the Second Coming, the Restoration of the Jews, and the Great Pyramid. Only one sentence remains in my memory: 'Then the Lord arose: the British Government decided to send troops to Egypt.'

involved. A still increasing population supported increasingly on foreign food; an industrial and commercial lead that was steadily lessening; the longest of frontiers guarded by the smallest of armies; communications encircling the world, but threaded on coaling stations that a venturesome squadron might annihilate in an afternoon; Australians snarling at the German flag in the Pacific; Newfoundland threatening to join the United States; English and Dutch eyeing one another for the mastery of South Africa; West Africa undelimited; China collapsing; Russia in search of an open sea; markets closing or opening as new tariffs are set up or spheres of influence staked out: what policy, one may ask, was possible in such a world, except the seeming no-policy of maintaining the frail Concert of Europe, of easing all contacts, with Germany in Africa, with France on the Mekong; and making the Fleet invincible at all costs? Isolation, splendid or not, was forced on the England of Rosebery and Salisbury as it had been chosen by the England of Canning and Palmerston, and isolation in that tense encroaching time bred a temper by turns self-critical and arrogant, reckless and earnest, and a diplomacy which the foreigner might read as a stony and unscrupulous egoism, or a flurried search for friends in a universally hostile world.

Yet all through this turmoil we hear the insistent note of a growing Imperial unity under the Crown. What formal bonds still linked England to the Colonies were rapidly parting, and there were none to link them to each other. Whether elements so disparate would fall apart by mutual consent, or reunite in a new order; of what shape or nature that order would be – a Customs Union or Union for Defence, with representation at Westminster or without – such topics might be debated in peace, but who could say what answer the strain of war might give? The Empire stood in such a precarious equipoise of parts that only some inner cohesion of feeling or purpose could create a habit of unity, and the one thing common to all subjects of the Queen was that they always had been subjects of the Queen. Her reign stretched out of memory, giving to the youngest of democracies its share in a majestic and immemorial tradition.

When we think of all the forces, all the causes, at work in the sixty-three years of her reign; with how few of them she was in sympathy, how few she understood; we must find it ironically strange that Victoria should, by the accident of a youthful accession and a long reign, have been chosen to give her name to an age, to impose an illusory show of continuity and uniformity on a tract of time where men and manners, science and philosophy, the fabric of social life and its directing ideas, changed more swiftly perhaps, and more profoundly, than they have ever changed in an age not sundered by a political or a religious upheaval. If the Queen, and not Prince Albert, had died in 1861, we might have set against each other the Victorian and Edwardian ages, and seen in the contrast the most striking example in our history of pacific, creative, unsubversive revolution. But upon the English race Fate had imposed the further, ecumenical function of Empire: and for all time that we can foresee, great nations in all Continents will look back, for the origins of their polity, and their institutions, to the years when they were first united in freedom, or the hope of freedom, under the sceptre of Victoria.

There are in our nineteenth-century history certain moments of concentrated emotion which seem to gather up the purposes of a whole generation. One is the determination which, fifteen years after Waterloo, drove England past all barriers into a resolute Liberalism. Another is the passion of goodwill and confidence which swept the country in 1851. A third is the second Jubilee. The homely and somewhat slipshod festivities of 1887[1] were for domestic enjoyment and were indeed overshadowed by the ensuing misfortunes of Miss Cass.[2] The magnificence of 1897 was an Imperial defiance. After Cyprus, Egypt,

---

[1] The Office of Works put the decoration of the Abbey into the hands of an undertaker, Banting. Thinking that the Coronation Chair looked shabby, he gave it a lick of brown paint and a coat of varnish, supplying missing crockets out of stock. The Bantings are the only undertakers who have found a place in *O.E.D.*, *D.N.B.*, and Hansard.

[2] A sempstress of irreproachable character who went out on Jubilee night to post a letter and was arrested for soliciting. Chamberlain took up her cause: the adjournment of the House was carried against the Government: the policeman prosecuted for perjury.

Burma, Nigeria, Uganda, Baluchistan, Rhodesia: what with chartered companies and protectorates, an area fifty times as large as Britain had in ten years been added to the Queen's Dominions. Some Nemesis was due, and Nemesis had already shown its hand. The Committee of Inquiry into the Jameson Raid had closed its proceedings abruptly. No one knew why, and every one thought the more.

The rash annexation of the Transvaal in 1877 and its precipitate abandonment in 1881 had left on either side a sentiment of apprehension and humiliation, which might have subsided into such a friendly indifference as commonly prevailed between the Empire and the other Republic on the Orange River. But in 1886 gold was discovered on the Witwatersrand; in 1888 Rhodes amalgamated the Kimberley Diamond Companies, and in 1889 the South African Company was incorporated. In the person of Rhodes, all the Imperialisms of the age seem to exist in a confused, inextricable embodiment. Of the stock and origin which has bred so many conquerors, he went out from his father's rectory in Hertfordshire to grow cotton in Natal, to hunt for diamonds and keep up his classics, and to nourish two ambitions. One was to become a graduate of the University of Oxford: the other to federate the Empire, an Empire so vastly enlarged that it could impose its Peace on all the nations of the world. He was barely thirty-six when, thrusting past the raids and outflankings with which Germany, Portugal, and the Transvaal were seeking to enclose the Cape Colony, he had carried the frontier from the Orange River to the Zambesi.

But in England, where Empire meant either the self-government of kindred communities, or the just rule of a superior caste, this new African venture had awakened many misgivings. Names of a kind not greatly honoured, Beit, Joel, Barney Barnato, were too conspicuous on its foundation stones. Serious men were apt at times to wonder whether more was not at stake than the suzerainty of the Queen; whether, if the safety of the Empire required the extinction of the Republics, the integrity of the English character was not bound up with the resistance they might offer to the tactics of the company promoter and the morals of the mining camp. A stain was left on the year of Jubilee; a discord had made itself heard, growing louder through the disasters and ineptitudes of the South African War, till it merged into the triumph song[1] of Liberalism reunited and victorious, but with a small, vigorous, and disconcerting auxiliary operating on its left flank. The Imperialism of the nineties had burnt itself out in the Mafeking bonfires, and the Conservative overthrow of 1905 recalled in its grounds and its magnitude, the defeat of 1880. But in twenty-five years much had happened that could not be undone. The Empire was a thing in being. Germany had thrown down her challenge at sea.

The Victorian age was over. The old queen was dead. She had lived long enough. The idol of her people, she had come to press on the springs of government with something of the weight of an idol, and in the innermost circle of public life the prevailing sentiment was relief.[2]

31

In January 1874 a number of Liberals met in London to congratulate the Emperor William I and Bismarck on the strong action they were taking against the Catholic Church in Germany. Lord Russell signified his support and was honoured with a letter of thanks from the Emperor, saluting him as the Nestor of European Statesmen. In the following winter, the *Deutschland* sailed from Bremen, having on board certain Franciscan nuns, exiles under the laws which the Liberals of

---

[1] *The Churchman and the Brewer, we will drive them from the land,*
For the Nonconformist children are marching hand in hand.
[2] Sir Charles Dilke wrote: 'The Accession Council (of Edward VII), attended almost solely by those who had reached power under her reign, was a meeting of men with a load off them.'

London, with the Vatican Decrees still fresh in their memory, so heartily approved.

> She drove in the dark to leeward,
> She struck – not a reef or a rock
> But the combs of a smother of sand: night drew her
> Dead to the Kentish Knock.

As life is short and knowledge boundless, is there any canon by which we can determine whether, in the history of Victorian England, Lord Russell's letter or Gerard Hopkins's poem better deserves to be recorded?

Philosophies of History are many, and all of them are wrecked on the truth that in the career of mankind the illuminated passages are so brief, so infrequent, and still for the most part so imperfectly known, that we have not the materials for a valid induction. Of historic method, indeed, nothing wiser has ever been said than a word which will be found in Gibbon's youthful *Essay on the Study of Literature*. Facts, the young sage instructs us, are of three kinds: those which prove nothing beyond themselves, those which serve to illustrate a character or explain a motive, and those which dominate the system and move its springs. But if we ask what this system is, which provides our canon of valuation, I do not believe we can yet go further than to say, it is the picture as the individual observer sees it.

If we trespass across this boundary, we may find ourselves insensibly succumbing to one of the most insidious vices of the human mind: what the Germans in their terse and sparkling way call the hypostatization of methodological categories, or the habit of treating a mental convenience as if it were an objective thing. 'Painting', Constable once said, 'is a science of which pictures are the experiments.' That there is a painter's eye, an attitude or disposition recognizable as such in Giotto and Gauguin, no one will question. Yet Giotto and Gauguin confronted with the same object will make very different pictures, of which no one can say that one is truer than the other: and to impose an Interpretation of History on history is, to my mind, to fall into the error, or to commit the presumption, of saying that all Virgins must look like Piero's, or that, if we were sufficiently enlightened, we should see all chairs as Van Gogh saw them.

History is the way that Herodotus and Fra Paolo and Tocqueville and Maitland, and all those people, saw things happening. And I dwell on the name of Maitland partly because, outside his own profession, England has never done justice to that royal intellect, at once as penetrating and comprehensive as any historian has ever possessed: but more because no other English writer has so perfectly apprehended the final and dominant object of historical study: which is, the origin, content, and articulation of that objective mind which controls the thinking and doing of an age or race, as our mother-tongue controls our speaking; or possessed, in so full a measure, the power of entering into that mind, thinking with its equipment, judging by its canons, and observing with its perceptions.

Capacity like that is no more imitable than the capacity which hung the dome of St Paul's in the sky. But one need not travel far in England to discover that, not Wren's genius, but Wren's way of thinking about brick and stone, the uses they can be put to, the spaces they can be made to enclose, was once the possession of craftsmen innumerable. Some day we may recover the builder's eye which we lost a hundred years ago. Some day we may acquire, what as a race we have never possessed, the historian's eye. Is it worth acquiring? I think it is. Any serious and liberal habit of mind is worth acquiring, not least in an age which the increase of routine and specialism on one side, the extension of leisure and amusement on the other, is likely to make less liberal and less serious. But if I needed another argument, I should say: Look at Ireland. There we have the great failure of our history. When I think of the deflexion and absorption of English intelligence and purpose by Ireland, I am inclined to regard it as the one irreparable disaster of our history; and the ground and cause of it was a failure of historical perception: the refusal to see that time and circumstance had created an Irish mind; to learn the idiom in which that mind of necessity expressed itself; to understand that what we could never remember, Ireland could never forget. And we live in an age which can afford to forgo no study by which disaster can be averted or eluded.

This may seem an unduly grave conclusion to a slight work. But one must be in earnest sometimes, especially when one's theme is the waning of a great civilization. As I see it, the function of the nineteenth century was to disengage the disinterested intelligence, to release it from the entanglements of party and sect – one might almost add, of sex – and to set it operating over the whole range of human life and circumstance. In England we see this spirit issuing from, and often at war with, a society most stoutly tenacious of old ways and forms, and yet most deeply immersed in its new business of acquisition. In such a warfare there is no victory, only victories, as something is won and held against ignorance or convention or prejudice or greed; and in such victories our earlier and mid-Victorian time is rich. Not so the later. Much may be set to the account of accident, the burden and excitement of Empire, the pressure and menace of foreign armaments, the failure of individual genius, the distraction of common attention. But, fundamentally, what failed in the late Victorian age, and its flash Edwardian epilogue, was the Victorian public, once so alert, so masculine, and so responsible. Compared with their fathers, the men of that time were ceasing to be a ruling or a reasoning stock; the English mind sank towards that easily excited, easily satisfied, state of barbarism and childhood which press and politics for their own ends fostered, and on which in turn they fed: 'and we think, with harms at the heart, of a land where, after Titanic births of the mind, naught remains but an illiberal remissness', of intelligence, character, and purpose.

That time has left its scars and poison with us, and in the daily clamour for leadership, for faith, for a new heart or a new cause, I hear the ghost of late Victorian England whimpering on the grave thereof. To a mature and civilized man no faith is possible except faith in the argument itself, and what leadership therefore can he acknowledge except the argument whithersoever it goes? But the great age is not so far behind us that we must needs have lost all its savour and its vigour. It takes some effort to think of England, in this autumn of 1936, as in any special sense the home of the disinterested mind, as very noticeably illuminated by the lights of argument and reason. But

> Carisbrooke keep goes under in gloom;
> Now it overvaults Appledurcombe:

and if they go out here, what ages must pass before they shine again?

1936

Note. — The floruit is taken as the year in which the person named reached 35. The small figures in the floruit column give the date of death; in the next, of birth.

Floruit	Died	Publications
1830 Arnold[42] Carlyle[81] Rowland Hill[79] Barry[60]	Hazlitt[78]	Lyell's *Principles of Geology*; Tennyson's *Poems chiefly Lyrical*; Milman, *History of the Jews*; Moore, *Life of Byron*.
1831		Peacock, *Crotchet Castle*.
1832 Thirlwall[75] Lyell[75]	Scott[71] Bentham[48] Crabbe[54]	Bulwer, *Eugene Aram*; *Penny Magazine* (–45); Austin, *Province of Jurisprudence*; H. Martineau, *Illustrations of Pol. Econ.* (–34); Tennyson's *Poems*.
1833	A. H. Hallam[11] Wilberforce[59]	*Sartor Resartus*.
1834 Stanley (Derby)[69]	Coleridge[72] Irving[92] Malthus[66] Lamb[95]	*Last Days of Pompeii*.
1835 Pusey[82] Macaulay[59] Chadwick[90] Hudson[71] Decimus Burton[81]	Mrs. Hemans[93] Cobbett[62]	Thirlwall, *Hist. of Greece* (–47); *Paracelsus*; *Midshipman Easy*.

Art and Architecture	Public Affairs	Other Events
	Fall of the Wellington Government. Grey P.M. Committee on London Cabs	July Revolution. Manchester and Liverpool Railway.
Travellers' Club (Barry)	Mrs. Partington Burning of Bristol.	British Association. Faraday's electro-magnetic current.
	Reform Act.	
	Committee on Open Spaces (large towns). Committee on Agriculture. Factory Act. Abolition of Slavery.	Keble's Assize Sermon.
	New Poor Law. Houses of Parliament burnt. Grey resigned; Melbourne P.M. Whigs dismissed; Peel P.M. Committee on Inebriety. Criminal Law Commission (-49)	Fox Talbot's first photograph.
Select Committee on Arts and Manufactures	Whigs return: Melbourne P.M. Municipal Reform Act.	

	Floruit	*Died*	*Publications*
1836	Newman[90] Shaftesbury[85] W. Barnes[86] D'Orsay[52] Mrs. Carlyle[66]	James Mill[73] Godwin[56]	*Boz*; *Pericles and Aspasia*; Porter's *Progress of the Nation* (–43); *Pickwick*; Pugin's *Contrasts*.
1837	H. Martineau[76] Landseer[73]	Constable[76] Grimaldi[79] Soane[53]	*French Revolution*; Hallam, *Literature of Europe* (–39); *Oliver Twist*; McCulloch's *British Empire*.
1838	Lytton[73] Borrow[81] Whitworth[87]		*Nicholas Nickleby*; *Proverbial Philosophy* (–42); Lockhart's *Life of Scott*; Gladstone on Church and State; Lane's *Arabian Nights*; Froude's *Remains*.
1839	Disraeli[81] Cobden[63] Kay-Shuttleworth[77]		*Voyage of the Beagle*.
1840	Ainsworth[82] F. D. Maurice[72] Brassey[70]	Lord Holland[73]	*Old Curiosity Shop*; *Ingoldsby Legends*; *Barnaby Rudge*; *Sordello*.
1841	J. S. Mill[73] Mrs. Browning[61] Cornewall Lewis[63]		*Heroes*; *Punch*; *Tract XC*; *Bells and Pomegranates* (–46)
1842		Arnold[95]	*American Notes*; *Lays of Ancient Rome*; Tennyson's *Collected Poems*.

Art and Architecture	Public Affairs	Other Events
Fitzwilliam (Basevi). Reform Club and Highclere (Barry). Landseer's *Chief Mourner*. London Art Union.		
	Negro Emancipation completed. Durham in Canada. Committee on Trade Unions. Registrar-General's First Report.	s.s. *Archimedes*. London & Birmingham Railway. *Sirius* crossed Atlantic.
St George's Hall, Liverpool (Elmes).	Bedchamber Plot. Penny Postage Act. Birmingham Riots. Royal Commission on Police. First Factory Inspectors' Report.	Aden annexed.
Trafalgar Square (Barry). Houses of Parliament begun. Landseer: *Dignity and Impudence*. Mulready's Envelope.	Opium War. Bombardment of Acre. Health of Towns Committee.	P. & O. incorporated. New Zealand annexed.
Houses of Parliament (Decoration) Committee. Royal Exchange (Tite).	Fall of Whig Government. Peel P.M. Factory Committee. Handloom Weavers Committee.	R.M.S.P. Company.
	Income Tax. Ashley's Act (Women and Children in Mines). Chartist Riots. Truck Committee. Ashburton Treaty. Committee on Town Housing. Sanitary Condition of Labouring Population (Chadwick).	Hong Kong annexed.

	Floruit	Died	Publications
1843	Manning[92]	Southey[74]	*Past and Present*; *Martin Chuzzlewit*; Macaulay's *Essays*; Liddell and Scott; *Modern Painters*, I; Mill's *Logic*; *Bible in Spain*; *Song of the Shirt*; *Last of the Barons*.
1844	Gladstone[98] Darwin[82] Kinglake[91] Lady Eastlake[93] Fanny Kemble[93] Monckton Milnes[85] Tennyson[92]		*Coningsby*; *Vestiges of Creation*; *Cry of the Children*; Barnes's *Poems of Rural Life*; Stanley's *Life of Arnold*.
1845	M. Tupper[80] Mrs. Gaskell[65] Armstrong[80]	Lady Holland[70] Sydney Smith[71] Mrs. Fry[80] Barham[88] Hood[99] Grey[64]	Carlyle's *Cromwell*; *Jeames de la Pluche*; *Sybil*; *Mrs Caudle's Curtain Lectures*; *Essay on Development*.
1846	Thackeray[63] Fitzgerald[83] Liddell[98] Bright[89]	Haydon[86]	Grote's *Greece* (–56); Lear, *Book of Nonsense*; Rawlinson, *Behistun Inscription*; Strauss's *Leben Jesu* (trans.).
1847	Dickens[70] Browning[89] Smiles[04] Pugin[52]	Franklin[86] O'Connell[75]	*Trancred*; *Eothen*; *Princess*; *Comic Hist. of England*; *Jane Eyre*; *Vanity Fair*; *Wuthering Heights*.
1848	Aytoun[65] Livingstone[73]	Emily Brontë[18] Marryat[92] Melbourne[79] G. Stephenson[81]	*Dombey*; Layard's *Nineveh*; Mill's *Political Economy*; *Yeast*; *Mary Barton*; *Pendennis*.
1849	C. Reade[84]	Anne Brontë[20] Maria Edgeworth[67] Brunel[69] Etty[87] Lady Blessington[89]	*Household Words*; *Strayed Revellers*; *David Copperfield*; *Seven Lamps*; *Rig Veda* (trans. –73); Macaulay's *History* (–61); *The Germ*; *The Caxtons*; *Scottish Cavaliers*.

Art and Architecture	*Public Affairs*	*Other Events*
St. George's Soutwark (Pugin). Lincoln's Inn (Hardwick). Cartoons for Houses of Parliament.	Rebecca Riots. Clontarf meeting. Smoke Abatement Committee. Rural Allotments Committee.	Disruption of Church of Scotland. Newman left St Mary's.
	Bank Charter Act. Railway Act. Royal Commission on Health of Towns. Metropolitan Improvements Committee (–51).	Rochdale Pioneers.
	Railway Mania. Maynooth Grant. Potato failure.	
Cruikshank's *Bottle*.	Potato famine. Repeal of Corn Laws. Russell P.M. Andover Workhouse Scandal. Railway Navvies Committee.	*Daily News.* Evangelical Alliance.
Jenny Lind in England. British Museum (Smirke). Great Hall at Euston (Hardwick).	Fielden's Factory Act. Bank crisis. Smithfield (Removal) Committee.	Hampden controversy. Chloroform first used. Franklin expedition.
P.R.B.	Fleet Prison demolished. Public Health Act.	European Revolutions. Gorham Case.
Doyle's *Manners and Customs*. Millais: *Isabella*.	Repeal of Navigation Acts. Free Libraries Committee (–52).	Punjab annexed.

Floruit	*Died*	*Publications*
1850 Church[90] Trollope[82]	Peel[90] Wordsworth[70] Jeffrey[73]	*In Memoriam* (1833–); *Alton Locke*; *Prelude* (posthumous).
1851 C. Brontë[55] Elwin[00] C. Newton[94]	Mrs. Shelley[97]	H. Spencer's *Social Statistics*; *Cranford*; *Stones of Venice*; *Lavengro*; *Casa Guidi Windows*; *Life of Sterling*.
1852 Jowett[93] Layard[94] G. H. Lewes[74] Helen Faucit[98]	Wellington[89] Pugin[12] Moore[79] J. Doe and R. Roe	*Empedocles on Etna*; *Esmond*; Hayward's *Art of Dining*; *Bleak House*; *Oxford and Cambridge Magazine*.
1853 Eliza Cook[89] Froude[94]		*Verdant Green*; *Hypatia*; *The Newcomes* (–55); *Villette*; *Scholar Gipsy*; Haydon's *Autobiography*; *Heir of Redclyffe*.
1854 Clough[61] C. Kingsley[75] Q. Victoria[01] George Eliot[80] Frith[09]	C. Kemble[75]	Milman, *Latin Christianity*; *Angel in the House* (–62); *Hard Times*; *Firmilian*.
1855 H. Spencer[03] P. Albert[61] Mansell[71] Miss Nightingale[10]	C. Brontë[16] Rogers[62]	*Westward Ho!*; *Men and Women*; *The Warden*; *Mecca and al-Medinah*; *Maud*; *North and South*.

Art and Architecture	Public Affairs	Other Events
Millais: *Carpenter's shop*.	Don Pacifico. Papal Aggression.	Gold in California.
Landseer: *Monarch of the Glen*.	Ecclesiastical Titles Act. Window tax repealed. Great Exhibition. Dismissal of Palmerston. H. Mann's Report on Church Attendance.	French *Coup d'État*. Gold in Australia. Bibby Line. Livingstone reached Zambesi.
Brown: *Work*. Keene's first drawing in *Punch*. Millais: *Huguenots*. Ophelia.	Common Law Procedure Act. Derby P.M.; Disraeli Ch. of Ex. Aberdeen P.M.; Gladstone Ch. of Ex. New Houses of Parliament opened. Draining and Sewerage of Towns Report. Cholera Report (40/9).	
Millais: *Order of Release*. Frith: *Ramsgate Sands*.	Competitive exam. for I.C.S. Northcote-Trevelyan reforms for H.C.S. Death Duties. Charity Commission.	
Doyle's *Brown, Jones, and Robinson*. Illustrated Tennyson (Millais, Rossetti, &c.).	Crystal Palace at Sydenham. Alma, Inkermann, Balaclava. Drink Traffic Report. Cholera Report (54).	Working Men's College.
Brown: *Last of England*. Church in Gordon Square (Brandon). Leighton: *Cimabue*.	Palmerston P.M. Fall of Sebastopol. Limited Liability Act. Metropolitan Board of Works. Adulteration of Food Committee. Met. Communications Committee. Cathedral Commission.	*Daily Telegraph*.

	Floruit	Died	Publications
1856	Burton[90] Buckle[62] Dion Boucicault[90] Madox Brown[93]	W. Hamilton[83]	*Daisy Chain*; Froude's *History*, I and II; *Opium Eater* (final version: first 1822); Lady Eastlake on *Modern Painters* (Quarterly); *It is Never too Late to Mend*; F. W. Robertson's *Sermons* (–63).
1857	M. Arnold[88] T. Hughes[96] Mrs. Lynn Linton[98]	D. Jerrold[03]	*Aurora Leigh*; *Coral Islands*; *Two Years Ago*; *Virginians*; Buckle's *History*, I; *Little Dorrit*; *Barchester Towers*; *Guy Livingstone*; *John Halifax*; *Tom Brown*; *Romany Rye*; *Scenes of Clerical Life*.
1858	Max Müller[00] C. Yonge[01] Freeman[92] Patmore[96]	R. Owen[71]	*Defence of Guinevere*; *Ionica*; *Three Clerks*; Mansell's *Limits of Religious Thought*; Wallace and Darwin on Natural Selection (simultaneous).
1859	Wilkie Collins[89]	J. Austin[90] Leigh Hunt[84] De Quincey[85] Macaulay[00] D. Cox[83] H. Hallam[77]	*Origins of Species*; *Adam Bede*; Smiles's *Self-Help*; *Richard Feverel*; *Tale of Two Cities*; *Omar Khayyám*; *Mill on Liberty*; (*Four*) *Idylls of the King*.
1860	Huxley[95] Blackmore[00] Birket Foster[99] Ballantyne[94]		*Woman in White*; *Mill on the Floss*; *Cornhill*; *Notes on Nursing*; *Unto this Last*; *Great Expectations*; *Evan Harrington*; *Essays and Reviews*.

G.M. Young

Art and Architecture	Public Affairs	Other Events
Millais: *Autumn Leaves*. Millais: *Blind Girl*. Mausoleum of Halicarnassus. Hunt: *Scape-goat*.	Peace of Paris. Life Peerage controversy.	Bombardment of Canton. Speke on Victoria Nyanza.
Millais: *Sir Isumbras*. Dorchester House (Vulliamy); Decorations (Stevens). Oxford Union frescoes.	Defeat and return of Palmerston. Indian Mutiny. Divorce Act. Bank Crisis. Military Education Commission.	
Exeter College Chapel (Scott). Frith: *Derby Day*. Stevens: Wellington Monuments.	Conspiracy to Murder Bill. Defeat of Palmerston. Government Buildings Report. Derby P.M. India transferred to Crown. Jews admitted to Parliament. Property qualification for M.P.s removed.	s.s. *Great Eastern*. Ottawa capital of Canada. Oxford and Cambridge Locals.
Red House, Bexley. Millais: *Vale of Rest*. Landseer's Lions in Trafalgar Square.	Derby defeated; Palmerston P.M. Gladstone Ch. of Ex.	Franco-Austrian War. Livingstone on Lake Nyassa.
du Maurier's first picture in *Punch*. Whistler: *At the Piano*.	Cobden treaty with France. Volunteer movement. Museums Committee (Sunday opening).	Annexation of Savoy. Garibaldi in Sicily and Naples. Burning of Summer Palace. Brown's armour plate. Source of Nile discovered.

Floruit	Died	Publications
1861 Bagehot[77] R. H. Hutton[97]	P. Albert[20] Mrs. Browning[06] A. H. Clough[19]	*Silas Marner*; *Golden Treasury*; *Framley Parsonage*; *Philip*; *Cloister and Hearth*; *Gryll Grange*; *Science of Languages*; *Mrs Beeton*; Maine's *Ancient Law*.
1862 Speke[64]	Buckle[21]	*Modern Love*; Derby's *Homer*; *Goblin Market*; *Ravenshoe*.
1863 Meredith[04] Rossetti[82] Lightfoot[89]	Lyndhurst[72] Thackeray[11] Whately[87]	*Man's Place in Nature*; Kinglake's *Crimea*; Gardiner's *History*, I and II; *Water Babies*; *Romola*; Lyell's *Antiquity of Man*.
1864 Millais[96] S. R. Gardiner[02]	Landor[75]	*Enoch Arden*; *Wives and Daughters*; *Apologia*; *Small House at Allington*; *Dramatis Personae*.
1865 Christina Rossetti[94]	Aytoun[13] Leopold I[90] Cobden[04] Eastlake[93] Mrs. Gaskell[10] Greville[94] Lincoln[09] Palmerston[84] Paxton[03] Wiseman[02]	Carlyle's *Frederick the Great*; Livingstone's *Zambesi*; Lubbuck's *Prehistoric Times*; *Our Mutual Friend*; Gilbert's *De Profundis*; *Atalanta in Calydon*; *Chastelard*; *Essays in Criticism*; Mill's *Hamilton*; *Sesame and Lilies*; *Alice in Wonderland*; Lecky's *Rationalism*; *Fortnightly Review*; *Pall Mall Gazette*.
1866 Mark Rutherford[13] Calverley[81]	Gibson[90] Keble[92] Whewell[95] Ann Taylor Mrs. Carlyle[01]	Froude's *History*; Stanley's *Jewish Church*; *Felix Holt*; *Hereward the Wake*; *Poems and Ballads* I; *The Dream of Gerontius*; *The Prince's Progress*; *The Crown of Wild Olive*; Baker's *Albert Nyanza*; *Contemporary Review*.

Art and Architecture	Public Affairs	Other Events
Morris & Co. founded. Whitehall (Scott).	Trent incident. Elementary Education: Newcastle Commission. Elementary Education: Revised Code.	Victor Emmanuel king of Italy. American Civil War.
Frith: *Railway Station.*	Lancashire Cotton Famine (–64).	Colenso controversy.
Whistler: *Symphony in White.*		Taiping rebellion.
Albert Memorial (Scott.)	Rural Housing Report. Public Schools Commission (Clarendon).	Schleswig-Holstein. Geneva Convention.
Madox Brown's *Work.* St Pancras (Scott).	Fenian Conspiracy. Insurrection in Jamaica. Union Rating Act. Russell P.M.	Cattle Plague. Commons Preservation Society. Antiseptic Surgery.
Law Courts. *Beata Beatrix*	Report of Jamaica Commission. Suspension of Habeas Corpus Act (Ireland) Adullamites. Hyde Park Riots. Stoppage of Overend and Gurney. Derby P.M. Disraeli Ch. of Ex.	

	Floruit	*Died*	*Publications*
1867		Sarah Austin[93] Faraday[94] Earl of Rosse[00] Alexander Smith[30] Archibald Alison[92]	*The Early Years of H.R.H.* *the Prince Consort; Last* *Chronicle of Barset; Song of* *Italy; The Life and Death of* *Jason; Thyrsis;* Bagehot's *English Constitution;* Freeman's *Norman Conquest* (–79); Froude's *Short* *Studies* (–83); *Under Two* *Flags; Vittoria.*
1868		Brewster[81] Raja Brooke[03] Brougham[78] Charles Kean[11] Milman[91]	*Leaves from the Journal of* *Our Life in the Highlands;* *The Moonstone;* Dilke's *Greater Britain; Earthly* *Paradise* (–70).
1869	Morris[96] Acton[02] Seeley[95] du Maurier[96] Whistler[03]	Derby[99]	Campbell's *Lives of the* *Chancellors; The Holy Grail;* *Rugby Chapel; Culture and* *Anarchy; Lorna Doone;* Lecky's *European Morals;* Mill's *Subjection of Women;* *Nature; Academy.*
1870	Samuel Butler[02]	Dickens[12] Maclise[11]	*Hereditary Genius; Grammar* *of Assent; Mystery of Edwin* *Drood; Lothair; St Paul and* *Protestantism;* Huxley's *Lay* *Sermons;* Spencer's *Principles of Psychology* (–72); *Historical Manuscripts* *Commission; Evening* *Standard;* Rossetti's *Poems.*
1871	Gilbert[11] Chamberlain[14]	De Morgan[06] Sir J. Herschel[92] Grote[94] Mansell[20]	*Battle of Dorking;* *Balaustion's Adventure; Prince* *Hohenstiel Schwangau; Songs* *before Sunrise; Through the* *Looking-Glass;* Darwin's *Descent of Man;* Jowett's *Plato; Harry Richmond; Fors* *Clavigera* (–87); *Fleshly* *School.*

Art and Architecture	Public Affairs	Other Events
	Reform Act. Disraeli P.M.	Trial of Fenians at Manchester. Marx *Kapital*, I.
Slade Professorships and Bequest.	Abyssinian Campaign. Gladstone P.M.	Prosecution of Eyre.
	Irish Church Act.	Vatican Council. Girton.
Millais: *Boyhood of Raleigh.*	Irish Land Act. Fenian Amnesty. Elementary Education Act. Franco-German War.	First School Board Elections – Mrs Garrett Anderson and Miss Emily Davies elected. Civil Service thrown open.
First Impressionist Exhibition in France. Slade School.	Abolition of Purchase.	Voysey Case. Tichbourne Case. Newnham College.

Floruit	Died	Publications
1872 Swinburne[09] J. R. Green[83]	Mazzini[06,08, or 09] Maurice[05] Mrs. Somerville[80]	Darwin's *Expression of the Emotions*; *Fifine at the Fair*; *Middlemarch*; *Erewhon*; Morley's *Voltaire*; Bagehot's *Physics and Politics*; Read's *Martyrdom of Man*; *Idylls of the King* (complete).
1873 Lecky[03] Morley[23]	Bulwer Lytton[03] Macready[93] Mill[06] S. Wilberforce[05] Mrs. Gatty[09] Landseer[03] Livingstone[10]	*Autobiography of* Mill; *Studies of the Renaissance*; *Literature and Dogma*; Stubbs's *Constitutional History* (–78); Morley's *Rousseau*; *Lombard Street*.
1874 Pater[94] Ouida[08]		*Greville Memoirs* (–87); Schliemann's *Troy*; Farrar's *Life of Christ*; *Bothwell*; *Far from the Madding Crowd*; Green's *Short History*; Thomson's *City of Dreadful Night*.
1875 J. A. Symonds[93] Hardy[28]	Kingsley[19] Lyell[97] Alfred Stevens[17] Thirlwall[97]	Tennyson's *Queen Mary*; *The Inn Album*; Dowden's *Shakespeare*; *Life of Prince Consort* (–80); Symonds's *Renaissance* (–86).
1876 Stanley[04]	Harriet Martineau[02]	*Life of Macaulay*; *History of English Thought in the Eighteenth Century*; *Daniel Deronda*; Tennyson's *Harold*; Swinburne's *Erectheus*; *Hunting of the Snark*; *Beauchamp's Career*; *Sigurd*; Spencer's *Sociology* (–96).
1877	Bagehot[26] Motley[14] Kay-Shuttleworth[04] Mrs. Norton[08] Brigham Young[00]	*Autobiography of Harriet Martineau*; *The New Republic*; *The Unknown Eros*; Meredith's *Idea of Comedy*; *Truth*; *XIXth Century*.

Art and Architecture	Public Affairs	Other Events
Walker's *Harbour of Refuge.* Albert Memorial Whistler: *Old Battersea Bridge.*	Ballot Act.	
		Moody and Sankey. Remington Typewriter.
Millais's *N.W. Passage.*	Ashantee War. Indian Famine. Disraeli P.M. Public Worship Regulation Act.	
Hermes of Praxiteles discovered. Burne-Jones: *Mirror of Venus.*	Acts for Improving Artisans' Dwellings. Acts for Amending Labour Laws.	Visit of Prince of Wales to India.
Leighton's *Daphnephoria.*	Bulgarian Atrocities.	
Dicksee's *Harmony.* Watts's *Love and Death.*	Empress of India.	Ibsen's *Pillars of Society.* Annexation of Transvaal. Russo-Turkish War.

Floruit	*Died*	*Publications*
1878 Henry James[16] Doughty[26]	Cruikshank[92] Gilbert Scott[11] Earl Russell[92] G. H. Lewes[17] Mrs. Grote[92]	Lecky's *History of the Eighteenth Century*; *Through the Dark Continent*; *English Men of Letters*; *Poems and Ballads*, II; *La Saisiaz*; Morley's *Diderot*; *Return of the Native*.
1879 Bridges[30]	W. K. Clifford[45] Panizzi[97] Butt[12] Lord Lawrence[11] Rowland Hill[95] Clerk Maxwell[31] Roebuck[01]	Balfour's *Principle Doubt*; Spencer's *Principles of Ethics* (−93); Arnold's *Mixed Essays*; Gladstone's *Gleanings*; *The Egoist*.
1880	George Eliot[19]	Pollock's *Spinoza*; Tennyson's *Ballads*; *Endymion*; *The Trumpet Major*; *John Inglesant*; Henry George's *Progress and Poverty*.
1881	Carlyle[95] Spedding[10] Disraeli[04] Stanley[15] Borrow[03] Trelawny[92] Street[24]	Taylor's *Anthropology*; Carlyle's *Reminiscences*; Morley's *Cobden*; *Virginibus Puerisque*; Rossetti's *Ballads and Sonnets*; Swinburne's *Mary Stuart*; *Portrait of a Lady*; Jowett's *Thucydides*; O. Wilde's *Poems*; *Mark Rutherford's Autobiography*.
1882	Harrison Ainsworth[05] Linnell[92] Longfellow[07] Rossetti[28] Darwin[09] Emerson[03] Garibaldi[07] Pusey[00] Trollope[15]	Seeley's *Natural Religion*; *Tristram of Lyonesse*; *Vice Versa*; Arnold's *Irish Essays*; Froude's *Carlyle* (−84); *Treasure Island*; *New Arabian Nights*; *All Sorts and Conditions of Men*.

Art and Architecture	Public Affairs	Other Events
Whistler *v.* Ruskin. Millais's *Yeoman of the Guard.* Maddox Brown: Manchester Town Hall (–93).	Berlin Congress. Afghan War.	Microphone.
Millais's *Mrs. Jopling.*		Zulu War.
Truro Cathedral. Burne-Jones: *Golden Stairs.* Burne-Jones: *Cophetua.*	Gladstone P.M. Bradlaugh's Claim to Affirm. Ground Game Act.	
	Irish Land Act. Married Women's Property Act.	Majuba. Boycotting.
	Phoenix Park Murders.	Bombardment of Alexandria. First Rowton House.

Floruit	Died	Publications
1883 A. J. Balfour[30]	Derwent Coleridge[00] Fitzgerald[09] Colenso[14] Wagner[13] Marx[18]	Mrs. Carlyle's *Letters*; Trollope's *Autobiography*; *Expansion of England*; Meredith's *Joy of Earth*; Galton's *Human Faculty*; *South African Farm*; Shaw's *Unsocial Socialist*.
1884 Henley[03]	Charles Reade[14] Mark Pattison[13] Fawcett[33] Calverley[31]	*Ferishtah's Fancies*; Tennyson's *Becket*; Toynbee's *Industrial Revolution*; Vernon Lee's *Euphorion*; *Life of George Eliot*; Rogers's *Six Centuries of Work and Wages*; *O.E.D.* (−28).
1885 Stevenson[94] Maitland[06]	Gordon[33] Victor Hugo[02] Shaftesbury[01]	*Dictionary of National Biography*; Mark Pattison's *Memoirs*; Martineau's *Types of Ethical Theory*; *Praeterita*; *Tiresias*; Burton's *Arabian Nights*; *King Solomon's Mines*; *Diana of the Crossways*; *Marius the Epicurean*.
1886	Caldecott[46] Cardwell[13] Sir Henry Taylor[00] Forster[18]	Swinburne's *Victor Hugo*; Dowden's *Shelley*; *Oceana*; *Locksley Hall*, II; Anson's *Law of the Constitution* (−92); *Little Lord Fauntleroy*; *Mayor of Casterbridge*; *Departmental Ditties*; Dicey's *Law of the Constitution*; *English Historical Review*.
1887 George Moore[33] Asquith	Mrs. Henry Wood[20] Stafford Northcote[18] Richard Jefferies[48] Jenny Lind[20]	*Study in Scarlet*; *Allan Quatermain*; Pater's *Imaginary Portraits*; Hill's *Boswell*.

Art and Architecture	Public Affairs	Other Events
		Fabian Society. Maxim Gun.
Art Workers' Guild.	Royal Commission on Housing of the Poor. Franchise.	
Mikado. Watts's *Hope*; *Love and Life.*	Dynamite Explosions. Fall of Khartoum. The Unauthorized Programme. Salisbury P.M.	
New English Art Club.	Gladstone P.M. Home Rule Bill. Liberal Split. Salisbury P.M. Lord Randolph Churchill's Resignation.	
Sargent: *Carnation, Lily.*	Queen's Jubilee. Trafalgar Square Riots.	Independent Labour Party.

Floruit	Died	Publications
1888	Lear[12] Maine[22] Matthew Arnold[22]	*Essays in Criticism*, II; *Arabia Deserta*; *American Commonwealth*; *Soldiers Three*; *Plain Tales from the Hills*; *A Reading of Earth*; *Wrong Box*; *Robert Elsemere*; Bellamy's *Looking Backward*.
1889	Bright[11] Eliza Cook[18] W. Allingham[24] Martin Tupper[10] Browning[12] Wilkie Collins[24]	*Appreciations*; Tennyson's *Demeter*; *Asolando*; Swinburne's *Poems and Ballads*, III; *Master of Ballantrae*; *Three Men in a Boat*; *Sign of Four*; *Lux Mundi*.
1890	Earl of Carnarvon[31] Chadwick[00] Newman[01] Liddon[29] Burton[21] Church[15] Boehm[34]	Booth's *Darkest England*; Stanley's *Darkest Africa*; *Golden Bough*, I; Gilbert's *Operas*, I; James's *Principles of Psychology*.
1891 Wilde[00] G. B. Shaw	Bradlaugh[33] Granville[15] Moltke[00] Lowell[19] W. H. Smith[25] Parnell[46] Earl Lytton[31] Kinglake[09]	Church's *Oxford Movement*; Sidgwick's *Elementary Politics*; Marshall's *Principles of Economics*; *News from Nowhere*; *Sherlock Holmes*, I; *Tess*; *One of our Conquerors*; *Dorian Gray*; *Intentions*.
1892 Gissing[03]	Manning[08] Spurgeon[34] Miss Clough[20] Freeman[23] R. Lowe[11] Renan[23] Woolmer[26] Gibson[17] Tennyson[09]	Curzon's *Persia*; *Death of Oenone*; *Barrack-Room Ballads*; *Peter Ibbetson*; *Countess Cathleen*.

Art and Architecture	Public Affairs	Other Events
New Gallery started.	Select Committee on Sweating. Parnell Commission.	Death of William, German Emperor, Death of Frederick, German Emperor.
	Dock Strike. Armenian Atrocities.	*Doll's House* acted. *The Kreutzer Sonata.* Booth's *Life and Labour* (–97). *Fabian Essays*, I.
		Baring Collapse. Parnell Divorce.
Fildes's *Doctor*.	Labour Commission. Newcastle Programme.	Baccarat Case.
	Gladstone P.M.	

Floruit	Died	Publications
1893	Fanny Kemble[09] J. A. Symonds[40] Jowett[17] Maddox Brown[21] Lady Eastlake[10] Tyndall[20]	Francis Thompson's *Poems*; Pater's *Plato and Platonism*; L. Stephen's *Agnostic's Apology*; *Dodo*; *Appearance and Reality*; *Sherlock Holmes*, II; *The Odd Women*; *Many Inventions*; *Catriona*; *Celtic Twilight*.
1894 Francis Thompson[07] Conan Doyle[30] Havelock Ellis	Lord Bowen[35] Sir Henry Layard[17] Pater[39] Froude[18] R. L. Stevenson[50] Christina Rossetti[30]	Kidd's *Social Evolution*; Webb's *History of Trade Unionism*; *Salome*; *Trilby*; *Dolly Dialogues*; *Jungle Book*; *Lord Ormont and his Aminta*; *Esther Waters*.
1895 Barrie Inge	Seeley[34] Randolph Churchill[49] Huxley[25] Pasteur[22]	*Vailima Letters*; Max Nordau's *Degeneration*; *The Foundations of Belief*; Yeats's *Poems*; Pater's *Miscellaneous Studies*; *Jungle Book*, II; *The Golden Age*; *Jude the Obscure*; Grant Allen's *The Women Who Did*; Purcell's *Life of Manning*.
1896	Lord Leighton[30] Verlaine[45] Tom Hughes[22] George Richmond[10] Morris[34] du Maurier[34] Coventry Patmore[23]	*The Seven Seas*; *A Shropshire Lad*; *Gaston Latour*; *Works of Max Beerbohm* I; *Weir of Hermiston*; *Daily Mail*.
1897	Mrs. Oliphant[28] Barney Barnato[52] Jean Ingelow[26] Hutton[26] F. W. Newman[05] Henry George[39] F. T. Palgrave[24] T. E. Brown[30]	Webb's *Industrial Democracy*; *The Will to Believe*; *Essay on Comedy*; *Life of Tennyson*.

Art and Architecture	Public Affairs	Other Events
	Defeat of Home Rule Bill.	Loss of *Victoria*.
Aubrey Beardsley in *Yellow Book*.	Lord Rosebery P.M. Harcourt's Death Duties.	Dreyfus Trial.
New Buildings of National Portrait Gallery. Westminster Cathedral.	Cordite Defeat. Salisbury P.M. Armenian Atrocities. Jameson Raid. Venezuelan Crisis.	Chino-Japanese War
Kelmscott *Chaucer*. Clausen: *Man with the Scythe*.		
Tate Gallery. Wallace Bequest.	South African Committee. Diamond Jubilee	Penrhyn Strike. Engineer's Strike.

Floruit	*Died*	*Publications*
1898 Lloyd George	Lewis Carroll[33] F. Tennyson[08] Aubrey Beardsley[74] Gladstone[09] Burne-Jones[33] Bismarck[15] Helen Faucit[17] William Black[41]	*Wessex Poems*; Webb's *Problems of Modern Industry*; *Plays Pleasant and Unpleasant*; *War of the Worlds*; *Ballad of Reading Gaol*.
1899	Birket Foster[25]	Yeats's *Wind Among the Reeds*; Browning *Letters*; *Letters of R. L. Stevenson*; Havelock Ellis's *Psychology of Sex*; *Irish R.M.*; *When the Sleeper Wakes*; Mackail's *Life of Morris*.
1900	James Martineau[05] Ruskin[19] Duke of Argyll[23] Henry Sidgwick[38] Max Müller[23] Wilde[56] Blackmore[25]	Symons's *Symbolist Movement*; L. Stephen's *English Utilitarians*; *Daily Express*.
1901 Wells	Charlotte Yonge[23] Creighton[43] Stubbs[25] Besant[36] Westcott[25] Empress Frederick[40] Kate Greenaway[46]	*Plays for Puritans*; Hardy's *Poems of the Past and Present*; Meredith's *Reading of Life*; *L.C.C. Survey of London*, Vol. I; *Kim*; *Erewhon Revisited*.
1902 Galsworthy[33] Arnold Bennett[31] Baldwin	Rhodes[53] Lord Acton[34] Samuel Butler[35] Zola[40]	W. James's *Varieties of Religious Experience*; Bryce's *Studies in History and Jurisprudence*; *Just so Stories*.

Art and Architecture	Public Affairs	Other Events
Sargent's *Asher Wertheimer*.	Fashoda Incident.	S. Wales Coal Dispute. Spanish-American War.
	Boer War.	Dreyfus Case.
Wallace Gallery opened.	Queen's Visit to Ireland.	Freud's *Traum-Deutung*.
	Australian Commonwealth. Death of Queen Victoria. Accession of Edward VII. Taff Vale Case.	
	S. African Peace.	

Index

Abercromby, James, 1st Baron, Dunfermline, 33
Aberdeen (George Hamilton Gordon), 4th Earl of, 83
Abney, Sir William, 175 n.
Acland, Sir Thomas Dyke, 31
Acton, Sir John, 1st Baron, 184
Acts of Parliament:
Artisans' Dwellings Act (1875), 133 n.
Ballot Act (1872), 111
British North America Act (1867), 109
Clerical Subscription Act (1865), 126 n.
Education Act (1870), 105, 111
Education Act (1902), 123, 182
Employers and Workmen Act (1875), 129
Factory Act (1833), 51, 54
Factory Act (1847), 50, 129
Food and Drugs Act (1875), 133 n.
Insurance Act (1911), 182 and n.
Irish Land Acts, 111, 136 n., 137, 138
Merchant Shipping Act (1854), 109 and n. 1
Merchant Shipping Act (1875), 133 n.
Mines Act (1842), 54
Municipal Reform Act (1835), 44
Police Act (1839), 40
Police Act (1856), 40
Protection of Property Act (1875), 129–30
Public Entertainments Act (1875), 133 n.
Public Health Acts, 50 and n., 60
and n. 2, 131, n. r, 133 n.
Public Worship Regulation Act (1874), 127
Reform Act (1832), 44
Reform Act (1867), 185
Reform Act (1885), 145
Smoke Nuisance (Metropolitan) Act (1853), 61
Tithe Commutation Act (1836), 70
Trade Union Act (1825), 129
Union Chargeability Act (1865), 176
Adelaide, Queen, 45 n.
Agnew, Sir Andrew, 53
Albert, Prince Consort, 31, 45 n., 57, 77, 82, 83, 95, 146,147, 150, 175, 191
Althorp, Lord. See Spencer, John Charles, 3rd Earl
Arch, Joseph, 176
Armstrong, William George, 1st Baron, 169
Arnold, Matthew, 107, 125, 162, 170
Thomas, 12, 15, 71 n.2, 72, 73 and n., 78, 79 n., 89, 90, 101, 105, 106, 129, 152, 164 n. 3, 155, 173, 180
William, 73 n.
Ashley, Lord. See Shaftesbury
Asquith, Herbert Henry, 1st Earl of Oxford and Asquith, 152, 164 n.3
Austin, Mrs. (née Sarah Taylor), 3

Bacon, Francis, 7 n. 3, 18
Bagehot, Walter, 14, 18 n., 90, 98, 150, 158, 162
Baines, Edward, 65